THE VALUE
OF A HUMAN LIFE

THE VALUE OF A HUMAN LIFE

Ritual Killing and Human Sacrifice in Antiquity

edited by
Karel C. Innemée

PALMA 26

PAPERS ON ARCHAEOLOGY OF THE
LEIDEN MUSEUM OF ANTIQUITIES

PALMA: Papers on Archaeology of the Leiden Museum of Antiquities (volume 26)

Published by Sidestone Press, Leiden
www.sidestone.com

Layout & cover design: Sidestone Press
Photograph front cover: Tophet de Salammbô, Tunisia by Patrick Giraud (CC BY-SA 2.5)
Photograph back cover: Pylon of Medinet Habu by Jacobus van Dijk

Volume editor: Karel C. Innemée

ISBN 978-94-6426-056-4 (softcover)
ISBN 978-94-6426-057-1 (hardcover)
ISBN 978-94-6426-058-8 (PDF e-book)

ISSN 2034-550X

Contents

Preface

Birth and death, the beginning and the end of a human life, are moments that are surrounded by myths and rituals in all cultures. Where the moment of birth usually announces itself and is surrounded with joy, the moment and the way a human life ends, by natural causes or not, can be unpredictable and is rarely met with positive emotions. Among the unnatural causes of death ritual killing takes a special place. Throughout history and all over the world people have been killed in a ritual way for a variety of reasons. Without exception, ritual killings have provoked emotions of various kinds, first of all to the ones directly involved. Victims, executioners, and bystanders must have been emotionally affected, although few reliable eyewitness accounts are known. The reactions of others who were not witnesses or directly involved are often expressions of horror, rejection and condemnation. Those 'others' could be contemporaries belonging to other cultures or religions, but also scholars studying these phenomena (anthropologists, historians, archaeologists) have often expressed their emotions and may have even let them stand in the way of an unbiased view on ritual killing.

Closely related to this is the atmosphere of horror and sensation surrounding ritual killing and human sacrifice, which has been been the reason that they became the subjects of countless films and novels, ranging from cheap horror stories to literary works like Gustave Flaubert's *Salammbô* (1862). For scholars it has not always been easy to correct caricatures and distortions of history that were the result.

Much has been said and written about ritual killing and human sacrifice and this volume is a modest contribution to the discussions surrounding the subject. It is the result of a symposium held on 11 April 2015 at the Rijksmuseum van Oudheden in Leiden, organised in collaboration with the Egyptological society *Huis van Horus*. It coincided with an exhibition about Carthage and was aimed at a wide audience of scholars and interested laypeople, with the intention to present the phenomenon in general and a number of case-studies of ritual killing, in Punic society and other cultures. This publication does not claim by any means to be exhaustive; it is a selection of essays, elaborations of the papers presented at the symposium, by scholars who, each in their field, shed light on questions surrounding ritual killing, and aimed at general readership. They try to do so by presenting the material in a way as unbiased as possible, trying to leave emotions aside, and with a critical look at conclusions and opinons from a recent past.

Karel Innemée

Chapter 1

Human sacrifice and ritual killing, defining the field

Karel C. Innemée[*]

1.1. Introduction

Every day people get killed by other people. Usually this is the result of conflict, crime, and other forms of aggression, or capital punishment. In most cases these deaths are involuntary. Death in general is surrounded by emotions, and whether it concerns cases of 'orchestrated' endings of a human life that are committed within the framework of the law, such as executions of criminals and euthanasia, or accidents and natural deaths as a result of old age, the knowledge that a border is irreversibly crossed, makes it difficult for any human being to switch these emotions off.

Euthanasia is nowadays one of the few situations where there is mutual consent concerning the deed of terminating a person's life, but in spite of this, opposition against it is still widespread and many of the opponents consider it a crime against the will of God. Emotions in the discussion surrounding its acceptability can run high.

Justifiable homicide in general is a problematic subject. Apart from certain cases of self-defence by a citizen which can result in the death of an attacker, it is generally regulated by the state monopoly on violence, which includes the right of the police to carry and use fire-arms, the right of military actions which result in deaths and, in a number of countries, capital punishment as a sanction for certain crimes. Whereas death penalty was widespread before 1900, it has met with growing resistance since the end of the Second World War, resulting in its abolition in numerous countries. In 2018 fifty-four countries worldwide practiced capital punishment.[1] Apart from the USA, those were mainly Asian and African countries, including a number of Islamic states where *sharia* law sanctions death penalty.

Killing of a human being as a result of a ritual, with or without a religious background, has become extremely controversial in modern society and is forbidden in general. Sati, the Hindu ritual in which a widow is supposed to throw herself on the funerary pyre of her husband, is now legally forbidden, but in spite of such legislation it took place until far into the twentieth century.[2] It may have been one of the last kinds of rituals in which a human life was taken in a religious context.[3]

---

[*]University of Amsterdam, University of Divinity, Melbourne

1   Based on information from https://en.wikipedia.org/wiki/Capital_punishment_by_country (accessed 15-12-2020).
2   The fact that still in 1987 a Sati Prevention Act was issued in India is an indication that the custom survived until recently. http://legislative.gov.in/sites/default/files/A1988-03_0.pdf (accessed 23-10-2020).
3   Excluding death penalty as a result of *sharia* (Islamic law).

Killing as an act of criminal violence stands in sharp contrast to ritual killing. If we consider a ritual 'a religious or solemn ceremony consisting of a series of actions performed according to a prescribed order'[4], then in the case of ritual killing there is no uncontrolled outburst of emotion, but a calculated and orchestrated set of actions that leads to the intended result. There is no question of trespassing the law for the gain of an individual or a group of individuals. On the contrary, as in the case of capital punishment, the sequence of actions is the result of conventions or rules and serves the purpose of fulfilling an obligation. At least, this is what seems to be the case upon the first superficial viewing of the phenomenon.

Much has been written about ritual killing and human sacrifice in past decades, from anthropological and archaeological point of view. This is not in the last place because of what is called *Lust am Grauen* (pleasure of horror) in German, even though many of those who consider themselves serious scholars would never admit to this. If death in general is surrounded by emotion, even more is ritual killing, and in many cases these emotions can be an obstacle to reaching an objective and balanced conclusion to questions surrounding this subject. In numerous publications the adjectives used betray the conscious or unconscious emotions of the author towards the subject.[5] Or, as Alberto Green puts it:

> Almost always the idea of such a practice evokes emotional reactions that obstruct the calm consideration of the evidence. Some have been led by biblical and classical accounts, and possibly also by their own devotion to monotheistic religions, to believe that human sacrifice was commonplace in the ancient world, and to be expected of pagans. Others are influenced by partisan feelings to deny that their favourite ancient people could have been capable of such "barbarity".[6]

Green was not the first one to be aware of this hurdle. More than a century earlier, the Dutch Protestant minister H. Oort, writing about human sacrifice in biblical Israel, had no problem in accepting that human sacrifice was practiced there, while he realised that most of his contemporaries could hardly believe that God's chosen people were able of doing such a thing.[7]

Jacobus van Dijk points at the 'partisan feelings' mentioned by Green when he writes:

> Human sacrifice has long been, and perhaps still is, a somewhat controversial subject among Egyptologist. The ancient Egyptians have often been considered too civilised for such barbaric custom.[8]

In order to overcome our own possible biases and come to a better understanding of the various forms and aspects of ritual killing, we could ask ourselves what causes an emotion of abhorrence when it comes to discussing the subject. Is there, in what we call the modern world, a general consensus when it comes to human dignity? If that is the case, it may be just a thin layer of varnish over a variety of opinions and approaches that exist as a result of the enormous diversity in cultural, religious, and political systems worldwide.

The Universal Declaration of Human Rights was accepted by the General Assembly of the United Nations in 1948. Although no member states of the UN voted against it, there was, however, no unanimous acceptance: the Soviet Union and a number of its satellite states, Saudi Arabia, and South Africa abstained. In other words, it is less than a century ago that the international community embarked on a road towards a definition of human rights and dignity, and the ways of defending them. Only Saudi Arabia abstained due to certain articles being presumed to contradict *sharia*-law, but in practice we know that this was, and still is, the tip of the iceberg of religious and cultural diversity that prevents a worldwide consensus on the rights and dignity of the human individual. Most scholars studying the subject of ritual killing probably agree on the most basic principles in the UDHR, and it is especially two of the first and most fundamental articles that are in contradiction with the ideas behind ritual killing of humans. Article 1 says: "All human beings are born free and equal in dignity and rights." This condemns slavery, or the situation where one human is property of another one, with the consequence that the free individual can decide about the fate of the person whom he or she owns. Article 3 states: "Everyone has the right to life, liberty and security of person."[9] This article explicitly excludes the right of one person to take the life of another. Since both articles are so much associated with 'civilised societies' in the mind of many people, it may be difficult to accept that some of the societies that we consider to be our cultural ancestors, did not share these values. Two other factors might play a role in a (sub)conscious resistance to accepting ritual killing in

---

4   https://en.oxforddictionaries.com/definition/ritual (accessed 5-11-2018).

5   For instance in Bremmer's *The Strange World of Human Sacrifice*, 1; apart from the word 'strange' in the title, the editor writes in his introduction: "Undoubtedly, the most fascinating and horrifying variety of sacrifice remains human sacrifice.".

6   Green, *The Role of Human Sacrifice*, 19.

7   Oort, *Het Menschenoffer in Israel*, 1-7.

8   Van Dijk, 'Retainer sacrifice', 135.

9   The citations have been taken from http://www.un.org/en/universal-declaration-human-rights/index.html (accessed on 6-5-2017).

other societies. First of all, it goes almost without saying in the modern world that ownership ends with the death of a person. Taking one's possessions to a hereafter is not considered a realistic idea anymore. The second point is that the existence of a hereafter may be a dogma that plays a role in many of the major world religions, but with a growing agnosticism and secularisation it is not a matter of fact anymore for many individuals. In consequence, death is considered the end of a human life rather than a transition to a more elevated and better form of living. The chasm between agnostic and fundamentalist religious attitudes towards death couldn't be clearer than in the case of suicide terrorists who have been taught that death is a mere step to Paradise. Transposing oneself into the world of thought of a Muslim fundamentalist may be as difficult as a getting into the mind of a believer in an ancient society that one studies as a scholar. Yet, in order to approach the subject of ritual killing with an open and unbiased mind, it is necessary to realise that in other societies, in other times and places, some or all of the following presuppositions should be accepted as realities, however contradictory they may seem with our values:

- People are not equal and not necessarily free;
- People can be owned by other people, and in that case have no (full) physical integrity;
- Owners of un-free people have the liberty to dispose of them at will;
- Physical death is not the end of life, but a transition to another state of being;
- In a continued life in the hereafter the deceased is still in need of possessions, servants and commodities.

An example of a scholarly discussion where not only facts, but also a great deal of emotion seems to have played a role is the question concerning child sacrifice in Carthage. Since decades there has been a fierce dispute on the question whether the infants buried in the *tophet* of Carthage were sacrificed or were merely still-born or died shortly after birth.[10] One of the excavators of the site, Lawrence Stager, initially accepted the idea of burials of intentionally killed children,[11] called this interpretation into question in later publications, but, like many scholars, has adhered to this conclusion in recent texts.[12] Others are outspoken in their negation of child sacrifice in Carthage.[13] That the differences of opinion go deeper than just a different interpretation of

facts may be felt in certain passages of publications but was explicitly formulated by Josephine Quinn (Oxford) in an interview about child sacrifice in Carthage for The Guardian:

> The feeling that some ultimate taboo is being broken is very strong. It was striking how often colleagues, when they asked what I was working on, reacted in horror and said, 'Oh no, that's simply not possible, you must have got it wrong.'[14]

Researchers may even have the un- or subconscious tendency to identify themselves with the object of their studies and project a 'civilised' way of thinking and behaving on ancient societies. In consequence, they may take what they see as an accusation of 'barbaric' behaviour as a reason to deny the practicing of human sacrifice.[15]

1.2. Allegations and accusations of ritual killing

While we should be careful to deny the occurrence of ritual killing on emotional grounds, a degree of scepticism concerning allegations of human sacrifice and other forms of ritual killing is justifiable in certain situations. It is a well-known fact that accusations of barbaric behaviour were made in countless cases when a society, or a group in a society, wanted to portray a group of 'others' as barbarians, in some cases with the clear intention to use such a portrayal as a justification for war or violence. An example may be the alleged human sacrifices by the Celts mentioned by Roman authors. According to Strabo (64/63 BCE – 21 CE) in his *Geography* (4.1.13):

> The Romans put a stop both to these customs and to the ones connected with sacrifice and divination, as they were in conflict with our own ways: for example, they would strike a man who had been consecrated for sacrifice in the back with a sword, and make prophecies based on his death-spasms; and they would not sacrifice without the presence of the Druids. Other kinds of human sacrifices have been reported as well: some men they would shoot dead with arrows and impale in the temples; or they would construct a huge figure of straw and wood, and having thrown cattle and all manner of wild animals and humans into it, they would make a burnt offering of the whole thing.[16]

---

10   See Garnand in this volume.
11   Stager and Wolff, 'Child sacrifice in Carthage', 31-46.
12   Stager, *Rites of Spring*.
13   For instance, Ribichini, 'Beliefs and Religious Life', 141. More recently: Schwartz et al., 'Skeletal remains', http://journals.plos.org/plosone/article/file?id=10.1371/journal.pone.0009177&type=printable (accessed 7-5-2017).

14   https://www.theguardian.com/science/2014/jan/21/carthaginians-sacrificed-own-children-study (accessed 7-5-2017).
15   Quinn in the interview mentioned in note 14: "We like to think that we're quite close to the ancient world, that they were really just like us – the truth is, I'm afraid, that they really weren't."
16   Koch and Carey, *The Celtic Heroic Age*, 18.

Julius Caesar (*c.* 15 March, 44 BCE) writes in *De Bello Gallico* (6.16):

> The whole nation of the Gauls is greatly devoted to ritual observances, and for that reason those who are smitten with the more grievous maladies and who are engaged in the perils of battle either sacrifice human victims or vow to do so, employing the Druids as ministers for such sacrifices. They believe, in effect, that, unless for a man's life a man's life be paid, the majesty of the immortal gods may not be appeased; and in public, as in private, life they observe an ordinance of sacrifices of the same kind. Others use figures of immense size, whose limbs, woven out of twigs, they fill with living men and set on fire, and the men perish in a sheet of flame. They believe that the execution of those who have been caught in the act of theft or robbery or some crime is more pleasing to the immortal gods; but when the supply of such fails they resort to the execution even of the innocent.[17]

So far there is no archaeological evidence to confirm the practices as described by Strabo and Caesar, although it cannot be excluded that occasionally ritual killing took place among Celtic tribes. The truth behind the bodies found in bogs, simply murdered or ritually killed, is a subject of ongoing discussion.

1.2.1. Accusations of child sacrifice and blood libel

The Roman accusation of child sacrifice against 'barbarians', especially the people of Carthage can be seen in this light. Even when writing in retrospect, discrediting the Punics was part of the rhetoric to justify a war against them. Diodorus Siculus, Quintus Curtius, Plutarch, described the way the Carthaginians sacrificed their children. To quote Diodorus:

> They also alleged that Cronus had turned against them inasmuch as in former times they had been accustomed to sacrifice to this god the noblest of their sons, but more recently, secretly buying and nurturing children, they had sent these to the sacrifice; and when an investigation was made, some of those who had been sacrificed were discovered to have been supposititious.[18]

Plutarch's account is one of the most elaborate:

Would it not then have been better for those Gauls and Scythians to have had absolutely no conception, no vision, no tradition, regarding the gods, than to believe in the existence of gods who take delight in the blood of human sacrifice and hold this to be the most perfect offering and holy rite? Again, would it not have been far better for the Carthaginians to have taken Critias or Diagoras to draw up their law-code at the very beginning, and so not to believe in any divine power or god, rather than to offer such sacrifices as they used to offer to Cronos? These were not in the manner that Empedocles describes in his attack on those who sacrifice living creatures: "Changed in form is the son beloved of his father so pious, who on the altar lays him and slays him. What folly!

> No, but with full knowledge and understanding they themselves offered up their own children, and those who had no children would buy little ones from poor people and cut their throats as if they were so many lambs or young birds; meanwhile the mother stood by without a tear or moan; but should she utter a single moan or let fall a single tear, she had to forfeit the money and her child was sacrificed nevertheless; and the whole area before the statue was filled with a loud noise of flutes and drums took the cries of wailing should not reach the ears of the people.[19]

Accusations of ritual killings were a favourite instrument of slander, not only against political enemies outside the borders, but could also be used against groups within society. If the killing of a human being can be considered abhorrent, then the accusation of killing a young, innocent child for the purpose of a religious ceremony is an even more gruesome and effective way to discredit an opponent. Early Christians were accused of child sacrifice and cannibalism and, interestingly enough, they uttered similar accusations against Jews and, in certain cases, even against heterodox groups.[20] Accusations against early Christians are not very explicit and have never led to formal charges by authorities, but from the *Apology* of Tertullian it is clear against what kind of rumours he reacts: accusations of cannibalism and incestuous intercourse during Christian rituals.

> Monsters of wickedness, we are accused of observing a holy rite in which we kill a little child and then eat it; in which, after the feast, we practise incest, the dogs– our pimps, forsooth, overturning the lights

17 *De Bello Gallico*, translation H.J. Edwards, Loeb Classical Library 72, 341.
18 *The Library of History*, 20.14., translation Russel M. Geer, Loeb Classical Library 390, 179.

19 *Moralia* II, *De Superstitione* 13,1, translation Babbitt, Loeb Classical Library 222, 493.
20 Roig Lanzillotta, 'The Early Christians and Human Sacrifice'; Bremmer. 'Early Christian Human Sacrifice'.

and getting us the shamelessness of darkness for our impious lusts. This is what is constantly laid to our charge, and yet you take no pains to elicit the truth of what we have been so long accused.[21]

The grounds of the accusations remain unclear, but at least two reasons could be found. First, the presumed ritual killing of adults or children in other non-Roman cults and the otherness of the Christian cult which made it prone to suspicion as a *superstitio*; second, the misunderstanding of the metaphors of the Eucharist.[22] Possibly as a reaction, once Christianity had been legalised and open confrontations by Christians towards non-Christians became more and more frequent, similar accusations were made by Christian authors. For instance, in the anonymous hagiography of Makarios of Tkôw 'pagans' are accused of sacrificing Christian children in their temples, a topic that recurs in various other sources.[23]

Curiously enough, not only 'pagans' but also certain heterodox movements were accused of similar atrocities by mainstream Christians, sometimes in very explicit descriptions of the presumed rituals of promiscuous sex and infanticide.[24] Epiphanius of Salamis, in his zeal to hunt down everyone and everything outside the boundaries of orthodoxy, goes to the extreme of describing how in the Gnostic sect of the Borborites children who are conceived in promiscuous intercourse during the rituals are aborted, cooked, and eaten by the members of the sect.[25] One might think that once such accusations had become a stereotype first used against, and later by Christians, they would lose their credibility over time. The contrary is true. During the Middle Ages there were countless cases of 'blood libel', or accusations against Jews concerning ritual killing of Christian children, mostly young boys, who were presumed to have been crucified or ritually slaughtered in order to use their blood for the preparation of matzes consumed during the celebration of Passover. Famous are the cases of William of Norwich (2 February 1132 – 22 March 1144) and 'Little' Hugh of Lincoln (1246 – 27 August 1255)[26], who were officially venerated as martyrs after their presumed death by crucifixion by Jews. One of the first documented

cases where the ritual use of the victim's blood was part of the accusation, was the death of Simon of Trent killed on March 21, 1475.[27] He was canonised as well, and it was not until 1965 that he was removed from the *Martyrologium Romanum*. False accusations of blood libel are by no means restricted to the Middle Ages. When in 1946 in the Polish town of Kielce the little Henryk Błaszczyk disappeared for several days, and told after his sudden return that he had been held by Jews, who were planning to ritually murder him, a pogrom broke out in which 42 people were lynched.[28] It is therefore not surprising that, when accusations of ritual killing of small children are uttered, historians and archaeologists tend to raise their eyebrows first and take nothing for granted, especially when the accusations in question concern the group or culture that is the object of their studies.[29]

1.3. Definitions

In the foregoing paragraphs the terms 'human sacrifice' and 'ritual killing' have been used without properly defining them. Some scholars prefer not to distinguish between them, as Àgnes Nay and Fransesca Prescendi do in their introduction to *Sacrifices humains. Dossiers, discours, comparaisons*:

> Dans ce contexte, nous ne distinguons pas les «sacrifices humains» des «meurtres rituels», c'est-à-dire des mises à mort ritualisées dans ou hors contexte religieux, les confins des uns et des autres étant flous et parfois impossibles à établir faute de documentation précise.[30]

Indeed, the exact motivation and thoughts behind material remains that archaeologists interpret as traces of ritual killings may often remain obscure, but that should not prohibit us from drawing up a theoretical framework within which distinctions can be made. In case of written sources, moreover, their content does give us the possibilities to identify the differences.

Numerous definitions have been given for the word 'sacrifice'[31], and a discussion concerning the history of the

---

21 *Apology* 7, 1; see also 8,2-3, 7, where he describes the Christian 'crimes' as a parody.

22 Dölger, 'Sacramentum infanticidii', 227, gives in total five possible reasons, but includes also actual initiation rituals of Gnostics, thereby presuming that certain Gnostic groups did perform such rituals. A further, critical examination of such allegations can be found in Henrichs, 'Pagan ritual and the Alleged Crimes of the Early Christians'. See also McGowan, 'Eating People'.

23 Frankfurter, *Religion in Roman Egypt*, 20; Nock, 'Greek Novels and Egyptian Religion', 169-175; Van der Vliet, 'Spätantikes Heidentum', 108.

24 Lanzillotta, 'The early Christians and human sacrifice', 95-97.

25 *Panarion* 26.5.5-6, translation by Frank Williams.

26 For this and other cases see Utz, 'The Medieval myth of Jewish ritual murder'.

27 Po-Chia Hsia, *Trent 1475*, 94.

28 Engel, 'Patterns Of Anti-Jewish Violence'.

29 The allegations of the QAnon movement, made recently, show that (antisemitic) blood libel is apparently still a favourite way to discredit opponents.

30 Nagy and Prescendi, *Sacrifices humains*, 7.

31 Hubert and Mauss' work *Sacrifice: its Nature and Function*, although first published in 1898, is still considered an authoritative study; here, the following definition is given: "Sacrifice is a religious act which, through the consecration of a victim, modifies the condition of the moral person who accomplishes it or that of certain objects with which he is concerned." (*Sacrifice*, 13).

phenomenon, which is impossible to summarise here, has been going on since decades. Sacrifice is widely associated with killing and according to René Girard has its root in a desire that is mimetic. He postulates that a desire by a person for something is imitated from someone else's desire, and that all conflict originates in such a mimetic desire. In a next step this antagonism, instead of the desire for the object, is copied and a common enemy is sought. The resulting antagonism and aggression between groups is then channelled towards a scapegoat, which is killed. The brutal elimination of the innocent victim would reduce the appetite for violence that possessed everyone a moment before, and leave the group suddenly appeased. The origin of sacrifice is explained by his scapegoat mechanism and religion would have been necessary in human evolution to control the violence that comes from mimetic rivalry.[32]

In the same year when Girard published his *La Violence et le sacré*, Walter Burkert's *Homo Necans* (1972) appeared. For Burkert, concentrating on Greek culture, sacrifice is also closely connected with killing, in the first place of sacrifial animals. "Grunderlebnis des 'Heiligen' ist die Opfertötung. Der homo religiosus agiert und wird sich seiner selbst bewußt als homo necans."[33] Nevertheless, there are reasons to argue that not every sacrifice is the result of killing of an animal or human being, while not every case of ritual killing can be called a sacrifice. Some authors distinguish more sharply than others between 'human sacrifice' and 'ritual homicide'.[34]

The etymology of the word 'sacrifice' is a combination of Latin *sacer* ('sacred' or 'damned') and *facere* ('to make'), and this could be freely translated as 'to set apart from the profane world' be it in positive or negative sense. Cristiano Grottanelli defines sacrifice as "l'offrande d'un bien ou d'une prestation (ou la renonciation à un bien) en faveur d'une sphère autre, qui peut être extrahumaine, et le meurtre d'une victime pour le bien de cette sphère supérieure"[35], which implies that the killing of a living creature is a form of sacrifice, but not the only one.

If an object or a creature is sacrificed, *i.e.* moved into another sphere, a parallel reality that can be the world of the divine or the hereafter, this transfer can be realised by 'dematerialising' the sacrifice. In the case of killing a sentient being (and burning, if it concerns a holocaust sacrifice), this is a necessary step to achieve this dematerialisation. What may seem to be a destructive act is in fact (meant as) a form of communication between two levels of reality. Killing a human being can be done as part of a ritual or in a ritualised way, but this does not imply automatically that it is a form of sacrifice. In the following paragraphs a number of forms of ritual killing of human beings will be discussed with the intention to show the differences and the possible motivations behind them.

1.3.1. Retainer sacrifice

Archaeological evidence from cultures all over the world shows that people, often belonging to the elite, were buried in the company of others, and that these others did not always die of natural causes, but were killed by violence, poison, or might have been buried alive after having been drugged. In most cases written evidence concerning the circumstances of burial and the identity of subsidiary burials is lacking. Some of the earliest cases of such burials, dating back to the fourth millennium BCE, are known from Nubia. In Kadada and Kadruka a number of tombs contained additional burials of individuals who were apparently killed to accompany the main burial.[36] One of the remarkable cases was the burial of a woman, to which a male companion had been added. We have no idea what was the relationship between these two individuals and whether the man was subordinate to the woman, or joined her voluntarily and as an equal in her transition to another world. Later cases of the so-called retainer sacrifice in the Nile Valley do suggest that the people buried in subsidiary tombs were subordinate to the person of the main burial. The kings of the First Dynasty (ca. 3100-2890 BCE) in Egypt were buried in Abydos and around most of the royal tombs in that location subsidiary burials have been found, ranging in number from a few dozen to several hundreds.[37] Subsidiary burials accompanied some of the tombs of the Second Dynasty (ca. 2890-2686 BCE), but after that the phenomenon disappears in Egypt. In Kerma, during the Classic Kerma period (ca. 1750-1500 BCE), it recurs in the so-called royal tombs excavated by George Reisner.[38] In one of the largest, tomb III, at least 322 people were buried with the main burial. In a much later period, after the collapse of the Meroitc Empire, there is a revival of the phenomenon in the elite tombs of Ballana and Qustul from the end of the fifth/beginning of the sixth centuries, where, again, the main burial is accompanied by the interments of people who were probably members of the household, as well as

---

32   Girard, *La violence et le sacré*.

33   Burkert, *Homo Nectans*, 9: "The basic experience of the 'sacred' is the killing of the sacrifice. The homo religiosus acts and becomes aware of himself as the homo necans".

34   Brelich (*Presupposti del Sacrificio Umano*, 6-14) makes a sharp distinction, while, for instance, Hughes (*Human Sacrifice in Ancient Greece*, 3-4) acknowledges the difference, but prefers to draw a less sharp line between the two phenomena.

35   Grottanelli, *Il sacrifcio*, 6, quoted from Nagy and Prescendi, *Sacrifices humains*, 7.

36   Reinold, 'Kadruka', 2-10, especially 4 and 9.

37   For general information about retainer sacrifice in Egypt and Nubia see Van Dijk, 'Retainer sacrifice'.

38   Reisner, *Excavations at Kerma* III, 61-528; Adams, *Nubia, Corridor to Africa*, 203-206.

horses.[39] Not only in the Nile Valley, but all over the world, examples of such mass burials have been found.

During the excavations at Ur by Leonard Woolley, sixteen elite/royal tombs from a round 2600 BCE were found that contained varying numbers of additional burials, ranging from twelve to as many as eighty.[40] The accompanying persons, most likely members of the royal household, included drivers of carts, grooms, and musicians -with their instruments-, lined up in order. The fact that cups were found with each of them suggests that they were taking poison or sedatives before being buried.

At certain moments in time the decision was taken to use substitutes instead of real people to accompany the deceased. One of the most spectacular examples is the terracotta army of emperor Qin Shi Huang, more than 8,000 life-size figures that were positioned around the tomb of the emperor.[41] In Egypt *ushabtis*, two- and three-dimensional representations of servants, cattle and other animals, given in the tomb, were meant to be turned real by means of magical spells that the deceased could use. Some scholars may have seen this substitution as a step forward on the path of civilisation, but there may have been other reasons for doing this. Killing several thousands of soldiers would have been a severe blow to the army. Sending a chief cook, a personal adviser and others from the close entourage of the king with him to the hereafter would leave his successor deprived of a valuable staff.

Such consideration is purely practical, but there may have been a more conceptual reason behind the phenomenon of substitution. In early dynastic Egypt divine kingship was already clearly developed and included the idea that the ruling king was Horus, an eternal embodiment, regardless from the person who acted as king. As a consequence, the staff in the royal court, servants, advisers, and the harem, would have been thought to belong to the *king*, not to the person who held that office for a given period. The concept of the 'body natural' and the 'body politic' of the king could have been a reason in that case.[42]

The act of killing people in order to send them on a journey to accompany a high-ranking person is usually called 'retainer sacrifice'. If we keep in mind the definition of Grottanelli, then there are serious reasons to doubt whether the term is justifiable. Indeed, people are transposed into another sphere, but not as a gift to the deceased.[43] In the same way that he or she is accompanied by lifeless possessions that are indispensable for continuation of life in the hereafter, so are his or her staff of servants sent on the journey, not as gifts, but as part of the belongings. Sacrifices to the dead, strictly speaking, are the offerings made after the funeral, as a regular flow of commodities that ensure lasting life on the other side. There is no reason to believe that humans were sacrificed as part of a funerary cult, at least not in the Near East. In almost all cases of the so-called retainer sacrifice, scholars have been speculating about the last moments of the 'victims': if they went voluntarily, or if their death was a gruesome anguish. Physical anthropological evidence can only indicate the way in which death was inflicted, not a person's state of mind just before and in the final moments. We will never know, but we can suspect that for many there was hope for a heavenly bliss that would have been out of reach for other mortals. Gruesome as it may seem to us now, then it may have been comparable to a medical intervention: a painful, unpleasant moment, after which all would be much better.

1.3.2. Ritual regicide

"Le roi est mort, vive le roi" is a well-known expression, though maybe not fully understood by many people. It means to say that a monarchy as an institution, be it divine kingship or not, is not dependent on the person who acts as king at a certain moment and that with his or her physical death a successor continues the line. Although the sentence was probably uttered for the first time in 1422, when Charles VII of France succeeded Charles VI, the idea behind it is much older.

If kingship is a continuum, a god-given institution that guarantees the stability of the state, an interregnum means a threat to this stability and a succession should preferably be a matter of hours. The *body politic* keeps functioning and the death and replacement of the *body natural* is subordinate to that. The origins of the concept of divine kingship are difficult to trace; there are reasons to believe that already in the predynastic period in Egypt it was the ideology that was to become the binding element in the formation of the state.[44]

Older than the idea that the ruler is an earthly manifestation of a god or a go-between between human society and the divine world must be the feeling that physical and mental qualities were criteria that qualified a leader of a group. As is still the case in groups of primates, the alpha male could maintain his position as long as he was mentally and physically fit. With the introduction of the idea of divine kingship, the importance attached to the physical fitness of the king did not disappear, but was

---

39   Emery, *The Royal Tombs of Ballana and Qustul*; Dann 'Changing patterns of violence', 189-200.

40   Woolley, *Ur Excavations* II, IV; Idem, *Excavations at Ur*. See also Theo Krispijn in this volume.

41   The total number is likely to be much higher, since only a part of the tomb has been excavated so far.

42   The concept was elaborated by Ernst Kantorowicz, writing about medieval kingship in England and France in *The King's Two Bodies*.

43   Testart, 'Doit-on parler de "sacrifice"?'.

44   Wilkinson, *Early Dynastic Egypt*, 183-186.

coupled to it, leading to the concept of the dual body of the king. The ancient Egyptian ritual of *heb-sed*, known from the earliest dynastic times, must have its roots in the prehistoric times, when a leader had to prove his qualities in order to have his position ritually confirmed and renewed.[45] In principle it was celebrated after thirty years of reign, when the king had reached an age at which most men start experiencing a waning of physical condition. Part of the ritual to be performed by the king consisted of running along a track, originally meant to show that his condition was still sufficient. In the time when the first evidence for this festival appears, it must already have been transformed from a real test into a ritual. There is no reason to believe that any king ever 'failed' the test in historic times. We can only speculate what would have been the consequences in a remote prehistoric period: a forced abdication or even a ritual death?[46] Ritual regicide in order to ensure a renewal or continuation of the monarchy may have been widespread in a remote past, but was turned into a symbolic ritual in many cases. The *sed*-festival, although not directly connected with regicide, may be a far cry of that.

The killing of kings in a ritual way, however, may have been widespread in a more recent past in more southern regions of the African continent. Diodorus Siculus mentions ritual regicide in his *Bibliotheca Historica*, when he writes about the kingdom of Meroë, Egypt's southern neighbour, and the reform by king Ergamenes:

> Of all their customs the most astonishing is that which obtains in connection with the death of their kings. For the priests at Meroë who spend their time in the worship of the gods and the rites which do them honour, being the greatest and most powerful order, whenever the idea comes to them, dispatch a messenger to the king with orders that he die. For the gods, they add, have revealed this to them, and it must be that the command of the immortals should in no wise be disregarded by one of mortal frame. And this order they accompany with other arguments, such as are accepted by a simple-minded nature, which has been bred in a custom that is both ancient and difficult to eradicate and which knows no argument that can be set in opposition to commands enforced by no compulsion. Now in former times the kings would obey the priests, having been overcome, not by arms nor by force, but because their reasoning powers had been put under a constraint by their very superstition; but during the reign of the second Ptolemy the king

of the Ethiopians, Ergamenes, who had had a Greek education and had studied philosophy, was the first to have the courage to disdain the command. For assuming a spirit which became the position of a king he entered with his soldiers into the unapproachable place where stood, as it turned out, the golden shrine of the Ethiopians, put the priests to the sword, and after abolishing this custom thereafter ordered affairs after his own will.[47]

Ergamenes is probably to be identified with the Meroitic king Arkamani, who ruled from the late third to early second century BCE.[48] There is no archaeological or textual evidence from other sources for ritual regicide in Nubia during the kingdom of Napata and Meroë, and Diodorus may have confused reports from elsewhere, possibly from regions farther south. That is not unlikely if we consider that ritual regicide was widespread in Africa, and was even practiced until relatively recent times. In several countries on the African continent, including Sudan, (ritual) regicide has been documented as a way to avoid an interregnum or a period of vulnerability for the leadership when a ruler started losing physical and/or mental qualities.[49] In southern Sudan, ritual regicide was practiced until the first half of the twentieth century, especially among the Shilluk[50], while among the Dinka the head of a tribe ('Master of the spear') would be buried alive.[51] Although Huntington and Metcalf call it 'neither suicide nor regicide' because of the mutual agreement between the master and his people, the fact is that also here the physical existence of the body natural is considered subordinate to that of the body politic, resulting in the death of the leader.

The view that the king as body politic symbolises, embodies, or even represents the tribe, group, or nation and its prosperity and safety, is the reason behind this phenomenon. In some cases this close association can also have as a consequence the punishment of the nation by a god for the misdoings of a king. This conclusion can be drawn from the Old Testament story of Achab. When he displeased Yahweh, the land was hit by a drought (1 Kings 17:1). When natural disaster would strike, or astronomical irregularities, such as an eclipse, would occur, the execution of the king could be used as a remedy,

45   Hornung and Staehelin, *Studien zum Sedfest*.

46   Compagno comes to the conclusion that there is no direct connection between the *sed*-festival and regicide ('Sur un régicide obscur', 136-147).

47   *Library of History* 3,6, translation Russel M. Geer, 101-102.

48   Török, *Between Two Worlds*, 389-390.

49   Already Frazer paid ample attention to ritual regicide (*The Golden Bough* (part III, *The Dying God*), 9-40). Though now outdated in many respects, the book presents a number of subjects that have been the starting point of further research. Hirschberg, (*Die Kulturen Afrikas*, 93-94), mentions numerous cases of ritual regicide in various countries, but without any annotation; De Heusch gives a better documented account ('La mort sacrificielle').

50   Schnepel, 'Continuity despite and through Death'.

51   Huntington and Metcalf, *Celebrations of Death*, 175-183.

at least in Babylon. Since eclipses could be calculated and predicted, in such cases the king would formally abdicate and a substitute, often a convicted criminal, would be appointed and executed after the eclipse.[52]

In conclusion, we can say that ritual regicide often shows that social and cosmic order are paramount to the life of an individual, even if, or rather, especially if that individual is the head of the community. In the cases where no substitute for a king to be killed was involved and the king or head of the tribe complied and cooperated in the procedure, it could be considered a form of self-sacrifice.

1.3.3. Ritual killing of enemies and capital punishment

That ritual killing occurred in Ancient Egypt, especially in early dynastic times, is an accepted fact. However, when examining the literature on this subject, it is remarkable that the term 'human sacrifice' is still used in a quite indiscriminate way. The Egyptologist Jacques Kinnaer remarks, when discussing human sacrifice:

> ... the three following practices should be distinguished:
> - The ritual killing of human beings as part of the offerings presented to the gods on a regular basis, or on special occasions.
> - Retainer sacrifice, or the killing of domestic servants to bury them along with their master.
> - The killing of convicted criminals or enemies of the country. Although criminals and enemies of the country may have been killed in a ritualised manner, this practice cannot be considered as real human sacrifice. It is therefore not discussed here.[53]

The last category, the execution of criminals and enemies of the country, deserves more attention. Herman te Velde argues that human sacrifice in the strict sense of the word was rare in Egypt, and that the sacrificing of humans to the goddess Mut during the Third Intermediate Period (ca. 1070-712 BCE) can be counted among the exceptions.[54] This case, however, concerns victims who were selected because of their red hair or other characteristics that were associated with Seth, the god of chaos. Under Amasis (ca. 600 BCE) such victims would have been replaced by wax statues. If indeed such rituals were performed, can we speak of 'human sacrifice'? The killing of criminals, enemies, and those associated with Seth, seems to be an act of restoring and maintaining order rather than a sacrifice.

First of all, we should distinguish between the execution of a death penalty and ritualised killing. A person convicted of a crime is an individual who has to face the consequences of his deed. On the other hand, fight against crime takes place at a higher and a more general level. Evil and Chaos, as opposed to Law and Order, are abstractions that can be personified in animals, humans or gods, and fighting these forces is an eternal struggle that can be represented in rituals. Here the scale is cosmic and supersedes the case of the individual criminal. The Egyptian myths of creation tell of the chaos of primeval matter (Nun), out of which the gods created a world based on order, truth, and justice (Maat, personified by the goddess of that name). The opposite forces of chaos and disorder, however, were always lurking to overthrow cosmic order and it was the king's duty to maintain order, both within society, at its borders, and on a cosmic scale. Egypt was believed to be organised according to Maat, but was surrounded by the forces of chaos, first of all the desert and its inhabitants (wild animals), and by its political enemies: Nubians, Lybians, Palestinians etc. On one hand there is the historical reality of battles to unite the Egyptian state and defend and maintain its territory; on the other, there are the rituals and depictions that represent this ongoing strife. The body politic of the king acts according to the paradigms of his duties and is represented as such, both in ritual and in representations, and, eventually, in representations of rituals. The hunting scenes of kings should be seen in this light, as well as the representations of ritual killings.

The palette of Narmer is a document that probably shows a ritual re-enactment of the struggle of a king in order to smite his enemies and create a state.[55] It is not clear to what events exactly the images refer, but it is clear that killing of the adversaries is done (or represented only) in a ritual way. The king smashes the skull of an enemy with a mace, an object that is both a deadly instrument in battle and becomes a sceptre that represents royal authority. This iconographical model, in modified ways, would be repeated endlessly throughout Egyptian history. The core of the message that these images convey is that the king is the guardian of cosmic and social order and that the powers of chaos will be defeated by him. An interesting set of such images, dating back to the Old Kingdom, are to be found in the region of the turquoise mines in the Wadi Maghara, in the south-western Sinai peninsula. Here a number of kings, among whom Djoser, Sekhemkhet, Snefru, and Khufu, left rock-tablets showing them smashing the skull of a foreigner, most likely referring to the indigenous inhabitants of Sinai.[56] The Egyptians, realising that they were venturing outside

---

52   See Krispijn in this volume.
53   Kinnaer, 'Human sacrifice'.
54   Te Velde, 'Human Sacrifice in Ancient Egypt', 131-132, discussing Yoyotte, 'Héra d'Héliopolis'.

55   Wilkinson, *Early Dynastic Egypt*, 68.
56   Lepsius, *Denkmäler* Abtheilung II Band III, 2, 39.

their 'organised' territory, must have left these tablets as a warning or message to the locals.

The front of temple pylons from the New Kingdom onwards has a more or less fixed and limited repertoire of themes, among which we find battle scenes with the king fighting his enemy from his chariot, and the king killing one or more enemies whom he grasps by the hair and kills with a mace or a scimitar. Often, he does this in front of a god. Such ritual executions were frequently depicted not only on public monuments, but also on private stelae.[57]

In the Egyptian perception of the world the borders between truth and reality, and between the image as a depiction of history or of a stereotype were fluid and the question remains whether such ritual killings were performed on real enemies or prisoners of war, and if so, how often it happened.[58] From archaeological evidence it is clear that, as in 'retainer sacrifice', substitutes were used. These included statues of kneeling, bound prisoners that could be decapitated, or statues with a hole in the chest or back into which a spear could be plunged. Following the abolishment of executions by Amasis, wax statues could be burnt, as mentioned above.

In the papyrus Jumilhac, a late Ptolemaic or early Roman text that deals with the myths and rituals of the seventeenth and eighteenth nomes of Egypt, the necessity of ritual killing of the enemy is clearly stated. If the ritual is not performed, the consequence will be the revolt of the foreign enemies. The formulation also implies that a substitute in wax or other material is used:

Si on ne décapite pas l'ennemi qu'on a devant soi (qu'il soit modelé) en cire, (dessiné) sur un papyrus vierge, ou (sculpté) en bois d'acacia ou en bois de hm3, suivant tous les prescriptions du rituel, les habitants du désert révolteront contre l'Égypte, et il se produira la guerre et la rébellion dans le pays tout entier.[59]

The scenes depicted on temple-pylons and stelae can be considered to be substitutes themselves, as the representations of offerings in tombs were substitutes that could be turned real through magic by the tomb-owner.

Although Kinnaer (see note 53) does not consider capital punishment a form of human sacrifice, there are some formulations that suggest ritual aspects to the execution of criminals, especially murderers and tomb-robbers. Impalement was apparently a profane way of execution, but in certain cases of burning the

terminology used was similar to that which was used for animal sacrifices.[60] Harco Willems, in his article on inscription 8 in the tomb of Ankhitifi at Mo'alla, discusses the phenomenon of execution of criminals as a form of human sacrifice. Potential tomb-robbers are warned in this text that their crimes will have serious consequences, and apart from death penalty they will be denied the right to be properly buried. However, "...the terminology for these killings is identical with that used for sacrifices. In Mo'alla inscription no. 8, the event is associated with a certain festival of the local god Hemen, during whose processions the criminal is said to be sacrificed.".[61] In spite of the use of the terminology that alludes to human sacrifice, there are reasons to doubt if we should use this term in the strict sense of the word. If we compare the burning of wax statues with the execution of criminals, for whom burial is not allowed, both procedures are aimed at the annihilation of the 'victim', not at a transposition to a sphere of the divine. Both fire and remaining unburied were guarantees for a 'second death'. The sacrifice to the divinity, one could say, does not consist in the killing of the victim or a substitute, but in restoring Maat by annihilation of an adversary of cosmic and social order. A similar mechanism can be observed when the king ritually kills a prisoner of war. In numerous representations in temples the king offers a statue of the goddess Maat to a god, showing that his works are aimed at maintaining cosmic order. The ritual killing of representatives of chaos: foreign enemies, criminals, wild animals, is therefore a deed of restoring or maintaining this order.

1.3.4. Human sacrifice

Sacrifice in the proper sense of the word can be defined as a transfer of property from the realm of the profane to the realm of the sacred, or as a gift offered to a 'superhuman recipient'. Violence can be involved in the process, but is not necessary. Inanimate objects can be sacrificed, as for instance in the cases of precious objects which were thrown into sacred wells.[62] Although, strictly speaking, a sacrifice can be anything, ranging from a flower to a herd of cattle, the term 'sacrifice' came to mean offering something of value, something that may or should be difficult for the owner to part with. In the case of human sacrifice this would imply that the 'giver'

---

57   Schulmann, *Ceremonial Execution and Public Reward*, 8-62.
58   See Van Dijk in this volume. In the case of military campaigns there are reasons to believe that such killing of prisoners of war took place at certain moments (Green, *The Role of Human Sacrifice*, 125-127).
59   Vandier, *Le Papyrus Jumilhac*, 130.

60   Muhlestein, 'Sacred Violence', 244-251.
61   Willems, 'Crime, Cult and Capital Punishment', 43.
62   This kind of sacrifice can be found in various parts of the world, such as Central America or Western Europe. The best-known example is the sacred well near Chichen Itza, where both precious objects and humans were sacrificed; Adams, *Prehistoric Mesoamerica*, 290. Similar sacrifices in sacred wells have been found elsewhere in the world; Varner, *Sacred Wells*, 11. The modern use of throwing coins into fountains may be a remnant of this practice.

is the owner of or has a full custody and authority over the victim, to such an extent that the victim has no say in the decision of sacrifice or is fully cooperative. Prisoners of war or slaves were categories of people who had no right of decision over their own body and therefore constituted easy potential victims.

More difficult than giving a slave or a prisoner is of course sacrificing one's own child. But apart from the personal barrier to overcome, how easy or legal was it to kill a child? Children, especially infants, had little legal protection and were not (or hardly) considered autonomous individuals in antiquity; these factors made them a category of potential sacrificial victims.[63] It is also remarkable that among the (mythological) victims of human sacrifice, especially in Greek narrative, a remarkably high number of young women and girls can be found. Polyxena and Iphigeneia of the ancient Greek tradition, but also the anonymous daughter of Jephthah in the Old Testament, are well-known examples.[64] This does not necessarily mean that in real life more women (if any) were sacrificed, but could illustrate the position of women in society in general, where their fate could be sealed by their fathers, or where they could voluntarily cooperate in the sacrifice to show their virtue and sacrifice themselves like men did on the battlefield in order to reverse the fate of the nation or kin for the better.[65]

We should of course distinguish between the different attitudes towards human sacrifice in various times and regions of the ancient Near East and the Mediterranean. In the Syro-Palestine region child sacrifice must have been more common than in elsewhere in the eastern Mediterranean.[66] Human sacrifice may have occurred incidentally in the Greek world, although here sources are ambiguous. The best-known cases of sacrifice are from mythology, like the aforementioned stories of Polyxena and Iphigeneia, and other, less famous stories.[67] The question is of course whether the mythological narratives are residues of historical events and practices or are fully made up and contain no reference to actual ancient rituals.[68] Archaeological evidence it scarce, even though now and then a shred of possible clue appears. The cult of Zeus of Mount Lykaion in the Peloponnese was surrounded with stories about human sacrifice and werewolf-like transformations of the people who had eaten of the sacrifial flesh, a clear example of mythology.[69] In

2016, however, archaeologists of the University of Arizona discovered a burial of a young male among the ashes of sacrificial animals near the altar on top of Mount Lykaion. The location is at least unusual for a normal burial and although the discovery is no solid evidence for human sacrifice, it raises questions for further research.[70]

Another rare case, although again not unanimously accepted as evidence, is a temple at Anemospilia on Crete, excavated in 1979, which must have collapsed during an earthquake around 1700 BCE and caught fire after that.[71] The position of the human remains found in the temple – a young man, two older men, and a woman who were killed by the collapsing building – were interpreted by the excavators as a freeze-frame fixed by the disaster while a human sacrifice was taking place. Was this an exceptional case of human sacrifice intended to avert further earthquakes?[72] Discussions about the possibility of human sacrifice in the Hellenic world have been fierce and emotional from time to time. Although not common, it looks as if it happened under exceptional circumstances. New food for thought was provided by the discovery in 2012 of what seems to be a comparable case of a human sacrifice at the Minoan palace of Kydonia (Crete): remains of a young woman found between those of sacrificial animals in the context of a building destroyed by an earthquake.[73]

Human sacrifice was not a part of the institutionalised cults in Rome, and was even forbidden by the Senate in 97 BCE. Such a prohibition, however, can be seen as an indication that human sacrifices were made, and indeed sources mention at least three cases when in situations of crisis during the Republic (509-44 BCE) pairs of Gauls and Greeks were buried alive in the Forum Boarium to placate the gods. The most famous instance was the one of 216 BCE after the Roman defeat at Cannae. Livy, describing the event about two centuries later, stresses its unusual character (*minime Romano sacro*) and the fact that it only took place after consulting the oracle of Delphi and the Sibylline Books.[74] During the Principate human sacrifice was not only forbidden, but also rejected as an act of barbarism, associated with 'others'. We have seen that especially child sacrifice was condemned and often used as an argument to discredit opponents. This is all the more remarkable if we realise that the value of a child's life was relative and a Roman *pater familias* had the *ius vitae*

63   For a general overview of the position children in late antiquity see Aasgaard, 'Children in Antiquity', 23-46.

64   Hughes, *Human Sacrifice*, 71-138.

65   Hughes, *Human Sacrifice*, 73-76.

66   For child sacrifice in the Punic world see Garnand in this volume.

67   Bremmer, 'Myth and Ritual', 59-65; Hughes, *Human Sacrifice*, 71-136.

68   Hughes, *Human Sacrifice*, 71-73.

69   Hughes, *Human Sacrifice*, 96-107; Bremmer, 'Myth and Ritual', 65-78.

70   Urbanus, 'Murder on the Mountain?'.

71   Hughes, *Human Sacrifice*, 13-17.

72   Sakellarakis and Sakellaraki 'Drama of Death'; Apart from this publication in National Geographic, no other, more scholarly publications were dedicated to this case, so that questions remain.

73   Vlazaki-Andreadaki, 'Sacrifices in LM IIIB'.

74   Titus Livius, *Ab Urbe Condita* XXII.57.2-7; For a discussion of these events see Schultz, 'The Romans and Ritual Murder' and 'Roman sacrifice', especially 60, 68-70, and Ndiaye, 'Minime Romano sacro'.

ac necis (the disposal of life and death) over his family, and could kill his child as long as he had a good reason (*iusta causa*) for this.[75] The killing or exposure of newborn children was common in the Graeco-Roman world and in an often quoted letter from a Roman citizen to his wife it is mentioned as a possibility in a surprisingly casual way:

> Know that I am still in Alexandria. And do not worry if they all come back and I remain in Alexandria. I ask and beg you to take good care of our baby son, an as soon as I receive payment, I will send it up to you. If you are delivered of child [before I get home], if it is a boy keep it, if it is a girl discard it. You have sent me word, 'Don't forget me.' How can I forget you? I beg you not to worry.[76]

There are no indications that in pharaonic Egypt infanticide was a common practice. Judaism and Christianity have traditionally always opposed abortion and infanticide and it must have been under Christian influence that it became a capital offence under Valentinian in 374. Seven years later, the Council of Constantinople underscored this by calling it a crime.[77]

When investigating the background of human sacrifice, we should also ask the question why and when such sacrifices were made. A general sub-division can be made between sacrifices that were made on a regular basis, according to a calendar of seasonal festivals, and sacrifices that can be considered incidental. The latter could be an extreme measure, applied when reconciliation with a 'superhuman recipient' required an unconventional sacrifice, such as the live interments in the Forum Boarium mentioned above.

1.3.4.1. Sacrifice of the first-born

Given that in many ancient societies children were considered a property of their parents, especially of the father, rather than autonomous human beings, it is not surprising that in societies where human sacrifice was practiced, child sacrifice was more common than the sacrifice of free adults.[78] On one hand this vulnerability of children made them more accessible victims; on the other, we should not underestimate the fact that having a child or children was (and still is in many societies in the Middle East) a matter of social status and a guarantee of care in old age. A childless couple had no future in old age, and a barren woman sank on the social ladder or could be divorced for her infertility.[79] In case of childlessness the man could conceive a child with a slave or handmaid, and consider it his legal heir. Such situations are known from the Old Testament, namely the cases of Abraham and Hagar (Gen. 16:4-15), and the handmaids Bilha (Gen. 35:25) and Zilpah (Gen. 39:9), with whom Jacob had children when Rachel and Leah could not conceive. The practice is also known from Mesopotamian sources.[80] The first-born child, especially when it was a son, was therefore a precious thing and its loss was a step downward on the 'social ladder'.[81] Sacrificing a child, especially the first-born, can therefore be thought of as giving away something of one's self, rather than just a cruel act of which an innocent 'other' is the victim. The sacrifice of Isaac, demanded from Abraham (Gen. 22: 1-19), remains an isolated case in the biblical narrative, although it may be representative of practices in ancient Near Eastern societies. The reason for the demand that YHWH made is not given, apart from the laconic statement 'that God did tempt Abraham'. It stands in contrast to the law given to Moses in Exodus, where YHWH demands the first fruits of the earth and the first born of both man and animal as a regular (annual) sacrifice. Exodus 22:27-29 is unambiguous about this, and it is only in Exodus 34:19-20 that the command is given to redeem the first-born son with the sacrifice of a sheep. Although this redemption makes it very unlikely that child sacrifice actually took place in the official religion of ancient Israel, there are enough reasons to believe that in unofficial ritual it played a role, possibly under the influence of the religious customs of neighbouring states.

An aspect that is rarely mentioned in the discussions concerning child sacrifice is the question what distinguishes a child's sacrifice from that of an adult. In general one could say that a present offered to someone should be something of a good quality and if this applies to presents given by one human to another, it almost goes without saying that a sacrifice to a divinity should be impeccable. This is one of the reasons that the ritual killing of criminals and prisoners of war cannot be seen as sacrifice in the usual sense of offering a present, since the 'victims' are defiled and it is rather their annihilaton that the offering consists of.[82] A number of passages in the Old Testament stress the requirement that all sacrificial animals should be unblemished and free of any defect.[83] In the case of a

---

75   Nótári, 'Some Remarks on ius vitae ac necis'.

76   P.Oxy 4.744 (1 BCE), translation after Lewis, *Life in Egypt under Roman Rule*, 54.

77   Radbill, 'A history of child abuse', 173-179.

78   For a general overview of the position of children in antiquity, see Aasgaard 'Children in Antiquity'.

79   White, 'The Legal Status of Barren Wives', 18-22; Stol, *Women in the Ancient Near East*, 160-163.

80   Van Seters, 'The Problem of Childlessness', 401-408; Grayson and Van Seters, 'The Childless Wife', 485-486.

81   Still today in many Arab countries parents are called father (Abu-...) or mother (Umm-...) of the first-born son.

82   This applies to the ritual killing of enemies like in Egypt; in the case of substituting a criminal for a king, like in Mesopotamia (see above 1.3.2.), the situation is more complicated.

83   Ex. 12:5, Lev. 1:3, 10, 4:3, 23, 28, 22: 24 and several other passages.

human sacrifice an infant would be the perfect specimen of a physically and mentally unblemished victim: innocent and without physical defects. The biblical passages insist on male animals, but in the only case that a female human victim occurs, the daughter of Jephthah (Judg. 11:37), the text stresses that she was a virgin, again a sign of 'purity'. Equally, Iphigeneia was a virgin. Although they were no infants anymore, the virginity of the daughters of Jephthah and Agamemnon was apparently a characteristic of the purity that is a first requirement for a victim.[84]

1.3.4.2. Occasional human sacrifice for reconciliation or rescue

'Extreme situations require extreme measures' – this is how the circumstances of certain cases of human sacrifice can be described. Exceptional events are more likely to become a subject of storytelling, mythology, and even historiography, while everyday routine belongs to the realm of common knowledge and is less likely to be recorded in written sources. The same applies to stories about human sacrifices that took place under exceptional circumstances, be it in fiction or reality. A common element in such stories is that the situation becomes so critical that only a divine intervention or the pacification of a deity can offer relief. In order to secure this, a human victim is sacrificed, in a number of cases even by the father of the victim. In the Bible only a few cases of human sacrifice (committed or avoided) are mentioned, and one of them is described in 2 Kings 3:26-27, where king Mesa of Moab decided to sacrifice his son and successor on the walls of the town of Kir-Chareset when it was besieged by king Jehoram of Judah. Although the biblical narrative does not mention a divine intervention, the sacrifice had the required result in the sense that the Judean army lifted the siege:

> And when the king of Moab saw that the battle was too sore for him, he took with him seven hundred men that drew swords, to break through even unto the king of Edom: but they could not. Then he took his eldest son that should have reigned in his stead, and offered him for a burnt offering upon the wall. And there was great indignation against Israel: and they departed from him, and returned to their own land.

In Greek mythology a number of such sacrifices occur and it is impossible to decide whether such stories refer to actual historical events or comparable cases in a remote past, or whether they should be seen as pure fiction. Seeing myths as 'repositories of obsolete cultural practices' is an attitude that is no longer adhered to, which does not exclude that in certain extreme cases human sacrifice was

practiced in ancient Greece.[85] The story of Iphigeneia is probably the most famous one, but numerous less well-known myths are known in which in most cases young women were the victims.[86]

1.3.5. Self-sacrifice and martyrdom

In the modern-day use, the meaning of the word 'sacrifice' includes a gift made by one person to another, to a god, or for the sake of a higher cause, which requires an effort from the giver, or a gift with which the giver can only part with difficulty. The term 'ultimate sacrifice' is often used for a deed whereby a person loses his or her life for a higher cause, and this implies that human sacrifice can be self-inflicted. Here we are in fact approaching, and even passing the limit of, the definition of sacrifice as a 'transfer of property from the realm of the profane to the realm of the sacred'. A person can put his or her own life at risk to save someone else, or die for the sake of his or her conscience, as in the case of hungerstrikers protesting against totalitarian regimes. In such cases there is often no 'recipient' of the sacrifice, apart from the fact that a community and/or an ideology could benefit from the death of a person often referred to as a martyr. Martyrdom, self-sacrifice, and the so-called 'noble death' are three categories that can overlap, but are by no means identical.[87] In recent years the world has been confronted with countless acts that were called 'self-sacrifice' or 'martyrdom' by Muslim radicals, but which were more commonly condemned as terrorism. Whether a death is noble or not, and whether a suicidal death or self-sacrice is an act of heroism, usually depends on the ideological point of view of the commenter or narrator, unless there is no ideology or religion involved, as in the case of a firefighter who puts his or her life at risk to save a victim. Human sacrifice may have occurred in ancient Greece and the Roman Republic on a sporadic base. Noble death and self-sacrifice, however, were well-known and respected in Graeco-Roman antiquity, although they are different phenomena that can have little in common. The death of the philosopher for reasons of principle, of which the self-poisoning of Aristotle is the most famous example, is of an entirely different category than the heroic death of a soldier who sacrifices his life to give victory to the others fighting with him. Jan Willem van Henten, who also mentions the sacrifice of Iphigeneia as an example of noble death, does not distinguish between the motivations behind these voluntary deaths.[88] The deaths of the philosopher and the military hero have no direct religious implications,

---

84   In chapters 5 and 6 the phenomenon of child sacrifice in Carthage and Israel will be dealt with in greater detail.

85   Hughes, *Human Sacrifice*, 71-73.

86   Hughes, *Human Sacrifice*, 73.

87   Van Henten, 'Noble Death and Martyrdom', 91-95.

88   Van Henten and Avemaria, *Martyrdom and Noble Death*, 9-41; Van Henten, 'Self-sacrifice and substitution'.

since they do not sacrifice themselves to a god, but first of all for the sake of a principle or the safety of others. In the play by Euripides, Iphigeneia eventually agrees to be sacrificed for the sake of her father's atonement for offences against Artemis, but also to enable the fleet to sail to Troy. An aspect of self-denial for the common sake and a religious dimension are combined in other stories as well. Livy (*Ab Urbe Condita* VII, 6) relates how at a certain moment in the year 362 BCE a bottomless sinkhole opened in the Forum Romanum. After failed efforts to fill it with earth, soothsayers announced that the gods want the most precious possession that Rome has to be thrown into the chasm. Marcus Curtius, a young soldier decided that this most precious thing is the arms and courage of Rome's men, and in full armour, mounted on his horse, he rode into the abyss, which closed itself, leaving only a pond, the Lacus Curtius, behind. It is just one of the explanations that were given in antiquity for the Lacus Curtius, but it seems related to a probably older story, presented by Pseudo-Plutarch in the *Parallela Minora*. In this narrative, a similar hole opened in the city of Celaenae in Phrygia and was closed after king Midas' son Anchurus rode into it.[89] In both stories an oracle conveys the demand of the gods for a sacrifice; Pseudo-Plutarch identifies the god as Jupiter in a slightly different version of the Marcus Curtius story that he also relates, while in the story of Anchurus an altar for the Idaean Zeus is erected after the incident.[90] These stories give an interesting combination of ingredients, in which human self-sacrifice is the main theme, not only as an example of a heroic/noble death, but also with the allusion that it is a god who demands such a sacrifice.

1.4. Concluding remarks

The ritual killing of humans has many different aspects and has occurred throughout history in many cultures and in various forms. A proper understanding of this phenomenon starts with a categorisation, for which a distinction between human sacrifice and ritual killing of other kinds is necessary. Although a ritual is in general an act or a sequence of acts that is performed in a strictly directed way, the ritual killing of humans is surrounded by emotions that belong, if not in the first place to the ones involved, then to the contemporaries from other cultures who witness the killing or have their opinion about it. A recurring response of outsiders is that of disapproval, the killing being considered a symptom or barbarity of the other culture, religion, or ethnic group. This can be an honestly felt objection against an unfamiliar custom, sometimes based on rumours or misinformation; it can also be a deliberate attempt to defame 'the other', not rarely to be used in a next phase as a justification for violence against this group of 'others'. These various emotions, and, as a result of them, deliberate or undeliberate distortions in the image of reality, make it difficult to draw a reliable picture of the actual events. The written sources concerning ritual homicide are almost never unbiased and eyewitness accounts are not available. An additional problem is that the lens through which modern scholars examine the material does not always sharpen this blurred image, as the researchers' own emotions can stand in the way of an unbiased analysis. A proper understanding of ritual homicide in all its forms and varieties requires a total detachment from emotions that accompany modern values and standards.

---

89 *Paralelli minori*, in Plutarch. *Moralia* IV, translation Cole Babbitt, 267.

90 The *Parallela Minora* also gives the story of Marcus Curtius in a slightly different form (see note 85). For an elaborate study on the Lacus Curtius and its background, see Riera Begué, *The Lacus Curtius.*

1.5. References

Aasgaard, Reidar, 'Children in Antiquity and Early Christianity: Research History and Central Issues', *Familia, Revista de Ciencias y Orientación Familiar* 33 (2006), 23-46.

Adams, Richard E.W., *Prehistoric Mesoamerica* (Norman, 1991).

Adams, W.Y., *Nubia, Corridor to Africa* (Princeton, 1984).

Albert, Jean-Pierre and Beatrix Midant-Reynes, eds, *Le sacrifice humain en Egypte ancienne et ailleurs* (Paris, 2005).

Brelich, Angelo, *Presupposti del Sacrificio Umano* (Rome, 1967).

Bremmer, Jan N., 'Myth and Ritual in Greek Human Sacrifice: Lykaion, Polyxena and the Case of the Rhodian Criminal', in Jan Bremmer, ed., *The Strange World of Human Sacrifice*, (Leuven, Paris, Dudley, MA, 2007), 55-79.

Bremmer, Jan N., 'Early Christian Human Sacrifice between Fact and Fiction', in Àgnes Nagy and Fransesca Prescendi, eds, *Sacrifices humains. Dossiers, discours, comparaisons*, (Turnhout, 2013), 165-176.

Burkert, Walter, *Homo Nectans, Interpretationen Altgriechischer Opferriten und Mythen*, (Berlin, 1972).

Compagno, Marallo, 'Sur un régicide obscur', in Jean-Pierre Albert and Beatrix Midant-Reynes, eds, *Le sacrifice humain en Egypte ancienne et ailleurs* (Paris, 2005), 136-147.

Dann, Rachael J., 'Changing patterns of violence at Qustul and Ballana in the post-Meroitic period. Part One: The Humans', *Der Antike Sudan, Mitteilungen der Sudanrchäologischen Gesellschaft zu Berlin* 18 (2007), 189-200.

Dijk, Jacobus van, 'Retainer sacrifice in Egypt and in Nubia', in Jan Bremmer, ed., *The Strange World of Human Sacrifice*, (Leuven, Paris, Dudley, MA, 2007), 135-156.

Diodorus Siculus, *The Library of History*, translation by Russel M. Geer, Loeb Classical Library 390 (Boston, 1954).

Dölger, Franz Joseph, 'Sacramentum infanticidii' in *Antike und Christentum* IV, (Münster in Wf, 1934), 188-228.

Emery, W.B., *The Royal Tombs of Ballana and Qustul*, 2 vols. (Cairo, 1938).

Engel, David, 'Patterns Of Anti-Jewish Violence In Poland, 1944-1946', *Yad Vashem Studies* Vol. XXVI (1998), 43-85, accessed 7-5-2017, http://www.yadvashem.org/odot_pdf/Microsoft%20Word%20-%203128.pdf.

Epiphanius of Salamis, *Panarion*, translation by Frank Williams (Leiden, 1987).

Frankfurter, David, *Religion in Roman Egypt, Assimilation and Resistance* (Princeton, 1998).

Frazer, J.G., *The Golden Bough, a Study in Magic and Religion*, III, *The Dying God* (London, 1911).

Girard, René, *La violence et le sacré* (Paris, 1972).

Grayson, A. K. and J. Van Seters, 'The Childless Wife in Assyria and the Stories of Genesis', *Orientalia*, nova series, 44.4 (1975), 485-486.

Green, Alberto, *The Role of Human Sacrifice in the Ancient Near East*, American Schools of Oriental Research Series 1 (Missoula, MT., 1975).

Grottanelli, C., *Il sacrificio* (Rome, Bari, 1999).

Henrichs, Albert, 'Pagan ritual and the Alleged Crimes of the Early Christians', in P. Granfield and J.A. Jungmann, eds, *Kyriakon, Festschrift Johannes Quasten*, (Münster in Wf., 1970), 18-35.

Henten, Jan Willem van, and Friedrich Avemaria, *Martyrdom and Noble Death, Selected Texts from Graeco-Roman, Jewish, and Christian Antiquity*, (London, New York, 2002).

Henten, Jan Willem van, 'Noble Death and Martyrdom in Antiquity', in Sebastian Fuhrmann and Regina Grundmann, eds, *Martyriumsvorstellungen in Antike und Mittelalter* (Leiden, Boston, 2012), 85-110.

Henten, Jan Willem van, 'Self-sacrifice and substitution in Geeek and Roman Literature', in Michael Hüttendorf, Wolfgang Kraus, and Karlo Meyer, eds, *«...mein Blut für Euch» Theologische Perspektiven zum Verständnis des Todes Jesu heute.* (Göttingen, 2018), 63-78.

Heusch, Luc de, 'La mort sacrificielle des rois africaines', in Jean-Pierre Albert and Beatrix Midant-Reynes, eds, *Le sacrifice humain en Egypte ancienne et ailleurs* (Paris, 2005), 148-155.

Hirschberg, Walter, *Die Kulturen Afrikas*, vol. 15 in Eugen Thurnher, ed., Handbuch der Kulturgeschichte (Konstanz, 1963).

Hornung, E. and E. Staehelin, *Studien zum Sedfest* (Basel, Geneva, 1974).

Hubert, Henri and Marcel Mauss, *Sacrifice: its Nature and Function* (London, 1964).

Hughes, D.D., *Human Sacrifice in Ancient Greece* (London, 1991).

Huntington, Richard and Peter Metcalf, *Celebrations of Death, the Anthropology of Mortuary Ritual* (London, New York, Melbourne, 1979).

Julius Caesar, *De Bello Gallico*, translation by H.J. Edwards, Loeb Classical Library 72, (Boston, 1917).

Kantorowicz, Ernst, *The King's Two Bodies: A Study in Mediaeval Political Theology* (Princeton, 1957).

Kinnaer, Jacques, 'Human sacrifice', *The Ancient Egypt Site*, 8-10-2014, accessed 13-5-2017, http://www.ancient-egypt.org/from-a-to-z/h/human-sacrifice.html.

Koch, John T. and John Carey, eds, *The Celtic Heroic Age* (Malden, Massachusetts, 1995).

Lepsius, Karl Richard, *Denkmäler* Abtheilung II, Band III (Berlin, 1949), 2, 39, accessed 15-6-2017, http://edoc3.bibliothek.uni-halle.de/lepsius/tafelwa2.html.

Lewis, Naphtali, *Life in Egypt under Roman Rule* (Oxford, 1986).

McGowan, Andrew, 'Eating People: Accusations of Cannibalism Against Christians in the Second Century', *Journal of Early Christian Studies* 2.4 (1994), 413-442.

Muhlestein, Kerry, 'Sacred Violence: When Ancient Egyptian Punishment was Dressed in Ritual Trappings', *Near Eastern Archaeology* 78.4 (2015), 244-251.

Nagy, Àgnes and Fransesca Prescendi, eds, *Sacrifices humains. Dossiers, discours, comparaisons* (Turnhout, 2013).

Ndiaye, Saliou, 'Minime Romano sacro, à propos des sacrifices humains à Rome à l'époque républicaine' *Dialogues d'Histoire Ancienne* 26.1 (2000), 119-128.

Nock, Arthur Darby, 'Greek Novels and Egyptian Religion', in *Essays on Religion and the Ancient World* I (Oxford, 1972), 169-75.

Nótári, Tamás, 'Some Remarks on ius vitae ac necis and ius exponendi', *Journal on European History of Law* 2 (2011), 28-38.

Oort, H., *Het Menschenoffer in Israel* (Haarlem, 1865).

Plutarch, *Moralia* II, *De Superstitione* 13,1, translation by Frank Cole Babbitt, Loeb Classical Library 222 (Cambridge MA, 1928).

Po-Chia Hsia, R., *Trent 1475: Stories of a Ritual Murder Trial* (New Haven, 1992).

Pseudo-Plutarch, *Paralelli minori*, in Plutarch, *Moralia* IV, translation by Frank Cole Babbitt, Loeb Classical Library 305 (Cambridge MA, 1936), 253-320.

Radbill, Samuel X., 'A history of child abuse and infanticide', in Suzanne K. Steinmetz and Murray A. Straus, eds, *Violence in the Family* (New York, 1974), 173-179.

Reinold, Jacques, 'Kadruka and the Neolithic in the Northern Dongola Reach' *Sudan and Nubia* 5 (2001), 2-10.

Reisner, G., *Excavations at Kerma* III, Harvard African Studies V (Cambridge, Mass., 1923) 61-528.

Ribichini, Sergio, 'Beliefs and Religious Life' in Sabatino Moscati, ed., *The Phoenicians* (Venice, 1988), 120-152.

Riera Begué, Pablo, *The Lacus Curtius in the Forum Romanum and the Dynamics of Memory*, MA thesis, Radboud University, Nijmegen, 2017, accessed 15-12-2020, https://theses.ubn.ru.nl/bitstream/handle/123456789/5181/Riera_Begu%C3%A9%2C_Pablo_1.pdf?sequence=1.

Roig Lanzillotta, Lautaro, 'The Early Christians and Human Sacrifice', in Jan Bremmer, ed., *The Strange World of Human Sacrifice* (Leuven, Paris, Dudley, MA, 2007), 81-102.

Sakellarakis, Yannis and Efi Sapouna-Sakellaraki, 'Drama of Death in a Minoan Temple', *National Geographic* 159(1981), 205-223.

Schnepel, Burkhard, 'Continuity despite and through Death: Regicide and Royal Shrines among the Shilluk of Southern Sudan', *Africa: Journal of the International African Institute* 61.1 (1991), 40-70.

Schulmann, Alan R., *Ceremonial Execution and Public Reward* (Göttingen, 1988).

Schultz, Celia E., 'The Romans and Ritual Murder' *Journal of the American Academy of Religion* 78, 2, (2010), 516-541.

Schultz, Celia E., 'Roman Sacrifice, Inside and Out' *Journal of Roman Studies* 106 (2016), 58-76.

Schwartz, Jeffrey H., Frank Houghton, Roberto Macchiarelli, Luca Bondioli, 'Skeletal remains from Punic Carthage do not support systematic sacrifice of infants', in *PloS ONE* 5.2 (February 2010), accessed 7-5-2017, https://doi.org/10.1371/journal.pone.0009177.

Stager, Lawrence and Samuel. R. Wolff. 'Child sacrifice in Carthage: religious rite or population control?', *Journal of Biblical Archeological Review* 10.1 (1984), 30-51.

Stager, Lawrence, *Rites of Spring in the Carthaginian Tophet* (Leiden, 2014).

Stol, Marten, *Women in the Ancient Near East* (Boston, Berlin, 2016).

Testart, Alain, 'Doit-on parler de "sacrifice" à propos des morts d'accompagnement?', in Jean-Pierre Albert and Béatrix Midant-Reynes, eds, *Le sacrifice humain en Égypte ancienne et ailleurs* (Paris, 2005), 34-57.

Török, László, *Between Two Worlds: The Frontier Region Between Ancient Nubia and Egypt 3700 BC – 500 AD* (Leiden, 2008).

Urbanus, Jason, 'Murder on the Mountain?', *Archaeology* November/December 2016, accessed 20-12-2020, https://www.archaeology.org/issues/233-1611/trenches/4921-trenches-greece-mt-lykaion-grave.

Utz, Richard, 'The Medieval myth of Jewish ritual murder: toward a history of literary reception', in *The Year's Work in Medievalism* 14 (1999), 22-43.

Varner, G.R., *Sacred Wells: A Study in the History, Meaning, and Mythology of Holy Wells & Waters* (New York, 2009).

Van Seters, John, 'The Problem of Childlessness in near Eastern Law and the Patriarchs of Israel', *Journal of Biblical Literature*, 87.4 (1968), 401-408.

Vandier, Jacques, *Le Papyrus Jumilhac* (Paris, 1961).

Velde, Herman te, 'Human Sacrifice in Ancient Egypt', in Jan N. Bremmer, ed., *The Strange World of Human Sacrifice* (Leuven, Paris, Dudley, MA, 2007), 127-134.

Vlazaki-Andreadaki, Maria, 'Sacrifices in LM IIIB: early Kydonia palatial centre' in *Pasiphae, Rivista di Filologia e Antichità Egee* 9 (2015), Actes du colloque international "le sacrifice humain dans le monde égéen et dans les civilisations périphériques", Milano, 27-28 octobre 2014, 27-42.

Vliet, Jacques van der, 'Spätantikes Heidentum in Ägypten im Spiegel der koptischen Literatur' *Riggisberger Berichte* 1 (1993), 99-130.

White, Kayla, 'The Legal Status of Barren Wives in the Ancient Near East', *The Priscilla Papers* 28.4 (2014) 18-22.

Wilkinson, Toby A.H., *Early Dynastic Egypt* (London, New York, 1999).

Willems, Harco, 'Crime, Cult and Capital Punishment (Mo'alla inscription 8)', *Journal of Egyptian Archaeology* 76 (1990), 27-54.

Woolley, C.L., *Ur Excavations: The Royal Cemetery*, II (London, Philadelphia, 1934).

Woolley, C.L., *Ur Excavations: The Early Periods*, IV (Philadelphia, 1955).

Woolley, C.L., *Excavations at Ur* (London, 1955).

Yoyotte, J., 'Héra d'Héliopolis et le sacrifice humain', *Annuaire de l'Ecole Pratique des Hautes Etudes* 89 (1980-81) 31-102, reprinted in Jean Yoyotte, *Histoire, géographie et religion de l'Égypte ancienne. Opera selecta* OLA 224 (Leuven, 2013), 1-75.

Chapter 2

Ritual killing of humans in ancient Mesopotamia

Theo J.H. Krispijn*

2.1. Introduction

There is a striking beauty in the ornamental objects found in the Royal Tombs of Ur in southern Mesopotamia. When seeing them for the first time, one is confronted with their unbelievable splendour, but one is horrified to realize that the people who used these objects were killed deliberately to join the princes and dignitaries in their tombs. What moved people to do this? Is this phenomenon particularly prevalent in Mesopotamia and Syria? These are some of the questions to be discussed in this article.

Not only do the royal graves need to be discussed, but also the killing of the substitute king in Mesopotamia deserves further consideration in the context of mortuary rituals. And what about the abuse and execution of prisoners-of-war depicted on cylinder seals from the Uruk period, the earliest period in the history of Mesopotamia? These are important questions to be raised when discussing the cultural history of the ancient Near East.

2.2. The archaeological evidence

2.2.1. The royal tombs of Ur

Sir Leonard Woolley, when excavating Ur, found among the many graves on the south side of the temple complex dedicated to the moon god Nanna. In the descending corridor adjacent to the tomb or in the tomb chamber itself he discovered the remains of servants who had been killed for the purpose of being buried here.[1]

These graves can be dated to a short period of the 25th century BCE. They are unique in southern Mesopotamia, although possible traces of such burials connected with ritual killings have been noticed in Kish.[2] The stratigraphy of the royal graves of Ur is extremely complex. Some graves overlap and parts of an underlying grave are lost. Recent research has clarified the conditions under which these deaths could have occurred.[3]

---

1   Woolley, *Royal Cemetery*, 33-42, 62-91, 112-124.
2   There were chariot burials in cemetery Y at Kish, sometimes with three chariots (Gibson Kiš B, 616-617). Due to the poor techniques of excavation at the time it is difficult to determine which skeletons to associate with the chariots and whether similar ritual human killing was involved here.
3   Moorey, 'Cemetery A'.

*Leiden University

Figure 2.1 Puabi's Headdress PG 800. After: Zettler, R.L. and Horne, L. Treasures of the Royal Tombs of Ur (Pennsylvania 1998), 91 Fig. 29. Courtesy of the Penn Museum, image no. 299835.

Woolley quickly gave the name 'Great Death Pit' to the grave PG 1237 (fig. 2.2) because of the large number of skeletons he found in the corridor adjacent to the tomb. Unfortunately, the tomb had been robbed leaving only the remains of three bodies in the tomb chamber. Although we do not know who was buried there, the valuable items of dress and the number of servants who had been deliberately killed make it clear that it is the grave of a very high dignitary if not of the king himself. The approach to the tomb was filled with 74 skeletons, mostly female. Alongside there were also the remains of soldiers, wagon drivers, and musicians with stringed instruments, singers with beautiful headdresses and other male and female servants.

In fact, three tombs can be distinguished at locations PG 789 (figs. 2.3-4) and PG 800 (fig. 2.5). The 'Death Pit' of 'servants' associated with PG 789 is often called the King's grave in the literature. Three skeletons were found in the tomb chamber, and in the corridor outside 63 skeletons. Most of these were of women, but also of soldiers with full accoutrements and chariots drawn by oxen, of

musicians with their instruments and singers with beautiful jewellery. PG 800 contained the body of Queen *Pû-abi* or *Pûm-abum*[4]; a seal found next to one of the two bodies there had the inscription "*Pû-abi* queen" (fig. 2.6).

In addition to the beautiful headdress there were jewellery and gold cups. Outside the tomb chamber in the corridor, which Woolley linked to this grave, 21 servants were found, including a lyre player (fig. 2.7) with his instrument, a wagon driver with his wagon drawn by mules, and a number of women with gold headdresses and rings.

Now we doubt whether this death pit belongs to PG 800. It is more likely that it belongs to a third lost grave chamber, and that PG 800 had no 'death pit' and is older than the actual 'death pit'.[5] The earthenware from the tomb chamber at PG 800 had been imported from the Habur region in the Middle Euphrates, as had some pieces from PG 1648.

Tomb PG 1648 (fig. 2.8 a-b) has a much smaller chamber than those discussed above. A reconstruction of that tomb based on Woolley's field notes[6] gives a better picture than that in the official publication.[7] In the stone coffin there was the almost totally perished body of a man with jewellery and pottery. Against his chest were the skeletons of at least four people: a girl, a woman, a boy and a man. In the same tomb the remains of more bodies were found.

2.2.2. Skeletal investigations of the 'Royal tombs' of Ur

In 2003 experts from the British Museum and the Natural History Museum in London re-examined the skeletons of the Royal tombs. They largely confirmed earlier findings[8], but reinterpreted them, highlighting a number of interesting phenomena rarely apparent in other skeletons.[9] Some of the male skeletons are very robust, especially those in PG 1648, and show traces of deformation as a result of bearing heavy loads and enduring hard work from an early age. The teeth and molars were worn, showing that their diet was restricted to almost only cereal products. These were not members of the social elite here, but rather slaves or prisoners-of-war who had been given as servants in the grave. The singers, adorned with beautiful headdresses, from PG 1237, on the other hand, were pretty young girls with fine teeth. Some (but not all) skulls in the 'death pits' were dented from a sudden impact. The servants must have

---

4   Marchesi, 'Royal Tombs of Ur', 175, 177, 194.
5   Zimmerman, 'Two Tombs or Three'.
6   Molleson and Hodgson, 'Human Remains', 100-105.
7   Woolley *Royal Cemetery*, 133-134.
8   Keith, 'Human Remains 1927', 'Human Remains 1934' and unpublished.
9   Molleson-Hodgson, 'Human Remains' and Baadsgaard et al., 'Human Sacrifice'; Baadsgaard et al., 'Bludgeoned'.

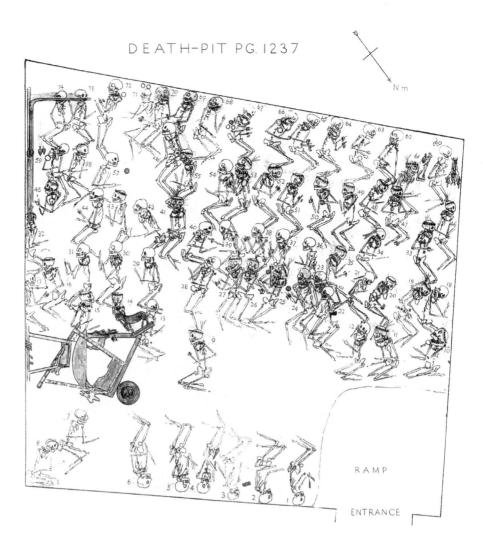

Figure 2.2 Plan of PG 1237, the 'Great Death Pit'. After: Zettler, R.L. and Horne, L. Treasures of the Royal Tombs of Ur (Pennsylvania 1998), 24 Fig. 24. Courtesy of the Penn Museum, image no. 141592.

been deliberately killed, which can be deduced from the size of the dent that shows that the final blow was given when the servant was still alive).[10]

Woolley found a large copper kettle and cups beside the bodies of the servants and concluded that they had voluntarily surrendered themselves to death and that they must have taken a lethal drink from the cups that were filled from the copper kettle.[11] This hypothesis has been challenged. Charvát wonders if this is a reburial[12]; Sürenhagen does not exclude burials from different periods[13]; Baadsgaard and Cohen point out that not all the skeletons had cups, and that a funeral ritual involved a bout of drinking.[14]

A number of skeletons also show traces of being exposed to heat and being treated with mercury sulphide. In antiquity heating or smoking was used as a method to counteract putrefaction; mercury sulphide is a preservative. So the corpses may have been exposed for a few days during the mourning rituals. Baadsgaard proposes various stages in the procedure. With a blow to the head from an axe the servants were killed outside the grave. The corpses were heated and treated with mercury sulphide. They were formally clothed as if they had participated in the funeral feast. The cups, the big pot and the musical instruments completed the picture.[15]

---

10   Baadsgaard et al., 'Bludgeoned', 143.
11   Woolley, *Royal Cemetery*, 36, 42.
12   Charvát, *Mesopotamia*, 224-226.
13   Sürenhagen, 'Royal Tombs'.
14   Baadsgaard, 'Bludgeoned'; Cohen, *Death rituals*, 80-93.
15   Baadsgaard, 'Human sacrifice', 38-39; see also Katz, 'Funerary Rituals', 174-182.

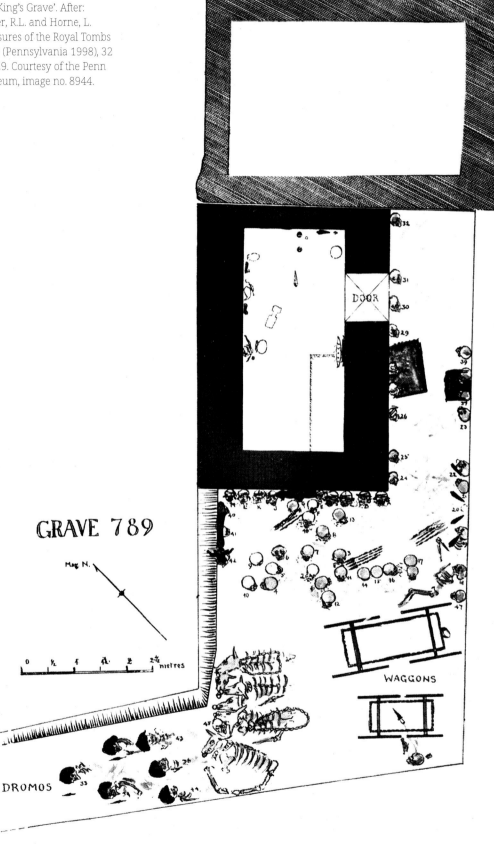

Figure 2.3 Plan of PG 789 the 'King's Grave'. After: Zettler, R.L. and Horne, L. Treasures of the Royal Tombs of Ur (Pennsylvania 1998), 32 Fig. 29. Courtesy of the Penn Museum, image no. 8944.

GRAVE 789

Mag. N.

0 ½ f 1½ 2 2½ metres

DOOR

WAGGONS

DROMOS

THE VALUE OF A HUMAN LIFE

Figure 2.4 An artist impression of the scene in PG 789 just before the death of the royal retainers. After: The Illustrated London News, June 23, 1928, 1172-1174 and Zettler, R.L. and Horne, L. Treasures of the Royal Tombs of Ur (Pennsylvania 1998), 38 Fig. 35. Wikimedia commons 14767118682.

2.2.3. The interpretation of ritual killing of humans in the Royal Tombs of Ur

Andrew Cohen proposes that the ritual originated from changes in state ideology.[16] In the early ED III period a new ideology gave the royal palace an important role. Votive gifts from that period show that the subjects of their king and master desired to see his kingship continue *post mortem*. Professionals performed a ritual around the dead ruler in which servants played a role in the ceremonial drinking. Seeing the richly decorated dead body of the ruler was an experience similar to seeing the image of a god. The presentation of funerary offerings represented the idea that the keeping the dead in the world of the living was beneficial. There might have been a direct association with fertility from witnessing sacrifices made in agricultural festivals. These sacrifices not only honoured the dead but also the living ruler. The new ruler was connected to his predecessor in this ritual. The ruler was buried with military attributes to reinforce the idea that he could also support his military successor. Because

the living ruler in these funeral rites was connected to the deceased predecessor and thus to the world of the gods, it gave him authority and access to the divine world.

Susan Pollock emphasizes the aspect of loyalty, one that leads to establishing interpersonal relationships, identity and obedience.[17] Premature death is the ultimate sign of loyalty in the funerary ritual. The human victims create this relationship.[18] Those sacrificed participate in an eternal meal (no storage vessels were provided) and thus participate in this relationship. In practice it is difficult to distinguish between the killing of prisoners-of-war and other socially acceptable executions. But a funerary execution transforms the victim to become someone in another world. Bruce Dickson explains the ritual killings of the servants from the conflict theory in combination with the idea of permanent structural violence.[19] The state trades off structural violence by providing protection to its subjects. Vulnerable, disposable and insignificant persons may be sacrificed.

---

16 Cohen, *Death rituals*.

17 Pollock, 'Death of a Household'.
18 Porter, 'Mortal Mirrors'.
19 Dickson, 'Kingship'.

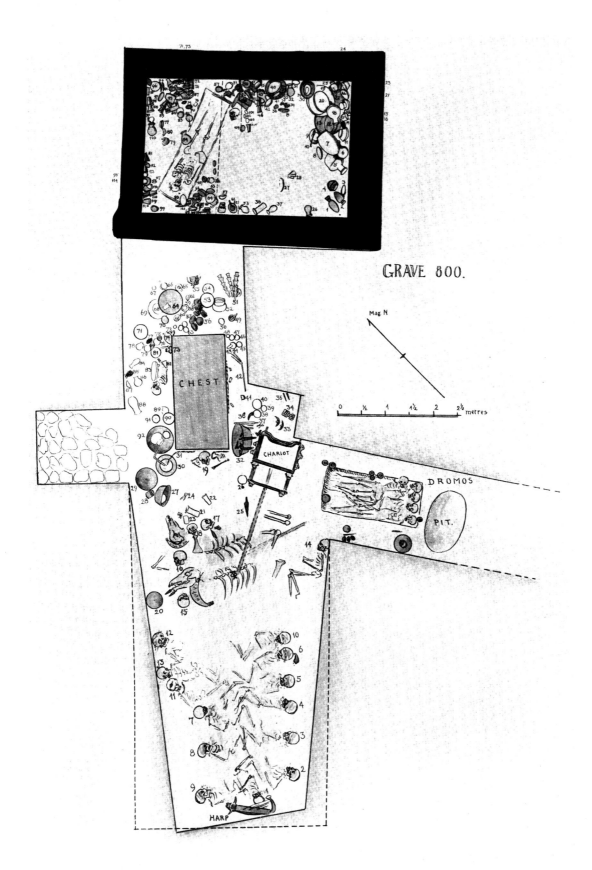

Figure 2.5 Plan of PG 800, Puabi's Tomb. After: Zettler, R.L. and Horne, L. Treasures of the Royal Tombs of Ur (Pennsylvania 1998), 34 Fig. 31. Courtesy of the Penn Museum, image no. 56378.

Figure 2.6 Impression of one of Puabi's seals. After: Zettler, R.L. and Horne, L. Treasures of the Royal Tombs of Ur (Pennsylvania 1998), 78 Fig. 46b. Courtesy of the Penn Museum, image no. 152075.

2.3. Excavated traces of ritual killing of humans in northern Mesopotamia

Tomb nr. 1 in Arslan Tepe (Malatya region, Turkey) (fig. 2.9) dates from the end of the third millennium BCE.[20]

It is a simple stone grave of which the roof had collapsed when found, the tomb of a young man aged 35-40. He must have been of high rank, since no less than 64 items, including much jewellery, were found in the grave. The remains of two young women, aged 16-18 years, without any jewellery, had been placed on the roof. No traces of violence were found on these skeletons. The upper parts of the skeletons of two young men, adorned with jewellery, were also found, and these had no traces of violence either. Were they all poisoned before being interred? The amount of dust in the grave suggests that it was only after a year that the roof was placed on the grave, on which the younger corpses were laid.

The excavations in Shioukh Tahtani (fig. 2.10), 150 km south of Arslan Tepe, also yielded a remarkable grave from the middle of the third millennium BCE.[21] It was the grave of a very young child of about two years old, which had been buried in a jar (found broken) and of an adult, buried with numerous funerary gifts and earthenware. From this we conclude that it was a high status tomb.

Next to the grave pit the excavator found the skeletons of two adults and another child, apparently additional burials. They had no funerary gifts but had been formally clothed, judging from the fact that cloak pins in the form of a cross were found. These special pins may be and indication for the special clothing these persons (who

Figure 2.7 Frontside of the Great Lyre from the 'Kings Grave' PG 789. After Zettler, R.L. and Horne, L. Treasures of the Royal Tombs of Ur (Pennsylvania 1998), 53 3. Courtesy of the Penn Museum, image no. 297042.

may have been ceremonially killed) would have been wearing at the funerary rituals.[22]

At Umm el-Marra there was also a special grave (no. 1) (fig. 2.11 a-c) from the end of the third millennium.[23] In it two young women had been buried with much jewellery, including a golden headband with a frontal disk, together with two infants.

Two men, one wearing a silver headband, had been buried in the same layer as well as another infant. Another body had been buried below. There were no traces of disease or violence detected and they all died at about the same time. This could be taken as evidence that the bodies placed beside the young woman were ritually killed.

---

20 Porter, 'Mortal Mirrors', 195-199.
21 Porter, 'Mortal Mirrors', 199-201.

---

22 Compare the man with the red cloak described in one of the Hittite examples of ritual human killing (KUB 9.8 Rev. 8; Kümmel, *Ersatzrituale*, 159).
23 Porter, 'Mortal Mirrors', 201-202.

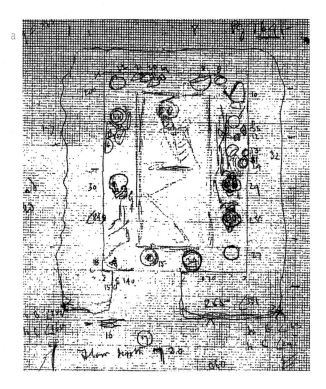

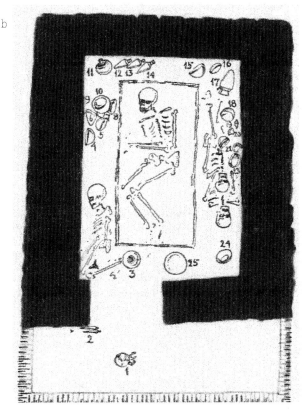

Figure 2.8 a-b Page from Woolley's field notebook and the official publication of PG 1648. After: Molleson and Hodgson, 'The Human Remains', 101 Fig. 6 and Woolley, *Royal Cemetery*, 133 Fig. 26.

2.4. Textual evidence of ritual killing

2.4.1. Prisoners-of-war

Probably one of the earliest mentions of ritually killing prisoners-of-war is in a text from Ebla, a long list of monthly textile allocations:

> 7 different types of garments for the three *badalums* from AN'arum who were killed (?) (Sumerian logogram TIL) in the temple of Hadda.
>
> (Ebla-Akkadian; Tell Mardikh / Ebla TM.75.G.2417; approx. 2400 BCE; II 14-III 2.)[24]

A campaign to the city of An'arum, which the vizier Ibrium undertook together with the king of Kakmium in his fourteenth year, is mentioned at the beginning of this text. That city was a city situated north of Ebla towards Harran. The person in highest authority there was called a *badalum*, a term perhaps originally concerned with trade and then for a city ruler. Ibrium conquered An'arum and received rewards on his return. Girra-Malik, who reported the victory to Ebla, is also mentioned among those who receive clothes. But how should we interpret the Sumerian logogram *TIL* in this passage? It could mean "to die" or "to be killed". Occasionally garments were presented to those who brought home the severed heads of enemies. So the three city rulers may have been killed in that way. It is interesting that they were not just killed but also presented (as sacrifices?) to Hadda, as ritual killings. This conforms to the practice of maltreatment and killing of prisoners-of-war. In the early iconography of the Uruk period we see depictions of prisoners-of-war on cylinder seals impressions from about 3300-3200 BCE[25]; they are also known from the Neo-Assyrian period and Urartian inscriptions.[26]

2.4.2. References to ritual killing in literary texts

Hardly any references to the ritual killing of humans are known from literary texts. An exception is a more or less direct reference to people who go with their king to the underworld, which occurs in the Sumerian text *The Death of Gilgamesh*. A richly decorated stone tomb was built on the dried out bed of the Euphrates, which would forever remain hidden under water. Then the text continues:

---

24 Biga, 'Sacrificio umano', 171.
25 Boehmer, *Uruk Siegelabrollungen*, 20-24, 27-29 and Fig. 12.
26 Klengel, 'Kriegsgefangene'.

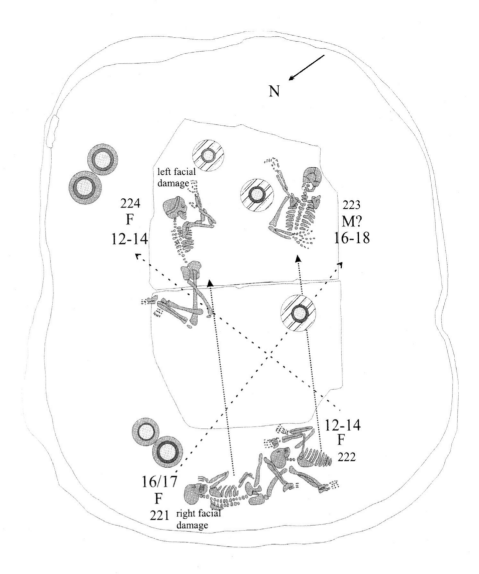

Figure 2.9 Human deposition on top of Tomb 1, Arslantepe. After: Porter, 'Mortal Mirrors', 197 Fig. 1. Courtesy of Dr. Anne Porter and Dr. Glenn Schwartz.

His beloved wife, his beloved children, his beloved favourite and junior wife, his beloved musician, cup-bearer and ......, his beloved barber, his beloved ......, his beloved palace retainers and servants and his beloved objects were laid down in their places as if ...... in the purified (?) palace in the middle of Uruk.[27]

Apparently several persons closely related to him were "laid down" in the tomb, an arrangement closely resembling the personnel of the court on the day of a palace inspection.

In the hymn about the death of King Urnamma, the founder of the Ur III dynasty, Urnamma and Gilgamesh are described as judges over dead soldiers and criminals in the netherworld:

---

27   Death of Gilgamesh Another version 1-7 (Sumerian, approx.1800 BCE) Translation: Electronic Text Corpus of Sumerian Literature (ETCSL) http://etcsl.orinst.ox.ac.uk/cgi-bin/etcsl. cgi?text=t.1.8.1.3&display=Crit&charenc=gcirc&lineid=t1813.p16#t1813.p16.

a   b   c

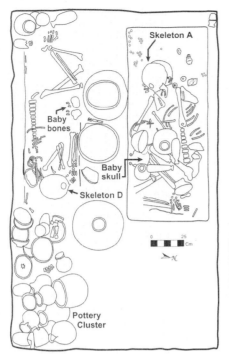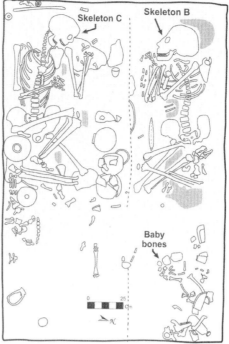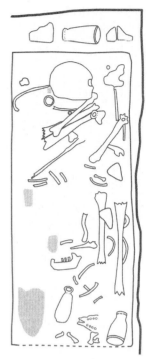

Figure 2.11a-c Three levels of Tomb 1 Umm el Marra. After: Schwartz, 'A Third Millennium Elite Tomb', Fig. 6, 19, 22. Courtesy of Dr. Anne Porter and Dr. Glenn Schwartz.

They seated Urnamma under the great canopy (*bara2*) of the Nether World and set up a dwelling place for him in the Nether World. At the command of Ereškigala all the soldiers who had been killed by weapons and all the men who had been found guilty were given into the king's hands. Urnamma was ......, so with Gilgamesh, his beloved brother, he will conduct the trials of the nether world and render the verdicts of the Nether World.[28]

Lines 139-140 are particularly interesting, saying that slain soldiers and executed criminals are 'put in the hands' of Urnamma, but unfortunately the following line is corrupted and gives no further help in understanding this passage. The Sumerian expression 'to put in the hands of' (*šu-šè sum*) can sometimes refer literally to handing over concrete objects. Therefore it is not inconceivable here that it refers to soldiers and criminals being added to the grave.

2.4.3. Ritual killing in Hittite texts

Hans Kümmel collected examples of ritual human killing in his book on the rituals for the substitute for the king. Most cases concern the killing of prisoners-of-war.[29]

When the troops are defeated by the enemy, the following sacrifice is made on the other side of the river: On the other side of the river you cut a man, a goat, a young dog and a young pig in half, placing one half on one side and the other half on the other side. To this end, you make a gate of hawthorn-wood and a rope on the top. Then the gate is burned on one side and on the other side. Then the (defeated) troops pass through (this gate).[30]

This does not explicitly mention prisoners-of-war, but that is likely from the context, since the troops of the defeated enemy are mentioned. In other examples of human sacrifice we find prisoners (including those of war) and other people mentioned together with young pigs, parts of dogs or other sacrificial animals.[31] In one text even human meat is prepared.[32]

---

28   Urnamma Hymn A line 136-144 (Sumerian approx. 1800 BCE) ETCSL with some deviations in italics http://etcsl.orinst.ox.ac.uk/cgi-bin/etcsl.cgi?text=t.2.4.1.1&display=Crit&charenc=gcirc&lineid=t2411.p17#t2411.p17.

29   Kümmel, *Ersatzrituale*, 150-168.

30   KUB XVII 28 IV 45-52, Late-Hittite approx. 1300 BCE; Kümmel, *Ersatzrituale*, 150-152.

31   Kümmel, *Ersatzrituale*, 152-164.

32   KUB 17.17 x + 3'-10 ', Kümmel, *Ersatzrituale* 156-158.

Figure 2.10 Crossed pins on burials at Sioukh Tahtani. After: Porter, 'Mortal Mirrors', 200 Fig. 2. Courtesy of Dr. Paola Sconzo.

A text written by the scribe Puliša is a magic ritual against an epidemic in the army camp, which involves a human being being sacrificed:

> As soon as he finishes the incantation, he lets a man as substitute for the gods ...., he lets two oxen for... .. To the protective god as a substitute sacrifice for the gods ... . is he going.[33]

2.4.4. Neo-Assyrian and Late-Babylonian texts about the substitute king

In the Neo-Assyrian period a substitute king was sometimes appointed if there was a threat to the king's life. If this substitute king died or was killed the threat disappeared. A chronicle of about 600 BCE records the remarkable history of Erra-imittī and Enlil-bāni, in which the ruling king dies and the substitute king continues to occupy the throne. This narrative is an echo from the ancient Babylonian period, approx. 1860 BCE.

> The king (of Isin) Erra-imittī (1874-1860 BCE) ordered Enlil-bāni, the gardener, to sit on the throne as the royal substitute (and) he put the crown of kingship on his head. Erra-imittī died in his palace while swallowing hot soup in little sips. Enlil-bāni (1860-1837 BCE), who sat on the throne, did not resign and was elevated to the royal office. (*Chronicle of the Old Kings*, Akkadian Late Babylonian, after 600 BCE) [34]

From the Neo-Assyrian royal correspondence of Esarhaddon (680-669 BCE) and Assurbanipal (669-627 BCE), eleven letters refer to a substitute king (*šar pūhi*), three of which concern his death:

---

33   KBO XV 1 IV 40'-44 ', Late-Hittite approx. 1300 BCE; Kümmel, *Ersatzrituale*, 144.
34   Glassner, Chronicles, 270-271, no. 40 lines 31-35.

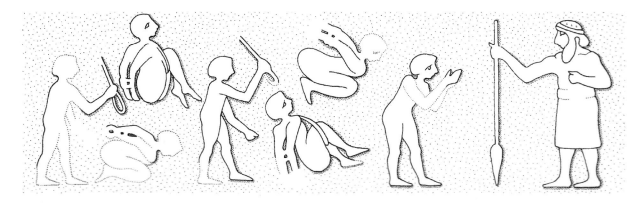

Figure 2.12 Maltreatment and killing of prisoners-of-war before the king of Uruk. After: Boehmer, *Uruk Früheste Siegelabrollungen*, Pl. 17 Nr 4 I-L. Courtesy of DAV Media Group.

Concerning the substitute king about whom the king, my lord, wrote to me: "How many days should he sit (on the throne)?". We waited for a solar eclipse, (but) the eclipse did not take place. Now, if the gods see each other on the 15th day, he may go to his fate on the 16th.[35]

The term "go to his fate" (*ana šimtišu alāku*) means "to die".

Another letter extends the death of the substitute king to the queen when evil omens arise:

Damqî, the son of the prelate of Akkad, who had ruled Assyria, Babylonia and all the countries, died with his queen on the night of the xth day as the substitute for the king, my lord, and for the sake of Šamaš-šumu-ukin [the brother of the king and gouvernor of Babylonia]. He went to his fate for their redemption. We prepared the burial chamber. He and his queen were decorated, treated, displayed, buried and wailed over.[36]

Thereafter rituals were performed meticuously. The letter also refers to a prophetess who said to Damqî that he would take over the kingdoms (of Esarhaddon) and that she had revealed to him 'the thief polecat' and that she had given him into his power. Apparently Damqî was planning to rebel. That was probably the reason he was appointed as substitute king.

2.5. Summary

Archaeological finds suggest that often ordinary young people like criminals and soldiers were ceremonially killed, most likely as substitutes for courtiers. Their bodies were conserved by heating and impregnated with mercury sulphide in order to prevent rapid decomposition during the funeral rituals. The bodies were displayed for a few days. The funerary gifts and pottery can be interpreted as burial-ritual offerings in which the conserved corpses of the servants played a part. In general, ritual human killing is found in northern Mesopotamia and Anatolia more frequently than in southern Mesopotamia. The relations between southern Mesopotamia and Syria might explain the unique findings in the tombs of Ur.[37]

On the basis of textual material, we can observe that in the death of famous rulers like Gilgamesh, his wife and children are also interred (Death of Gilgamesh). Fallen soldiers and executed criminals may also be placed in the grave of a prince (Urnamma A). The substitute king is said to "go to his fate", which cannot mean anything else but being killed, to safeguard the king from a predicted evil. Sometimes this substitute is a rebellious citizen (Damqī) or hostile city ruler (Ebla). Some Hittite texts mention the ritual killing of people, usually prisoners of war, besides other unusual sacrificial animals like dogs and pigs, as a sacrifice of atonement.

---

35   Parpola, *Letters*, no. 220 7-r. 3 parallel to no. 221 r. 2-3.
36   Parpola, *Letters*, no. 352 5-15.

---

37   For persons with Sumerian names in Mari see Gelb 1992, 132. Other indications for contact between northern and southern Mesopotamia are the bead of Mesanepada the son of Meskalamdug in the treasury of Mari (Frayne 2008, 391-392), the donated (?) Sumerian musician Ur-Nanše (Gelb, Mari and Kish, 132), and the Akkadian name of *Pû-abi* itself.

2.6. References

Baadsgaard, A., J. Monge, S. Cox, L. Zettler, 'Human sacrifice and intentional corps preservation in the Royal Cemetery of Ur', *Antiquity* 85 (2011), 27-42.

Baadsgaard, A., J. Monge, and L. Zettler, 'Bludgeoned, Burned and Beautified: Reevaluating Mortuary Practices in the Royal Cemetery of Ur', in Porter, A.M. and Schwartz, G., eds, *Sacred Killing, The Archaeology of Sacrifice in the Ancient Near East* (Winona Lake, 2012), 125-158.

Biga, M.G., 'Ancora sul sacrificio umano nel Vicino Oriente antico', in Loretz, O., Ribichini, S., W.G.E. Watson, and J.Á. Zamora, eds, *Ritual, Religion and Reason Studies in the Ancient World in Honour of Paolo Xella* (Münster, 2013), 167-174.

Boehmer, R.M., *Uruk: Früheste Siegelabrollungen,* Ausgrabungen in Uruk-Warka Endberichte (UEB) Band 24 (Mainz am Rhein, 1999).

Charvát, P., *Mesopotamia before History* (London, New York, 2002).

Cohen, A.C., *Death rituals, ideology, and the development of early Mesopotamian kingship: toward a new understanding of Iraq's royal cemetery of Ur* (Leiden, 2005).

Dickson, D. B., 'Kingship as Racketeering the Royal Tombs and Death Pits at Ur, Mesopotamia, Reinterpreted from the Standpoint of Conflict Theory', in J.A. Hill, Ph. Jones, and A. J. Morales, eds, *Experiencing Power, Generating Authority: Cosmos, Politics, and the Ideology of Kingship in Ancient Egypt and Mesopotamia* (Philadelphia, 2013), 311-330.

Frayne, D., *Presargonic Period (2700-2350 BCE),* Royal Inscriptions of Mesopotamia Early Series (RIME) Volume 1 (Toronto, 2008).

Gelb, I.J., 'Mari and the Kish Civilization', in G.D. Young, ed., *Mari in Retrospect* (Winona Lake, 1992), 121-202.

Gibson, M., 'Kiš B. Archäologisch', in D.O. Edzard, ed., *Reallexikon der Assyriologie und vorderasiatischen Achäologie* (RlA) Band 5, (Berlin, 1976-1980), 613-620.

Glassner, J.-J., *Mesopotamian Chronicles,* Writings from the Ancient World 19, (Atlanta, 2004).

Katz, D., 'Sumerian Funerary Rituals in Context', in N. Laneri, ed., *Performing Death Social Analysis of Funerary Traditions in the Ancient Near East and Mediterranean* (Chicago, 2007), 167-188.

Keith, A., 'Report on the Human Remains', in H.R. Hall and C.L. Woolley, *The Ur Excavations (UE) Volume I, Al-cUbaid,* (Oxford, 1927), 214-240 (Chapter XIII).

Keith, A., 'Report on the human Remains', in C.L. Woolley, *Ur Excavations (UE) Volume II, The Royal Cemetery,* (London-Pennsylvania, 1934), 400-410 (Chapter XXIII).

Klengel, H, 'Kriegsgefangene', in D.O. Edzard, ed., *Reallexikon der Assyriologie und vorderasiatischen Achäologie* (RlA) Band 6 (Berlin-New York, 1983), 241-246.

Kümmel, H.M., *Ersatzrituale für den hethitischen König,* in Studien zu den Boğazköy-Texten (StBoT), Herausgegeben von der Kommission für den Alten Orient der Akademie der Wissenschaften und der Literatur Heft 3 (Wiesbaden, 1967).

Marchesi, G., 'Who was buried in the Royal Tombs of Ur? Epigraphy and Textual Data', *Orientalia Nova Series (OrNS)* 73 (2004), 153-197.

Moorey, P.R.S., 'Cemetery A at Kish: Grave Groups and Chronology', *Iraq* 32 (1970), 86-128.

Molleson, Th., and D. Hodgson, 'The Human Remains from Woolley's Excavations at Ur', *Iraq* 65 (2003), 91-129.

Parpola, S., *Letters from Assyrian and Babylonian Scholars,* State Archives of Assyria, State Archives of Assyria (SAA) published by the Neo-Assyrian Text Corpus Project of the Academy of Finland in cooperation with Deutsche Orient-Gesellschaft Volume X (Helsinki, 1993).

Pollock, S., 'Death of a Household', in N. Laneri, ed., *Performing Death Social Analysis of Funerary Traditions in the Ancient Near East and Mediterranean* (Chicago, 2007), 209-222.

Porter, A., 'Mortal Mirrors: Creating Kin through Human Sacrifice in Third Millennium Mesopotamia', in A. Porter and G.M. Schwartz, eds, *Sacred Killing The Archaeology of Sacrifice in the Ancient Near East* (Winona Lake, 2011), 191-215.

Sürenhagen, D., 'Death in Mesopotamia: The Royal Tombs of Ur Revisited', in L. Al-Gailani Werr e.a., eds, *Of Pots and Plans. Papers on the Archaeology and History of Mesopotamia and Syria presented to David Oates in Honour of his 75th Birthday* (London, 2002), 324-338.

Woolley, C.L., *Ur Excavations (UE) Volume II, The Royal Cemetery* (London, Pennsylvania, 1934).

Zimmerman, P., 'Two Tombs or Three?', in R.L. Zettler and L. Horne, eds, *Treasures from the Royal Tombs of Ur* (Pennsylvania, 1998), 39.

Abbreviations

KBO = *Keilschrifturkunden aus Boghazköi* (Berlin 1921-).
KUB = *Keilschrifttexte aus Boghazköi,* (Leipzig 1916-).

Chapter 3

Ritual homicide in ancient Egypt

Jacobus van Dijk*

3.1. Introduction

Human sacrifice is not the first thing that comes to mind when one thinks of the culture of Ancient Egypt, and the question of whether any form of human sacrifice was ever actually practised there is still controversial today. For a long time it was thought (and many still think) that the ancient Egyptians were too civilized to practise such a barbaric custom. They were not to be compared with the Aztecs, for example, who have the bad reputation of practising particularly cruel forms of human sacrifice.[1] In discussions of this subject, a famous episode from a literary text from the early New Kingdom usually comes up. This text, known as the *Tales of Wonder from the Court of King Khufu* (Papyrus Westcar), contains a number of fairytale-like stories situated in the distant past, in the time of the Old Kingdom.[2] One of the narratives concerns a certain magician Djedi, who is rumoured to be able to reaffix a decapitated head and restore life to the victim. Pharaoh Khufu, or Cheops as he was known to the Greeks, the builder of the Great Pyramid at Giza, wants to have a demonstration of this and orders a prisoner to be brought to act as guinea pig, but Djedi refuses indignantly because, as he says, "it is forbidden to do such a thing to 'the noble cattle'", *i.e.* to human beings. A duck, a goose and a bull are then successfully used instead. In this tale, King Khufu is clearly depicted as a barbaric despot.

3.2. Retainer sacrifice

When discussing human sacrifice, we must differentiate between two main types: so-called *retainer sacrifice*, whereby servants or other subordinates are killed in order to be buried with their master and serve him in the afterlife, and true, *cultic human sacrifice*, whereby people – often but not always convicted criminals or captured enemies – are sacrificed as part of a temple cult (regular or otherwise) to satisfy the gods, maintain cosmic order, etc. About ten years ago, the *Religious Symbols* working group of the department of Religious Studies of the University of Groningen dedicated a symposium to *The Strange World of Human Sacrifice*, and in the resulting publication I wrote extensively about retainer sacrifice in Egypt and Nubia,[3] and I am therefore not going to dwell on that subject here. That form of human sacrifice was practised

---

*University of Groningen

1   Cf. Trigger, *Early Civilizations* 84. See also Jansen and Pérez Jiménez in this volume.
2   Lichtheim, *Ancient Egyptian Literature* I, 218-219; Parkinson, *The Tale of Sinuhe*, 114-115; Borghouts, *Egyptische sagen* 32-33.
3   Van Dijk, 'Retainer Sacrifice'. See also idem, 'Dodencultus en dodenpersoneel'.

in Egypt only during the formative phase of the Egyptian central state, during the First Dynasty, as well as during various periods in Nubia. It remains controversial, however, and there are still Egyptologists – mistakenly in my view – who doubt the existence of this practice. Incidentally, I would like to note that I do not share the objections to the use of the term sacrifice in this context raised in the introductory chapter of the present publication. The view that we are not dealing with sacrifices here, but merely with taking one's possessions with one to the other world seems to me to be a false dichotomy. We know virtually nothing about the ritual actions that accompanied retainer sacrifice, nor do we know whether the servants who were killed in order to follow their master to the hereafter were perhaps sacrificed during a ritual performed for a god, for example an early form of the god Osiris, with whom the divine deceased king may have been identified.

3.3. Human sacrifice as part of the temple cult

Far more controversial than retainer sacrifice is the cultic, ritual form of human sacrifice. The only more or less concrete indications we have date from the time of the First Dynasty, so from the same period in which retainer sacrifice was practised. They consist of a number of representations on wooden and ivory labels that seem to depict the killing of a kneeling figure in a ritual setting. The interpretation of this scene is extremely difficult given the lack of explanatory text and suitable parallels. It appears to be a royal ritual, but it is not clear at all on which occasion it would have been carried out. It is quite possible that we are dealing here with a ritual that took place during the funeral of the king; in other words, that it depicts an actual retainer sacrifice. The anthropologist and Egyptologist Bruce Trigger, mentioned above, has pointed out that retainer sacrifice and cultic human sacrifice often go hand in hand – when one is discontinued, the other disappears as well.[4] It would therefore appear to be unlikely from the start that cultic human sacrifice could have continued in Egyptian culture after the early dynastic period. Nevertheless, there are a few clues that point in that direction and need explaining.

In the Egyptian temples dating from the Graeco-Roman Period, we have numerous extensively described and illustrated rituals whereby the enemy of the god, of the king, of Egypt and thus of the order of creation, is destroyed. This enemy can take the form of an animal, such as a crocodile, a hippopotamus, a donkey or a pig, and sometimes even that of a human. This has led some Egyptologists to suppose that people were actually sacrificed to the gods in these late temples. This theory is strengthened by a number of classical authors who report that human sacrifice was practised in Egypt. For example, we read that the Egyptian king Busiris sacrificed foreigners (possibly referring to prisoners-of-war) to Zeus (Amun). In turn, he and his henchmen were killed by Hercules, a theme that also appears in Greek vase painting. Authors such as Plutarch and Diodorus record that 'Typhonic' or 'Sethian' people, who are distinguished by their blond or red hair or other physical characteristics, were used for this. (Typhon is the Greek name for Seth, the god who murdered Osiris, who during the Late Period gradually became a kind of devil in Egyptian religion.)

Such stories were apparently already doing the rounds, at least among the Greeks, in the days of Herodotus, who refers to them in Book II of his *Histories*. However, Herodotus, who actually travelled to Egypt and so does not simply repeat other writers, regarded these rumours as tall stories to which no credibility should be attached: "For me at least such a tale is proof enough that the Greeks know nothing whatever about Egyptian character and custom. The Egyptians are forbidden by their religion even to kill animals for sacrifice, except sheep and such bulls and bull-calves as have passed the test for 'cleanness' – and geese: is it likely, then, that they would sacrifice human beings?"[5] Later Greek and Roman authors report nevertheless that the Egyptians sometimes sacrificed humans, and John Gwyn Griffiths, who collected all of these sources, came to the conclusion that during the pharaonic period human sacrifice may have been very rare but not unknown, and that in the post-pharaonic era, particularly in the Roman Period, human sacrifice was practised regularly.[6] On the other hand there is a reference in Manetho (cited by Porphyry), who says in his *On Ancient Ritual and Religion* that the custom of sacrificing three men a day to the goddess Hera of Heliopolis was abolished by a certain Pharaoh Amosis (either Amasis of the 26th Dynasty or Ahmose of the 18th) and replaced by the ritual burning of three wax figurines.[7]

3.4. Killing the followers of Seth and Apophis

The French Egyptologist Jean Yoyotte has compared this classical tradition with the sparse Egyptian sources.[8] According to him, human sacrifice did occur from time

---

4   Trigger, *Early Civilizations*, 97-98.

5   Histories II, 45; de Sélincourt, 120; for a Dutch translation see Van Dolen, *Herodotos*, 154. Cf. Lloyd, *Herodotus Book II*, 212-214.

6   Griffiths, 'Human Sacrifice', 409-423.

7   Waddell, *Manetho*, 199-201.

8   Yoyotte, 'Héra d'Héliopolis', 31-102.

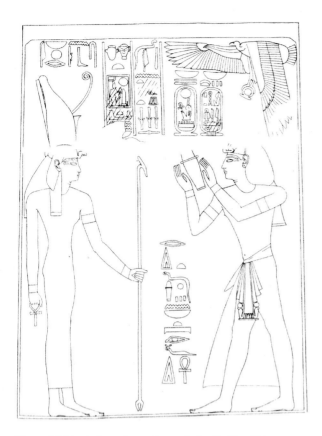

Figure 3.1 Mut *ḥrt snwt=s* as shown in the Re-Harakhty complex in the Temple of Seti I in Abydos. After: Calverley and Broome, *The Temple of King Sethos I*, Pl. 75, 9C (W).

Figure 3.2 Mut *ḥrt sn=s* carrying the mummy of her brother Osiris. After: De Garis Davies, *The Temple of Hibis*, Pl. 3 (vi).

to time, particularly in the Third Intermediate Period and later. The people who were sacrificed (or the images that represented them) were regarded as followers of Seth, the murderer of Osiris, or of Aphophis, the primeval snake who is the enemy of the sun god Re and who attempts to destroy the order of creation. These people were sacrificed as burnt offerings to the daughter of Re, the sun's eye, who protects him and destroys his enemies. This goddess is called Mut or Sakhmet in the Egyptian sources (and sometimes Hathor, Tefnut, Bastet, etc.) and is usually depicted in the form of a lioness. Manetho calls this goddess Hera of Heliopolis, and this Heliopolitan goddess is known in Egyptian sources as Mut *ḥrt snwt=s*, "Mut who is under her *snwt*" (fig. 3.1). The meaning of the word *snwt* is not clear here; it probably originally meant some sort of wooden poles or raised stones (stelae) that were placed at the entrance of a building to mark someone's property and to ward off enemies. It later also became the word used for the flagpoles raised in front of the pylon of a temple. At some point, the Egyptians themselves obviously no longer knew what "Mut who is under her *snwt*" meant: in the temple of Hibis from the Persian Period, and in several ritual texts from the Late Period, *Mut ḥrt snwt=s* was changed into Mut *ḥrt sn=s*, "Mut who is under (*i.e.* carrying)

her brother", and she is sometimes depicted carrying the mummy of Osiris (fig. 3.2); she is then obviously perceived as a form of the goddess Isis. In the Late Period, Re and Osiris were more than ever seen as aspects of one and the same god, and the connection with Heliopolis primarily points to a link with the sun god Re.

Mut *ḥrt sn(wt)=s* also appears in two spells from the *Book of Warding off the Evil One*, whereby both Apophis and Seth are meant. In a passage about Heliopolis, twenty enemies of the sun god are mentioned. They are followers of Apophis, "conspirators who are destined for the slaughter block of the gate of the Horizon". They, their children and grandchildren down to the present day, have taken on the appearance of the human inhabitants of Heliopolis. They are doomed and will burn on the braziers (*ꜥḫw*) of Mut *ḥrt sn(wt)=s*. The gods of Heliopolis are standing nearby and shout four times: "Re triumphs over Apophis, Osiris triumphs over the evil Seth!"[9] In another spell from the same book, the rebel is addressed as follows:

> You will be destroyed on the slaughter block (*nmt*) intended for Apophis, without your *ba* being able to escape, your body will be burnt on the braziers (*ꜥḥw*) of Mut *ḥrt sn(wt)=s* (...), who surrounds all those who behave as rebels. They will be consumed by the fire of the Eye of Re. 'Yes, they are your conspirators!', one says to Apophis. The Heliopolitans rise up to cause Re to triumph over Apophis, to cause Osiris to triumph over the evil Seth, to cause the king to triumph over his enemies.[10]

This text speaks unequivocally about the burning of human rebels, and such human sacrifices or ritual executions were performed within the framework of the solar cult in Heliopolis. In this context it is interesting that the writer Procopius of Caesarea, who lived in the sixth century AD, says that the Blemmyes and the Noubades, two southern tribes who lived in the region around Philae, were accustomed to sacrifice people to Helios, *i.e.* the sun god Re, in the Temple of Philae up until the Roman emperor Justinian, who converted to Christianity, ended this practice by closing down all the pagan temples. Junker has linked this comment by Procopius with the illustrations of ritual executions (known as *smꜣ sbiw*, "the killing of the rebel") on the temple walls at Philae,[11] and both he and Griffiths conclude from this that actual human sacrifices took place at Philae, at least in the Roman Period. It should thus come as no surprise that the following passage can also be read in the Temple of Philae: "May you (a certain god) place those who have evil intentions and who hate the king upon the braziers (*ꜥḥw*) of Mut *ḥrt sn(wt)=s*, after you have overcome the opponents of His Majesty".[12]

3.5. Ritual execution at the palace or temple gate

But there is another link that is very old indeed, as evidenced by the name Mut *ḥrt snwt=s*, namely with the façade of a building or the gate of a temple. The *snwt*, as has already been mentioned, stood near the entrance to a building, and this term is also used for the flagpoles in front of the pylon of a temple. In the introduction to the late (demotic) Instructions of Ankhsheshonqy,[13] it is related that the chief court physician Harsiese, together with a group of military men and other courtiers, hatched a plot to murder the king. But the evil plan was discovered in time and the pharaoh caused an altar with a copper brazier (*ꜥḥ ḥmt*) to be constructed near the palace gate, and on it Harsiese and his fellow conspirators were burnt. There is a similar passage in a Late Period hieratic literary papyrus, unfortunately in a very fragmentary context.[14] Here, too, people are executed on the orders of the king and placed on a brazier (*ꜥḥ*) in front of Mut *ḥrt sn(wt)=s* in Heliopolis. Even more fragmentary is a demotic literary papyrus from Saqqara, but here again Pharaoh orders that someone who has fallen from grace (in a conflict involving the priesthood and the army?) "should be placed upon the brazier with his family and his fellow [priests]" and the execution takes place "at the door of the palace".[15]

Interestingly, in the passages of the *Book of Warding off the Evil One* that we have just discussed, there is a reference to "the slaughter block (*nmt*) of the gate of the Horizon". Yoyotte, because of the association with Osiris, connected this location specifically with the entrance to the place where Osiris was mummified,[16] but it seems more likely to me to see this "gate of the Horizon" in more general terms as a reference to the place where the sun rises, *i.e.* the gateway in the pylon of the temple, which is after all a symbolic representation of the *akhet*, the two hills between which the sun rises.[17]

All of these passages give rise at least to the question of whether, perhaps under certain circumstances, people were indeed sacrificed near the gate to the temple or the palace. A number of years ago, Alan Schulman published a controversial book entitled *Ceremonial Execution and Public Rewards*.[18] It deals with two types of representation, one of which is explained by analogy with the other – a rather risky method, as we shall see. The first group is the well-known representation of a high official being rewarded by the king for outstanding services rendered by being given the 'gold of honour'.[19] The recipient of

9   Schott, *Urk.* VI, 63: 16-18, 65: 10-13.
10   Schott, *Urk.* VI, 77: 15, 79: 13.
11   Junker, 'Die Schlacht- und Brandopfer', 69-77.
12   Bénédite, *Le temple de Philœ*, 116: 19.

13   Smith, 'The Story of Ankhsheshonqi', 133-156; translations: Lichtheim, *Ancient Egyptian Literature* III, 163; Stricker, 'De wijsheid van Anchsjesjonq', 14.
14   pVandier 5, 12: G. Posener, *Le Papyrus Vandier*, 32-33 and 77.
15   Smith and Tait, *Saqqâra Demotic Papyri* I, 40-41 (Text 1, col. 14, 3-4 and 36). Cf. also Leahy, 'Death by Fire'.
16   Yoyotte, 'Héra d'Héliopolis', 99-101.
17   "Flagpoles (*snwt*) covered with white gold are set up before its façade, it resembles the horizon (*ꜣḫt*) in the sky in which Re arises", Helck, *Urk.* IV, 1649, 3-5. The roof over the gateway between the pylon towers is dedicated to the cult of the rising and setting sun, see e.g. *Medinet Habu* VI, Pls 430-433 and Stadelmann, 'šwt-*Rꜥw*', 159-178.
18   Cf. Schulman, *Ceremonial Execution*.
19   Binder, *The Gold of Honour*.

Figure 3.3 Votive stelae from Memphis, Newark 29.1788 (left) and Brussels E 2386 (right). After: Schulman, *Ceremonial Execution*, Pls 6 and 4.

this prestigious royal decoration naturally took great pride in it and had this very important event in his life immortalized in his tomb. The second group comprises a number of small stelae, most of which come from Memphis, the royal residence and administrative capital of Egypt. On them we see the owner depicted in obeisance in front of a gateway; in the gate can be seen a representation of the king destroying one or more enemies in front of a god, in these instances usually the god Ptah of Memphis (fig. 3.3). Schulman now concludes that, just like the award ceremony, this scene is also referring to a real, historical event, *i.e.* the ceremonial execution of prisoners-of-war as an offering to the god to thank him for a victory achieved by the king; Schulman postulates that the stela owner was given the privilege of being a witness to this event.

Critics, however, have rightly pointed out that there is not a single scrap of contemporary written or other evidence besides the stelae themselves to support this interpretation. It rests exclusively on the analogy with the reward scenes, but this analogy is not as secure as it may seem to be. During a reward ceremony, it is of course the person in whose tomb it is depicted who is the centre of attention; he derives enormous prestige from it, and this is the reason why it takes pride of place in the tomb decoration of the person in question. The depictions of 'ceremonial executions', on the other hand, appear on votive stelae; the person represented has left his stela at a temple and hopes as a result to receive favours from

the god, such as being healed of a disease, or being given children etc., or wishes to thank the god for similar favours that he already received. This is made very clear by the ears which are sometimes depicted on these stelae and which we know well from other types of votive stelae; they represent the benevolent hearing ear of the god.

The representation of the king who is destroying his enemy is an ancient motif in Egyptian iconography; the oldest examples date from as early as the Predynastic Period. The most familiar are the huge scenes on the façades of the temple pylons (fig. 3.4). These are purely symbolic representations showing the divine pharaoh as the maintainer and protector of cosmic order, ma‛at; maintaining cosmic order, after all, is what an Egyptian temple is all about. We also know that 'ordinary' people, unlike consecrated priests, were not permitted to enter the actual temple but were allowed to pray to the gods or the divine king or deposit votive offerings to them in the forecourt of the temple, in front of the pylon, where the colossal royal statues were objects of worship. Schulman's stelae must therefore be viewed in this context. The person depicted has dedicated his stela to the god of the temple (Ptah) and to the divine king who is depicted on the pylon of the temple while symbolically destroying the enemy in the presence of Ptah. The stelae do not depict an historical event, but rather show the setting in which the stela owner offers his prayers and his votive offering. Similar scenes of the king destroying his enemies are shown on the private stelae carved into the cliffs in the border area between

Figure 3.4 The King smiting the enemies before Amun on the Pylon of Medinet Habu. Photo: author.

Egypt and Nubia, for example at Abu Simbel. Although these stelae have a dated inscription, and therefore record a specific occasion, the texts do not ever mention the type of historical event that Schulman wants to see in them. Here, too, they are symbolic representations displaying the pharaoh as the protector of the borders of Egypt and the suppressor of the forces of chaos. None of these scenes, it should be noted, make any reference to goddesses like Mut or Sakhmet, let alone Mut ḥrt sn(wt)≈s, as one might have expected had they been depictions of real executions.

3.6. Altars near the temple gate

Schulman's claim thus holds no water, but his thesis that ritual executions took place near the gates of a temple or palace cannot simply be relegated to the world of fantasy, given the passages that we have examined earlier. Incidentally, it is rather surprising that Schulman in his book never refers to the studies by Griffiths and Yoyotte, or even to the classical authors. In this context, it is interesting that several temples from the Ptolemaic and Roman periods contain huge altars, which were usually erected immediately inside the pylon, in the first courtyard. Anyone who has been to Karnak will remember those in the temple of Amun (fig. 3.5). There were originally two of

them, but only the northern example is still in situ. They are very large, almost square altars with flat tops on which triangular blocks were originally placed at each of the four corners, creating a typical horned altar.

This is a type of altar that was imported into Egypt from Syria-Palestine, probably not before the Ptolemaic Period.[20] Behind the Amun temple, in the open space between the rear wall of the temple and what is known as the contra-temple, is one of the best-preserved examples, complete with 'horns' and with a stairway granting access to the upper surface of the altar (fig. 3.6).

In the temple of the goddess Opet, adjacent to the Khonsu temple, there is also one of these altars just inside the gate, missing its horns but with a stairway. It was excavated in the early 1950s by Alexandre Varille,[21] who says that traces of fire could still be seen on the upper surface.[22] Interestingly, a granite statue of the goddess Mut-Sakhmet, the goddess known as the "mistress of the slaughter block" (nbt nmt), was placed beside the altar

---

20 Quaegebeur, 'L'autel-à-feu'.
21 Varille, 'La grande porte du temple d'Apet à Karnak', 79-118; cf. p. 108, fig. 9, and Pls XVII-XVIII.
22 Varille, 'La grande porte', 109.

(fig. 3.7).[23] The scenes on the gateway immediately next to it record the destruction of the king's enemies before a god. On the left, the god says: "I will cause you to triumph over your enemies", and on the right: "I will cause the rebel to fall on your slaughter block (*nmt*)" (fig. 3.8).

In the temple of Mut, too, there used to be such an altar, again immediately inside the entrance gate. Unfortunately not much more of it remains than two huge loose blocks, on one of which is a graffito of a horned animal. Here, too, it can clearly be seen where the blocks that formed the horns of the altar were placed. We also know of similar huge

---

23   This statue is one of the several hundred statues of Mut-Sakhmet which originally stood in the mortuary temple of Amenhotep III on the Theban West Bank (Kom el-Hetan) and in the Temple of Mut in Karnak. On one of them the goddess is called *nbt snwt*, "mistress of the *snwt*" (Louvre A 4).

Figure 3.7 Altar with staircase and statue of Mut-Sakhmet inside the gate of the Opet Temple, Karnak. Photo: author.

altars at Medamud and Coptos.[24] Unfortunately, not a single one of these altars is inscribed; the only exception is an earlier altar from Medamud, the blocks of which were reused in the foundation of the (Roman) altar just mentioned and which is now in the Egyptian Museum in Cairo (fig. 3.9).[25] It has detailed reliefs showing all kinds of sacrificial animals and inscriptions derived from the traditional offering liturgy that unfortunately tell us nothing specific about this kind of altar.

Given the location of these huge open-air altars right beside the entrance gates to the temple, and the passages from Egyptian and classical texts, it seems likely that *if* people were actually sacrificed in an Egyptian temple, it would have been on these altars. Once again, however, unequivocal evidence is lacking. Numerous sacrificial animals are depicted on the Medamud altar in the Cairo Museum, but no humans. The few representations that we have of these altars also only show animals and never people. Even though the inscriptions on the gateway by the altar in the Opet temple speak of "enemies" and

the "rebel", the sacrificial animals depicted are bulls (see fig. 3.8).

The question thus again arises how literally we should take all these texts and descriptions. Sacrificial animals have been used as symbols of the enemies of the god and the king since the Pyramid Texts, if not earlier, and on these altars, too, it may have been animals being sacrificed that only in the religious vocabulary are being represented as human enemies. The punishing of the evildoers, *i.e.* those whose behaviour places them outside cosmic order (maʿat), and who thus prove that they belong in the world of the primeval chaos that rules outside the cosmic order, is also a motif that appears in numerous Egyptian religious texts and representations, most explicitly in the so-called Books of the Underworld in the royal tombs of the New Kingdom, such as the Amduat, the Book of Gates, the Book of Caverns, etc. In these books, the forces of chaos are permanently punished and killed, and great emphasis is placed on the doomed being cut into pieces and burnt or cooked in huge cauldrons.[26] It is a giant leap, however, from these representations of ancient Egyptian hell to a ritual practice of actual human sacrificial victims on earth.

---

24   Medamud: Bisson de la Roque, *Rapport sur les Fouilles*, 25-28, figs 20-21; Coptos: Traunecker, *Coptos*, Pl. Vb.

25   Cairo JE 54853 (see http://www.globalegyptianmuseum.org/record.aspx?id=15863; accessed 18 June 2016). See Bisson de la Roque, *Rapport (1926)*, 26-28, figs 22-23. It dates from the reign of Ptolemy III.

---

26   Hornung, *Altägyptische Höllenvorstellungen*; Van Dijk, 'Hell'.

Figure 3.8 Inscriptions describing the offerings in the reliefs on the interior side of the gate of the Opet Temple, Karnak. Photos: author.

Figure 3.9 Large altar of Ptolemy III from Medamud, Egyptian Museum Cairo JE 54853.

3.7. Execution as a last resort

In one of the Egyptian wisdom texts, the Instruction for Merikare, it is said that killing as a punishment is not "useful", thus counterproductive. "Punish with beatings and with imprisonment, so that the land remains in good order", says the writer, but he does make a clear exception for "the rebel whose plan is discovered".[27] Such a person must be expelled from society and killed, his name must be eradicated and his fellow perpetrators must be destroyed. And as we have already seen, Ankhsheshonqy also says that those who want to topple the divine pharaoh are burnt on an altar near the gate to the palace. Serious crimes such as conspiracy or the theft of temple equipment, *i.e.* the property of

---

27   Lichtheim, *Ancient Egyptian Literature* I, 100; Parkinson, *The Tale of Sinuhe*, 220.

the god, were punishable in Ancient Egypt with the death penalty,[28] and burning (dead or alive) was one of the most radical options; after all, the body was then destroyed for good and continued life in the hereafter made impossible.

In Moaʻlla in the Middle Kingdom, as Harco Willems has shown,[29] representatives of Apophis, the enemy of cosmic order, were sacrificed during the processional feast of the local god Hemen; in addition to the animal sacrifices made on that occasion (bull, hippopotamus, fish), criminals such as tomb robbers were also killed. This could be called a human sacrifice, because the victims were killed in a ritual setting in the presence of a god, but it is also possible to view this event as a legal issue, the implementation of the death penalty, an act that in the context of an ancient culture like that of the Egyptians more or less automatically took on a religious character. [30] After all there was no separation of 'church' and 'state'; the laws of the state were determined by *maʿat*, the cosmic order bequeathed by the creator god.

But even if we interpret such ritual executions as sacrifices to the god, we are still a long way from a regular practice of human sacrifice within the framework of the temple cult, even though Manetho says that the practice abolished by Pharaoh Amosis concerned three people a day.

3.8. Conclusion

In conclusion, it can be said that there is no proper hard evidence for the cultic practice of human sacrifice in the Egyptian temple cult. The crucial question still remains whether it was really human beings who were sacrificed and not symbolic substitutes, such as certain sacrificial animals[31] or wax or wooden statuettes of people,[32] as Manetho also records. The few bits of evidence that we have seem to point to individual, ritualized executions of criminals or rebels against the legal authority of the pharaoh rather than to regular sacrificial practices.

28 Cf. Muhlestein, 'Royal Executions', 181-208, who produces arguments for expanding the range of crimes punishable by execution even during the Middle Kingdom. In an inscription of Senwosret I in Tôd "priests who do not know how to worship", criminals (?, *bskw-ib*) who go about stealing, and "those who enjoy stirring up rebellion", in short, all those who have violated the temple domain are put on the brazier (*ꜥḥ*) where "they burn for him (the god) like torches", Barbotin and Clère, 'L'inscription de Sésostris Ier', 1-33, cols. 28-30.

29 Willems, 'Crime, Cult and Capital Punishment'.

30 On this problem see Muhlenstein, *Violence in the Service of Order*; idem, 'Sacred Violence' and Müller-Wollermann, *Vergehen und Strafen*, 195-196.

31 Cf. the passage in Pap. Leiden T 32 (col. IV: 4-5) which says that the ferocious Sakhmet and her emissaries are appeased by the smell of burnt offerings of goats and pigs and not, it may be emphasized, by sacrifices of human enemies. Cf. Herbin, *Le livre de parcourir l'éternité*, 57, 172 and cf. 363; Stricker, 'De Egyptische Mysteriën', 27.

32 Cf. Raven, 'Wax in Egyptian Magic'. As Raven points out, wax images symbolising the enemy are already attested in the Coffin Texts (Spell 37) from the Middle Kingdom.

3.9. References

Barbotin, C. and J.J. Clère, 'L'inscription de Sésostris Ier à Tôd', *BIFAO* 91 (1991), 1-33, cols. 28-30.

Bénédite, G., *Le temple de Philœ*, MMAF 13 (Paris, 1893).

Binder, S., *The Gold of Honour in New Kingdom Egypt*, ACE Studies 8 (Oxford, 2008).

Bisson de la Roque, F., *Rapport sur les fouilles de Médamoud (1926)* (Cairo, 1927).

Borghouts, J.F., *Egyptische sagen en verhalen* (Bussum, 1974).

Calverley, A.M., and M.F. Broome, *The Temple of King Sethos I at Abydos* IV (London, Chicago, 1958).

Dolen, H. van, *Herodotos: Het verslag van mijn onderzoek* (Nijmegen, 1995).

Dijk, J. van, 'Hell', in D.B. Redford, ed., *The Oxford Encyclopedia of Ancient Egypt*, Vol. 2 (New York, 2001), 89-91.

Dijk, J. van, 'Retainer Sacrifice in Egypt and Nubia', in J.N. Bremmer, ed., *The Strange World of Human Sacrifice*, Studies in the History and Anthropology of Religion 1 (Leuven, 2007), 135-155.

Dijk, J. van, 'Dodencultus en dodenpersoneel in het vroege Egypte', *Groniek. Historisch Tijdschrift* 42 no. 184 (2009), 369-382.

Garis Davies, N. de, *The Temple of Hibis in El Khärgeh Oasis* III (New York, 1953).

Griffiths, J.G., 'Human Sacrifice in Egypt: the Classical Evidence', *ASAE* 48 (1948), 409-423.

Herbin, F.R., *Le livre de parcourir l'éternité*, OLA 58 (Leuven, 1994).

Hornung, E., *Altägyptische Höllenvorstellungen*, ASAW 59: 3 (Berlin, 1968).

Helck, W., *Urkunden der 18. Dynastie*, Heft 20: *Historische Inschriften Amenophis' III.*, Urk. IV: 20 (Berlin, 1957).

Herodotus, *Histories*, II, 45, translation by A. de Sélincourt (Harmondsworth, 1954).

Junker, H., 'Die Schlacht- und Brandopfer und ihre Symbolik im Tempelkult der Spätzeit', *ZÄS* 48 (1911), 69-77.

Leahy, M.A., 'Death by Fire in Ancient Egypt', *JESHO* 27 (1984), 199-206.

Lichtheim, M., *Ancient Egyptian Literature: A Book of Readings, I: The Old and Middle Kingdoms* (Berkeley, Los Angeles, London, 1973).

Lichtheim, M., *Ancient Egyptian Literature III: The Late Period* (Berkeley, Los Angeles, London, 1980).

Lloyd, A.B., *Herodotus Book II: Commentary 1-98*, ÉPRO 43 (Leiden, 1976).

Medinet Habu VI. The Temple Proper, Part II: The Re Chapel, the Royal Mortuary Complex, and Adjacent Rooms with Miscellaneous Material from the Pylons, the Forecourts, and the First Hypostyle Hall, by The Epigraphic Survey, OIP 84 (Chicago, 1963).

Muhlestein, K., 'Royal Executions: Evidence Bearing on the Subject of Sanctioned Killing in the Middle Kingdom', *JESHO* 51 (2008), 181-208.

Muhlestein, K., 'Sacred Violence. When Ancient Egyptian Punishment was Dressed in Ritual Trappings', *Near Eastern Archaeology* 78: 4 (2015), 244-251.

Muhlestein, K., *Violence in the Service of Order: The Religious Framework for Sanctioned Killing in Ancient Egypt*, BAR International Series 2229 (Oxford, 2011).

Müller-Wollermann, R., *Vergehen und Strafen. Zur Sanktionierung abweichenden Verhaltens im alten Ägypten*, PÄ 21 (Leiden, Boston, 2004).

Parkinson, R.B., *The Tale of Sinuhe and Other Ancient Egyptian Poems 1940-1640 BC* (Oxford, 1997).

Posener, G., *Le Papyrus Vandier*, Bibliothèque générale 7 (Cairo, 1985).

Quaegebeur, J., 'L'autel-à-feu et l'abbatoir en Egypte tardive', in J. Quaegebeur, ed., *Ritual and Sacrifice in the Ancient Near East*, OLA 55 (Leuven, 1993), 329-353.

Raven, M.J., 'Wax in Egyptian Magic and Symbolism', *OMRO* 64 (1983), 7-47.

Schott, S., *Urkunden mythologische Inhalts*, Heft 1-2: *Bücher und Sprüche gegen den Gott Seth*, Urk. VI: 1-2 (Leipzig, 1929-1939).

Schulman, A.R., *Ceremonial Execution and Public Rewards. Some Historical Scenes on New Kingdom Private Stelae*, OBO 75 (Freiburg, Göttingen, 1988).

Smith, H.S., 'The Story of Ankhsheshonqi', *Serapis* 6 (1980), 133-156.

Smith, H.S. and Tait, W.J., *Saqqâra Demotic Papyri I (P. Dem. Saq. I)*, Texts from Excavations 7 (London, 1983).

Stadelmann, R., 'šwt-Rʿw als Kultstätte des Sonnengottes im Neuen Reich', *MDAIK* 25 (1969), 159-178.

Stricker, B.H., 'De Egyptische Mysteriën. Papyrus Leiden T 32' [II], *OMRO* 34 (1953), 13-31.

Stricker, B.H., 'De wijsheid van Anchsjesjonq', *JEOL* 15 (1957-1958), 11-33.

Traunecker, C., *Coptos. Hommes et dieux sur le parvis de Geb*, OLA 43 (Leuven, 1992).

Trigger, B.G., *Early Civilizations: Ancient Egypt in Context* (Cairo, 1993).

Varille, A., 'La grande porte du temple d'Apet à Karnak', *ASAE* 53 (1955), 79-118.

Waddell, W.G., *Manetho*, Loeb Classical Library 350 (Cambridge, Mass., London, 1940).

Willems, H.O., 'Crime, Cult and Capital Punishment (Moaalla Inscription 8)', *JEA* 76 (1990), 27-54.

Yoyotte, J., 'Héra d'Héliopolis et le sacrifice humain', *AnnÉPHÉ* 89 (1980-1981), 31-102; reprinted in *Histoire, géographie et religion de l'Égypte ancienne. Opera selecta*, OLA 224 (Leuven, 2013), 1-75.

Abbreviations

ACE = The Australian Centre for Egyptology

AnnÉPHÉ = Annuaire [de l']École Pratique des Hautes Études, Vᵉ Section, Sciences religieuses

ASAE = Annales du Service des Antiquités de l'Égypte

ASAW = Abhandlungen der Sächsischen Akademie der Wissenschaften, Philologisch-historische Klasse

BAR = British Archaeological Reports

BIFA = Bulletin de l'Institut Française d'Archéologie Orientale du Caire

ÉPRO = Études Préliminaires aux Religions Orientales dans l'Empire Romain

JEA = Journal of Egyptian Archaeology

JEOL = Jaarbericht van het Vooraziatisch-Egyptisch Genootschap Ex Oriente Lux

JESHO = Journal of the Economic and Social History of the Orient

MDAIK = Mitteilungen des Deutschen Archäologischen Instituts, Abteilung Kairo

MMAF = Mémoires publiés par les membres de la Mission Archéologique Française au Caire

OBO = Orbis Biblicus et Orientalis

OIP = Oriental Institute Publications

OLA = Orientalia Lovaniensia Analecta

OMRO = Oudheidkundige Mededelingen uit het Rijksmuseum van Oudheden te Leiden

Urk = Urkunden des ägyptischen Altertums

ZÄS = Zeitschrift für ägyptische Sprache und Altertumskunde

Chapter 4

Sacrifice and ritual killing of humans in the Etruscan world?

L. Bouke van der Meer*

4.1. Introduction

Did the Etruscans sacrifice and ritually kill human beings?[1] Opinions differ greatly.[2] To answer the questions there are four sources of information: ancient literature, iconography, archaeology, and epigraphy. Ancient authors mention Etruscan killings of humans from the fifth century BCE until the twelfth century AD. However, they may be biased, when they write about *barbaroi*, people who did not speak Greek. In addition, authors may describe events that had happened long, even centuries before their time. Visual representations are also problematic as they may have been influenced by or copied from Greek models.

4.2. Written sources

Let us start with the written sources. The father of ancient Greek history, Herodotus, describes in *Histories* 1.166-167.10 the 'Cadmean (that is an empty) victory' of the Phocaeans from Alalia (nowadays Aleria on Corsica) over the Etruscans around 540-535 BCE:[3]

> When these (Phocaeans) came to Kyrnos (Corsica), for five years they dwelt together with those who had come thither before (the Phocaeans in 565 BCE), and they founded temples there. Then, since they plundered the property of all their neighbours, the Tyrsenians (Etruscans) and Carthaginians made expedition against them by agreement with one another, each with sixty ships. And the Phocaeans also manned their vessels, sixty in number, and came to meet the enemy in that which is called the Sardinian sea: and when they encountered one another in the sea-fight the

---

1   A human sacrifice is dedicated to a deity, a superhuman being, a supernatural power, a deceased person, or ancestors (see Brelich, *Presupposti*; Bonnechere, *Sacrifice humain*; Hughes, *Human sacrifice*, 1-12). A ritual killing is not religious and happened more than once. For definitions of rituals (Greek nomos; Latin ritus, mos), see Van der Meer, *Etrusco ritu*, 1-12.

2   For positive views, see Bonfante, 'Human sacrifice', De Grummond, 'Lur', and Donati, 'Sacrificio umano'; for critical views, see Briquel, 'Sacrifice des prisonniers'; Steuernagel, *Menschenopfer*, 149-165, and for a negative view, see Di Fazio, 'Sacrifici umani'. The authors do not use all available data. This article is an update including recent archaeological discoveries.

3   For comments, see Bernardini, *Machè*; Thuillier, *Jeux*, 53-55; 426-427; 482-484; Weber, *Geschichte*, 57-61. Van der Meer, 'Greek and local elements'.

Phocaeans won a kind of Cadmean victory, for forty of their ships were destroyed and the remaining twenty were disabled, having had their prows bent aside. So they sailed in to Alalia and took up their children and their women and their other possessions as much as their ships proved capable of carrying, and then they left Kyrnos behind them and sailed to Rhegion (nowadays Reggio di Calabria). But as for the crews that were destroyed, the Carthaginians and Tyrsenians obtained much the greater number of them, and these they brought to land and killed by stoning. After this the men of Agylla (Caere, nowadays Cerveteri) found that everything which passed by the spot where the Phocaeans were laid after being stoned, became either distorted (*diastropha*), or crippled (*empèra*), or paralysed (*apoplekta*), both sheep and beasts of burden and human creatures: so the men of Agylla sent to Delphi desiring to purge themselves of the offence; and the Pythian prophetess bade them do that which the men of Agylla still (ca. 450 BCE) continue to perform, that is to say, they make great sacrifices in honour of the dead, and hold at the place a contest of athletics and horse (chariot?) racing'.[4]

Is there a core of truth in this story? According to some medical experts it is unlikely that touching the rotting corpses, inhaling their stench or drinking contaminated water could cause symptoms of distortion, crippling and palsy.[5] Water contamination would only have led to gastroenteritis. Maybe onlookers became hysterical, making spastic movements. However, Jean MacIntosh Turfa and Adrian Harrison now suggest that the three symptoms (suffering a stroke, becoming twisted and paralysed) were caused by airborne botulism spread by Clostridia spores or toxins from wounded and decomposing bodies during warm (sea) weather.[6] As for the introduction of new games after the Sea Battle some athletic games are indeed depicted at just this time in late archaic Etruscan tomb paintings in Tarquinia and on Etruscan vases. A nice example is the painted right wall of the Tomba delle Olimpiadi at Tarquinia (530-520 BCE; fig. 4.1), showing three runners moving to the left, a jumper without weights, and a discus thrower both moving to right, all male athletes, nude apart from their belts, and the bloody performance of Phersu (see below).

The left wall, however, shows horse chariot racing, including realistic accidents, and one of the entrance walls depicts two boxing men.[7] The Etruscans had already developed the tradition of horse races and boxing games since the beginning of the sixth century BCE, before the sea battle that is known as the Battle of Alalia. Etruscan horses were famous. According to Livy, Rome imported horses and boxers in the sixth century BCE when Etruscan kings ruled the city.[8] It seems that the stoning of the Phocaeans took place outside the city, since sheep and pack animals are mentioned. Herodotus does not explain why the prisoners of war were stoned. It was certainly not a Greek custom to do such things during a war.[9] The reason may have been punishment, revenge or a sacrifice in honour of the Etruscans who had died in the Sea Battle as Torelli and MacIntosh Turfa suggest.[10] Etruscans sent messengers to the oracle of Apollo in Delphi, probably because the victims were Greeks. Apollo was not only a god of light and healing but also could punish by sending a plague as an act of vengeance. For the Etruscans, who called him Apulu, he probably was also as a god of the underworld.[11] As for the place of stoning, there may be indirect archaeological evidence, although no mass grave has ever been found here. An almost square building (56 x 59.5 m) with a bipartite courtyard was built around 530-520 BCE at 150 m distance from a seventh century BCE tumulus with a diameter of sixty metres, the largest one in Caere, at a place called Montetosto, along the 13 km long and ca.10 metres wide road, built between 650 and 550 BCE, leading from Caere to the monumental harbour sanctuary in Pyrgi.[12] The building lies four kilometres from the city walls. Giovanni Colonna tentatively suggests that the building was used for the rituals in honour of the Phocaeans,[13] since, unlike similar sixth century BCE monumental palace-like buildings in Murlo (near Siena) and Acquarossa (near Viterbo), it had an altar in the centre of the first, inner courtyard.[14] In addition, a little terracotta head of an anxious, bearded black man (h. 9.5 cm) may have belonged to an *antepagmentum*[15]

4   Translation by G.C. Macauley, *The History of Herodotus*, with my additions between brackets.
5   For the impossibility of reconstructing the nature of ancient epidemics, see Leven, *Antike Medizin*, 219-221 s.v. (retrospektive) 'Diagnosis'; 258 s.v. 'Epidemie'.
6   Torelli, 'Delitto religioso'; MacIntosh Turfa and Harrison, 'Plague'.

7   Thuillier, *Jeux*, 125 fig. 17; 290-291, 379, 617-619 (Olimpiadi), 210 fig. 28; 215-217, 290, 302-303, 317-320, 411-412, 438-439, 445-449, 541-546, 555-557 fig. 57; 561 (Auguri).
8   Livy, *Ab urbe condita* 1.35.9: ...equi pugilesque ex Etruria maxime acciti ('...horses and boxers were mostly summoned from Etruria').
9   A case of stoning prisoners is mentioned by Plutarchus, *Philopoemen* 21.5: 'He (Philopoemen; 183/182 BCE) was buried, then, as was fitting, with conspicuous honours, and at his tomb the captive Messenians were stoned to death.' For comment, see Bonnechere, *Sacrifice humain*, 287; Hughes, *Human sacrifice*, 58-60.
10   MacIntosh, Turfa and Harrison, 'Plague', 9.
11   Cristofani, 'Achille e Troilo'.
12   For scepticism, see Briquel, 'Sacrifice des prisonniers', 93-95; Thuillier, *Jeux*, 487 n. 89.
13   Colonna, in Belelli Marchesini et al., *Santuario*, 10; Toreli, 'Delitto'.
14   Belelli Marchesini et al., *Santuario*, 150, pl. 17 (N).
15   A rectangular slab attached to the frontal short side of a wooden roof beam in a pediment.

Figure 4.1 Tomba delle Olimpiadi at Tarquinia, left and right wall. Courtesy Jean-Paul Thuillier.

Figure 4.2 Caeretan hydria from Cerveteri. After: Furtwängler and Reichhold, *Griechische Vasenmalerei*.

representing the victory of Heracles as civilising hero, over king Busiris and his Egyptian black assistants as is suggested by Colonna.[16] It was Busiris' custom to sacrifice foreigners to Zeus.[17] So the theme may have been meant as a warning not to sacrifice strangers. The Busiris theme is also visible on a Caeretan hydria, found at Cerveteri, dated to ca. 530-510 BCE (fig. 4.2).[18]

The building kept its original, sacred function until ca. 100 BCE when it was converted into a Roman villa rustica. Terracotta votives, among which anatomical ones, dated to the third and second centuries BCE confirm its religious function. The skeleton of a handicapped adult, probably a man, was found, lying with his head against a wall in the south-west corner of room H next to the anterior, main part of the courtyard. He had probably suffered from chondrodysplasia, an illness damaging the growth of bones.[19]

16   Belelli Marchesini et al., *Santuario*, 9, 36-37 (A.I.1), 150, pl. 18, 30.

17   Pherecydes (*Fragmente der griechischen Historiker* 3 F17); Apollodorus 2.5.11.

18   The hydria (now in Vienna, Kunsthistorisches Museum, inv. ANSA-IV-3576), shows Heracles, depicted as an African black, killing his victims near an altar. For other representations of Heracles killing Busiris, see Laurens, 'Busiris'.

19   Belelli Marchesini et al., *Santuario*, 8, 150, 156, 161-162 (analysis by W. Pantano), 192 pl. 10 (room H, inside wall 5 and 6).

He may have served as human victim during the foundation rite of the building.[20] The proximity to the barrow suggests that the rites had a funerary character like the games depicted in the Tomba delle Olimpiadi mentioned before. Herodotus' reference to Delphi may be trustworthy as Caere had a thesaurus there, a treasure house for storing gifts to Apollo, in the sixth century BCE, possibly built after the Sea Battle.[21] To conclude, Herodotus' story may contain some truth. Around 490-480 BCE Etruscans conquered the islands of Lipari, to the north of Sicily. Ovid (*Ibis* 465-6) reads: "...victima vel Phoebo macteris ad aras quam tulit a saevo Theudotus hoste necem."; "...or be sacrificed as a victim to Apollo at the altars, as Theudotus suffered death from a savage enemy." and late antique comments, scholia B and C on Ovid's poetic lines read: "Tyrrheni **obsidentes Liparium** castrum promiserunt Apollini, si faceret eos victores, fortissimum Liparensium ei sacrificare. Habita autem victoria promissum reddiderunt, immolantes ei quondam Theodotum."; "The Tyrrhenians [Etruscans] who besieged the fortification of Lipari promised to Apollo to sacrifice the strongest of the Liparian men if he let them win. After the victory, they kept the promise by sacrificing a man called Theodotus [which means given to god]." inform us on what may have happened.[22] A late echo of this story is transmitted by Tzetzes (*Chiliades* 8.891-892) who wrote in the twelfth century CE: "The Tyrrhenoi (Etruscans) were extremely violent and rather beastly; they even sacrificed human beings in the time of Hiero." The latter is Hieron I, tyrant of Syracuse, who defeated the Etruscan navy off the Greek colony of Cumae in 474 BCE. Most interesting is what Livy (7.15.9-10) tells us about a much later event, the war between Romans and Etruscans from Tarquinia in 358 BCE:

Eodem anno et a consulibus vario eventu bellatum; nam Hernici a C. Plautio devicti subactique sunt. Fabius collega eius incaute atque inconsulte adversus Tarquinienses pugnavit. nec in acie tantum ibi cladis acceptum, quam quod trecentos septem milites Romanos captos Tarquinienses immolarunt, qua foeditate supplicii aliquanto ignominia Romanis insignitior fuit.;

In the same year the consuls too, waged war with varying success. Gaius Plautius defeated the Hernici and reduced them to subjection; his colleague Fabius showed neither prudence nor skill in his battle with the Tarquinians. And yet the disaster experienced on the field was overshadowed by the fact that the Tarquinians sacrificed (immolarunt) three hundred and seven captured Roman soldiers, an act of savage cruelty that greatly emphasized the humiliation of the Roman People.

The sacrificial slaughtering of the prisoners of war took place on the forum of Tarquinia as becomes clear from the report on the events in 354 BCE (Livy 7.19.2-3):

Triumphatum de Tiburtibus; alioquin mitis victoria fuit. In Tarquinienses acerbe saevitum; multis mortalibus in acie caesis, ex ingenti captivorum numero trecenti quinquaginta octo delecti, nobilissimus quisque, qui Romam mitterentur; vulgus aliud trucidatum. nec populus in eos qui missi Romam erant, mitior fuit; medio in foro omnes virgis caesi ac securi percussi. id pro immolatis in foro Tarquiniensium Romanis poenae hostibus redditum.;

A triumph was celebrated over the Tiburtines (the inhabitants of Tibur, nowadays Tivoli), but in all other respects the victory was used with clemency. The men of Tarquinia were shown no ruth; many were slain in the field of battle, and out of the vast number taken prisoners three hundred and fifty-eight were selected – the noblest of them all – to be sent to Rome, and the rest of the populace were put to the sword. Neither were the people less stern towards those who had been sent to Rome, but scourged them all with rods in the middle of the Forum and struck off their heads with an axe. Such was the vengeance they exacted of their enemies for the Romans sacrificed on the forum of the Tarquinians.[23]

It is striking that in 358 BCE Etruscans slaughtered Roman war prisoners as sacrificial victims whilst four years later Romans killed the Etruscan war prisoners who belonged to aristocratic families with rods and an axe. The latter instruments were usually used by lictors, attendants who walked before a consul or another magistrate and could execute sentences of judgment, e.g. behead criminals. The killing in Tarquinia was religious, the second in Rome not. In both cases the killings took place on a forum. Unfortunately, Livy does not indicate to which deity the Etruscans made their sacrifice; maybe to Artum[es]

---

20 Future ^{14}C research, however, has to confirm the proposed date of the skeleton. So, there remains the possibility that the deceased was deposited in late antiquity when the building was already in ruins.

21 Strabo, *Geography* 5.2.3: 'Among the Greeks, however, this city (Agylla/Caere) was in good repute both for bravery and for righteousness; for it not only abstained from all piracy, but also set up at Pytho (Delphi) what is called the treasury (house) of the Agyllaeans.' For comment, see Thuillier, *Jeux*, 483-486.

22 Callimachus, *Aetia* (fragment F93 Pfeifer; 93 Harder). For comments, see Di Fazio, 'Callimachus'; Colonna, 'Apollon'; Briquel, 'Sacrifice des prisonniers', 102-104.

23 For a comment on Livy's texts, see Briquel, 'Épisode'.

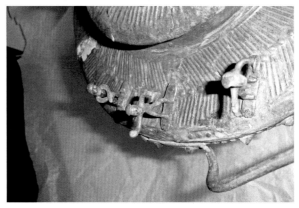

Figure 4.3 Bronze urn from Bisenzio, lid and shoulder. Photo: author.

Figure 4.4 Bronze urn from Bisenzio, shoulder, detail. Photo: author.

(Artemis), judging from an inscription on a bronze staff and terracotta deer heads from the Temple of the Ara della Regina. The forum lies just to the north of the temple.

4.3. Iconography

Let us now turn our attention to iconography. Most interesting is a bronze ash urn from tomb 22 in the Olmo Bello necropolis at Bisenzio, a settlement just to the west of the Lake of Bolsena. The urn, probably of a woman, is dated to ca. 730-700 BCE. On top of the lid sits a chained monstrous being which looks like the fetus of a dog (fig. 4.3).[24]

Nude, ithyphallic men who seem to threaten the animal with their spears march or dance around him. On the shoulder of the urn we see marching or dancing nude, ithyphallic men with hats, (lost) spears and shields, probably warriors, also moving in anti-clockwise direction. At the head of the procession a man pushes a bull towards a man who, holding a club in his left hand, is about to slaughter the animal with a raised spear in his right hand. At the rear a man, a captive, probably a prisoner of war, without hat, is walking with his hands bound in front (fig. 4.4).[25]

These funerary rituals had a symbolic, magical meaning. They are apotropaic, in other words meant to ward off evil, the power of death. The male erections allude to fertility, ongoing life after death. We may not exclude the possibility that the prisoner was due to be slaughtered like the bull at the head of the procession. This interpretation is reinforced by the paintings (fig. 4.5) of an Etrusco-Corinthian painted column krater, called 'Vaso dei Gobbi' (Vase of the Hunchbacks). It was found in tomb II of tumulus I in the Banditaccia necropolis (zone A) of Cerveteri, and dated to ca. 590-570 BCE.[26]

On the shoulder of one side of the vase a priest, a haruspex, judging from his hat with a short apex, leads a bull to the stairs of an altar on which sits a dressed male figure, probably a demon who extends his right hand, holding a round object; on the body at the other side a man carrying a dressed woman with outstretched hands is mounting similar altar stairs, followed by a woman and a horseman. On top of the altar is a bearded head with a snake (?) growing from its neck, probably a demon of death too. The head may belong to a man standing behind the altar extending his right hand to the victim. Although there are two mythological scenes at the right, showing Heracles meeting the centaur Pholos and Heracles fighting Geryon, the altar scene is probably not mythological like the sacrifice of Iphigenia in Aulis or of Polyxena, since the form of the altars is not Greek; the stairs look like those of seventh century BC tumulus I in Cerveteri (fig. 4.6), which holds a tomb in which the vase was found. Originally, the stairs led to an altar on top of the tumulus.[27]

---

24 Villa Giulia, Rome 57066. According to Donati, 'Sacrificio umano', 150, no 6 (orso) the animal is a bear. He holds that the scene represents a sacrifice in the context of hunting. The animal, however, is chained (to the shoulder of the vase). According to biologists of Leiden University it looks like the fetus of a dog. The scene may illustrate a symbolic sham fight. See Van der Meer, *Etrusco ritu*, 68-70, fig. 20 for another monstrous death demon, a *Mischwesen*, consisting of a human being, horse, bear and wolf. In Etruscan wall- and vase paintings a wolf may represent Apollo as an underworld god, see Cristofani, 'Achille e Troilo'.

25 An Etrusco-Corinthian vase (630-590 BCE) shows an interesting parallel: a nude male victim lying supine on a bed, extending his bound arms is threatened by a beast of prey. See Bonfante, 'Human sacrifice', 76 fig. 3. Usually, however, the hands of a prisoner are bound behind his back.

26 Cerveteri, Museo Nazionale 19539 (the vase was probably commissioned and made in Vulci; it is ascribed to the Circle of the Painter of the Knotted Tails). Donati, 'Sacrificio umano', 139 no. 16.

27 See now Prayon, 'Tomb', 76-79.

Figure 4.5 Etrusco-
Corinthian krater from
Cerveteri, details. Courtesy
Luigi Donati.

In addition, one of the step stones decorated with panel reliefs (ca. 580 BCE), probably belonging to the stairs of tomb L in the Monterozzi necropolis at Tarquinia, only shows sphinxes, griffins, a horseman, a panther, a winged man, and a tree-carrying centaur, but also a guardian leading a prisoner with his hands bound behind his back.[28] These pictures may suggest that humans were sacrificed during funerals. The Etruscan interest in human sacrifice also appears from a famous painting in the Tomba dei Tori at Tarquinia (ca. 540 BCE) showing Achilles holding a sacrificial axe instead of a sword in comparable scenes on Attic vases, standing in ambush behind a fountain building about to kill Troilus, the beautiful son of the Trojan king Priam. The fountain is an altar at the same time.[29] Shedding blood for the deceased must have been important as is shown by bloody scenes in the paintings of the Tomba degli Auguri ca. 520 BCE; fig. 4.7) and the Tomba delle Olimpiadi (ca. 510 BCE; fig. 4.1) at Tarquinia.

The paintings in the first tomb show, on the right wall, a man with a bearded mask, holding an aggressive Molossian dog at a leash and an inscription reading his name: Phersu.[30] The dog bites his opponent, a man with a white, round sack over his head, who tries to defend himself with a club. The outcome of the struggle is unclear; in the Tomba degli Auguri Phersu appears a second time, running, dancing or fleeing on the left wall but it is difficult to see whether this is before or after the bloody game. The Latin word *persona*, which means mask or person is derived from Phersu. The scenes show a kind of bloody theatre or an imitation of hunting. Interpretations differ. Some scholars interpret the fight as a forerunner of the much later Roman gladiatorial games that were held at funerals in Rome from 264 BCE onward,[31] though the latter, as we know, are of Campanian origin. Denise Emmanuel-Rebuffat compares the blindfolded man with Heracles who defends himself with his club against Cerberus, the watchdog of the underworld, though the Molossian dog does not have three heads. Anyhow, the scenes illustrate the need of blood.[32] This is in line with what is told by the Christian author Arnobius in his *Adversus nationes* (Against the Pagans) 2.62: '...Etruria libris in Acheronticis pollicentur, certorum animalium sanguine numinibus certis dato divinas animas fieri et ab legibus mortalitatis educi.' '...in Etruria they promise in the Libri Acherontici (the Books of the Underworld) that by giving blood of certain animals to certain divine powers souls become divine and are delivered from the laws of mortality.' Arnobius wrote his book in 303 CE but he quotes Labeo, who wrote in the time of the emperor Augustus. In the fourth century CE Servius, *In Vergilii Aeneidem Commentarii*. 3.168 quotes Labeo too: '...dicit Labeo in libris qui appellantur de diis animalibus: in quibus ait, esse quaedam sacra quibus animae humanae vertantur in deos, qui appellantur animales, quod de animis fiant.' 'Labeo says in the books which are called *De Diis Animalibus*: in which he says that there are certain sacrifices by which human spirits are changed into gods who are called animate deities because they originate

---

28   Prayon, 'Tomb', 78, fig. 3.

29   Cristofani, 'Achille e Troilo'; Camporeale 'Achle'.

30   Emmanuel-Rebuffat, 'Phersu'. Thuillier, 'Jeux', 338-340, 588-591.

31   Livy, *Periocha* 16; Valerius Maximus, *Factorum ac Dictorum Memorabilium Libri IX*, 2.4.7.

32   For the need for bloodshed, see Camporeale, 'Deified deceased', and Warden, 'Blood'.

Figure 4.6 Tumulus I (Banditaccia) at Cerveteri. After: Giglioli, *L'Arte etrusca*.

Figure 4.7 Tomba degli Auguri at Tarquinia, reconstruction. After: https://www.viaggioinbaule.it/tomba-degli-auguri-tarquinia-descrizione/phersu/.

from spirits.' The Tomba delle Olimpiadi shows Phersu and his victim to the right of three runners, a jumper and a discobolus which suggests that the scene belonged to the same funeral program. Phersu is depicted without dog and opponent in the Tomba del Pulcinella (ca. 510 BCE) and in the Tomba del Gallo (ca. 400 BCE) where he is dancing with a female and a male musician. It seems, therefore, that after ca. 510 BCE Phersu lost his cruel role. As for blood shedding, however, the reliefs of a horse-shoe-like grave-stone from Bologna, dated to ca. 400 BCE, are interesting.[33] One side shows a merchantman with the captain on board whose name is Vel Kaikna, the other side depicts in two friezes two men who seem to box (fig. 4.8).

Their left hands, however, are put in gloves with three or four sharp fork-like points. If the points were of metal, they certainly caused bloodshed. In the upper

frieze, from the right, come a dressed man leading a captive, and an umpire holding a *lituus* (staff) and leading a captive too. Probably the 'fork' fighters, (war) prisoners or slaves, were forced to shed blood during funeral games in honour of the deceased. The outcome of the duel is not clear. It seems that after ca. 350 BCE representations of mythological human sacrifices in tomb paintings, on stone sarcophagi from Southern Etruria, and urns from Northern Etruria substitute for real ones. Jacques Heurgon suggests that the reason may have been that human sacrifices were too expensive or that, hopefully, the mores had become more refined.[34] Frequent is the depiction of the Sacrifice of the Trojans by Achilles, a well-known scene partly inspired by Homer,

---

33 Sassatelli, 'Riflessioni'; Sassatelli and Govi, 'Ideologia'; Maggiani, 'Agoni'; Thuillier, *Jeux*, 223-225, fig. 30.

34 Heurgon, *Die Etrusker*, 345: 'Es scheint so, als habe man den Toten ein durch den Mythos verklärtes, bescheidenes Äquivalent für die Menschenopfer bieten wollen, die entweder aus finanziellen Gründen nicht möglich oder auch – was man lieber annehmen möchte – durch die Verfeinerung der Sitten abgeschafft waren'.

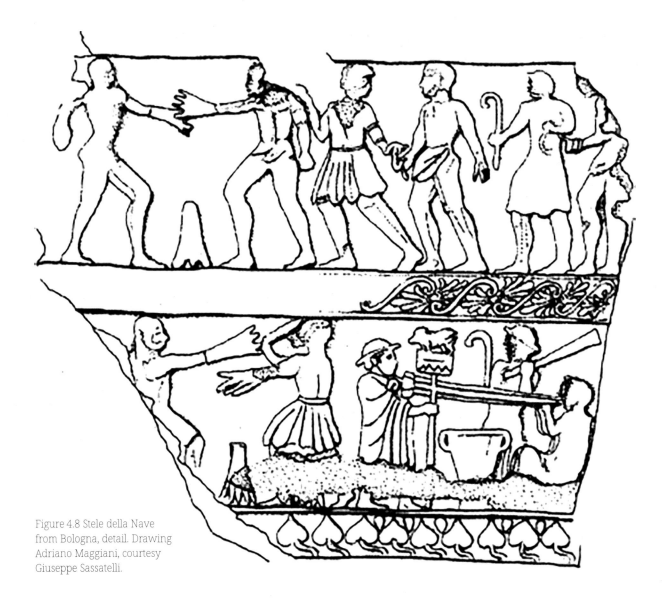

Figure 4.8 Stele della Nave from Bologna, detail. Drawing Adriano Maggiani, courtesy Giuseppe Sassatelli.

Iliad 23.19-23; 175-183,[35] on a Faliscan red-figure vase, in a tomb painting (see below), and on two stone sarcophagi, all dated to ca. 350 BCE, and on an alabaster ash urn from Volterra dated to ca. 200 BCE. The choice of the theme of the painting on the front of the so-called Priest sarcophagus from Tarquinia, made of Parian marble and of Carthagian type, but decorated by an Etruscan painter

in Tarquinia,[36] may have been triggered by the sacrifice of Romans on the forum of the city some years earlier, in 358 BCE. The sarcophagus from Torre San Severo (near Orvieto) shows Achilles cutting the throat of one of three nude Trojans in the presence of the shadow of Patroklos with the Etruscan Hades and Persephone as onlookers on one side (fig. 4.9); on the opposite side Achilles' son Neoptolemos is about to slaughter the almost nude Polyxena, daughter of Priam, king of Troy, in the presence of the shadow of his father Achilles (fig. 4.10).[37]

Both ghosts bear bandages around their heads and across their chests like deceased persons on Apulian red-

---

35   The scenes show the two Aiantes leading Trojan captives who are not mentioned by Homer in the context of the funeral. They were no brothers but often mentioned as acting together in the Iliad. Their different statures mentioned there too are visible in several Etruscan scenes. For a comment on Homer's description of the funeral of Patroklos, see Hughes, *Human Sacrifice*, 49-56; Bonnechere, *Sacrifice humain*, 229, 284-287. For Greek human sacrifices, see Bremmer, 'Myth and Ritual', 55-79. Homer does not approve of human sacrifice (Iliad 23, 176: '(Achilles) planned evil deeds in his heart).' Cf. *Iliad* 18.336-337; 357-359.

36   Van der Meer, *Myths*, 32-33, fig. 9.

37   Van der Meer, *Myths*, 29-31. The scene is not mentioned by Homer but probably inspired by the Ilioupersis. For the sacrifice of Polyxena in Greek literature and visual arts, see Bremmer, 'Myth and Ritual', 72-78; Hughes, *Human Sacrifice*, 61-62.

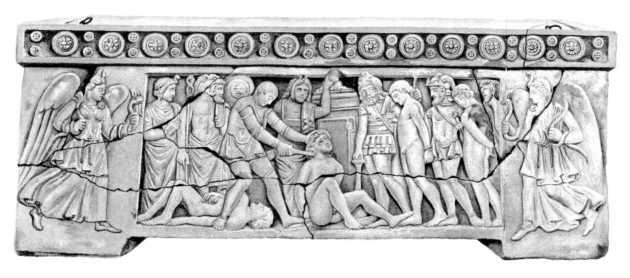

Figure 4.9 Sarcophagus from Torre San Severo, front. After: Monumenti Antichi, *Tav. I.*

Figure 4.10 Sarcophagus from Torre San Severo, back. After: Monumenti Antichi, *Tav. II.*

figure vases. The symmetry of the two compositions[38] and the themes prove that the Etruscans knew Greek myths and the fatal chain of the events. Interestingly, the scenes show local colour as the slaughters take place in front of Etruscan tombs instead of the pyre mentioned by Homer and depicted on an Apulian red-figure vase of the Dareios Painter and an engraved Praenestine bronze cista (ca. 340 BCE). Symmetry also plays a role in the paintings (with inscriptions) from the famous Tomba François at Vulci (ca. 340-310 BCE; now in the Villa Albani at Rome). The painted scene of the Achle's (Achilles') sacrifice of a *truials* (a man from Troja; a Trojan) in the presence of

hinthial Patrucles (the shadow of Patroklos), Achmemrun (Agamemnon), and the underworld gods Charun and Vanth on the left wall (fig. 4.11) is the counterpart of the right wall representing heroes from Vulci, who are about to slaughter their opponents from Velzna (Volsinii veteres/nowadays Orvieto), Sveama (Sovana), Psla (Pisa?) and Rome.

The latter is a man called Cneve Tarchunies rumach (the first Etruscan king of Rome, Lucius Tarquinius, from Tarquinia, or a member of his family). Half shields flanking the door opening in the rear cella invite us to associate both scenes. Among the Vulcian heroes is Macstrna, a name derived from the Latin word magister (military leader) who became, according to Livy, the second Etruscan king of Rome in 578 BCE after L. Tarquinius. The main person in the paintings, Vel Saties, pater familias of the tomb, who stands opposite Nestur (Nestor), thus comparing

---

38   The slaughter of the Trojan captives is flanked by female underworld deities (Vanth) and the slaughter of Polyxena by male underworld deities (Charun), in both cases on raised relief panels.

Figure 4.11 Painting from Tomba François, Vulci: Sacrifice of the Trojans. Drawing Carlo Ruspi, ca. 1850.

himself with a Greek wise old man, may have ordered the depiction of Vulci's glorious past to encourage fellow-citizens because of the threatening military aggression of Rome in Southern Etruria. As for other representations, the Sacrifice of Iphigenia in Aulis on Hellenistic urns from Chiusi, Volterra and from Perugia was even more popular, probably because it had a happy ending. Artemis/Diana, rendered as Vanth, the Etruscan goddess of death, brings a deer as substitute for Iphigenia who will be carried off to the country of the Taurians.[39] There are indications that even in the third to first centuries BCE human sacrifice was practiced, be it incidentally. A third century BCE sherd of a black-gloss bowl from a sanctuary at Cetamura del Chianti (near Siena), mentions Lur, a deity with infernal, martial, protective and oracular functions. Based on the engraved scene on the reverse of a bronze mirror (ca. 350 BCE), now in the Pushkin Museum of Fine Arts in Moscow, showing an inscribed sitting man holding a dagger, called Lur, with a severed head above him, a standing Tinia (Jupiter) holding a lightning bolt and an unnamed youth whose right

foot rests on a rock, Nancy de Grummond presumes that humans were sacrificed to Lur as a god of the underworld.[40] His name may be akin to the Latin adjective *luridus* (lurid), an epithet of Orcus, a Roman deity of the underworld.[41] A strange ritual, which caused a slow death, took place at Rome during sacrifices in 228, 216 and 114 BCE.[42] A pair of a Gaulish man and woman and a pair of a Greek man and woman were buried alive, probably intended as an apotropaic rite, to ward off enemies. Livy writes that it was 'not at all a Roman sacred ritual.'[43] As the Greeks and Gauls were enemies of the Etruscans in the fourth century BCE, the origin of this indirect killing of human couples may have

---

40   De Grummond, 'Lur', 311, fig. 5-7.

41   Van der Meer, *Liber linteus*, 97-98.

42   Schwenn, *Menschenopfer*, 148-154. Várhelyi, 'Specters'.

43   Other sources on 228 BCE are: Cassius Dio 12.50; Orosius 4.13.3; Scholion (ad) Lycophron 602; Plutarchus, *Life of Marcellus* 3.5-7 mentions that the ritual was prescribed by (Greek) Sibylline books; Zonaras 8.19; on 114 BCE: Plutarchus, *Quaestiones Romanae* 83 (or 283 F). Minucius Felix, Octavius 30.4: Ritus fuit … Romanis Graecum et Graecam, Gallum et Gallam in sacrificiis viventes obruere ('It was a Roman custom to bury alive a Greek man and woman, a Gaulish man and woman during sacrifices').

---

39   LIMC V, s.v. Iphigeneia; Van der Meer, *Liber linteus*, 40-41, figs. 11a and b (where a pig instead of a deer is sacrificed).

Figure 4.12 Sarcophagus from Tuscania. After: Van der Meer, *Myths and More.*

its roots in Etruria. In addition, in 216 BCE Rome was at war with Hannibal, not with Gauls or Greeks. Livy 22.57.6 writes about the events of this year when the disastrous battle of Cannae took place: 'Interim ex fatalibus libris sacrificia aliquot extraordinaria facta, inter quae Gallus et Galla, Graecus et Graeca in foro boario sub terram uiui demissi sunt in locum saxo consaeptum, iam ante hostiis humanis, minime Romano sacro, imbutum.'; 'In the meantime some extraordinary sacrifices were made on account of the Fatal Books, among which a Gaulish man and woman, a Greek man and woman were sent alive under the earth, to a place enclosed with stone(s), which was already soaked by human victims, not at all a Roman sacred rite.' The Fatal Books were Etruscan or Greek, not Roman.[44] Interestingly, Pliny writes in *Historia Naturalis* (28.12): 'boario vero in foro Graecum Graecamque defossos aut aliarum gentium cum quibus tum res esset etiamnunc nostra aetas vidi'; 'that on the Forum Boarium (in Rome), however, a Greek man and woman were buried or (pairs) of other people with whom was war then, sees now even our time (the first century CE).' The front of a sarcophagus of a female, called Thanchvil, from the Tomba dei Vipinana at Tuscania (ca. 310-300 BCE) may show the preparation of the burying alive of a nude, probably seated Gaulish pair, watched by Mars and Venus who appear or stand behind the altar in the centre (fig. 4.12).[45]

Even in the last centuries BCE human sacrifice may have taken place. During the Bacchanalia in Rome, which according to Livy were introduced from Etruria 'like the contagion of a disease,' unwilling initiates were

sacrificed as victims.[46] The Senate forbade the Dionysiac festivals in 186 BCE.[47] From the second century BCE dates a terracotta ash urn from Chiusi showing a bound man in front of the door of a tomb or the gate of the underworld. Larissa Bonfante interprets him as a captive destined for human sacrifice.[48] Laura Ambrosini, however, lists similar scenes on five other Chiusine terracotta ash urns and concludes that the bound persons, in two cases led by a custodian, represent cursed humans.[49] The size of the persons, however, seems to be in favour of Bonfante's interpretation. From the early first century BCE dates a Volterran urn showing the killing of a man in a grove, in the presence of Artemis/Vanth who sits in a tree (fig. 4.13).

Servants holding ritual vases give a realistic flavour to the probably non-mythological scene. Marjatta Nielsen suggests that the killing may have happened in the war between consul Sulla and the Etruscans around 80 BCE.[50] The Roman senate had prohibited the sacrifice of humans in 97 BCE.[51] The persisting practice in Etruria, however, may explain why Octavian, who later became emperor Augustus, is said to have sacrificed three hundred senators and *equites* on an altar erected to the Divus Julius Caesar in Perugia on the Ides of March in 41/40 BCE, as a revenge and in memory of the day when Caesar was murdered in 44 BCE.[52] Octavian punished the city because it had

---

44   Livy 5.15.11 (Etruscan books); 22.9.8 (the Xviri (sacris faciundis) consult Sibylline books).

45   Van der Meer, *Myths*, 54-57, fig. 27. Steuernagel, *Menschenopfer*, 28-29, 47-50. In a thiasus scene on the body of an engraved Praenestine cista, now in Chicago, Field Museum of Natural History inv. 25034 (B. Bordenache Battaglia, *Le ciste prenestine* I.1 (Roma, 1979), 77 no. 14, pl. 90) a woman grasps the hair of a frontally rendered girl (an initiand?) threatening her with a dagger. A maenad holds the girl's left hand.

46   Livy 39.13: ....pro victimis immolari. For a comment, see Van der Meer, *Etrusco ritu*, 120-126. For human sacrifice and the Greek Dionysiac cult, see Bonnechere, *Sacrifice humain*, 181-225.

47   *Corpus Inscriptionum Latinarum* I², 581.

48   Bonfante, *Sacrifice*, 77, fig. 5.

49   Ambrosini, 'Nuovi dati', 186-189, figs. 3a-d and 4, pl. VIa-b.

50   Nielsen and Rathje, 'Artumes', 287-288.

51   Pliny, *Historia Naturalis* 30.3.11: 'senatus consultum factum est, ne homo immoletur.' ('A decision of the Senate is made that no human being should be sacrificed').

52   Suetonius, *Augustus* 15.1: ... hostiarum more mactati (' ...they were killed like animal victims'). Seneca, *De Clementia* 11.1; Cassius Dio 48.14.4. Appian, *The Civil Wars* 5.48 and Velleius Paterculus 2.74 do not mention the sacrifice. For a critical comment, see Briquel, 'Sacrifice humain', 39-63.

Figure 4.13 Urn from Volterra. After: Körte and Von Brunn, *I rilievi delle urne etrusche* II.

harboured and supported the rebellious consul Lucius Antonius. It is not impossible that Octavian imitated an old Etruscan rite.

4.4. Archaeological evidence

Let us now turn to the archaeological, material evidence, first to skeletons in a non-funerary context that may prove the practice of human sacrifices from ca. 820 to 550 BCE. The monumental complex, also called sacred area, maybe first dedicated to an Artemis-like goddess and later on to Uni (Juno),[53] in Pian di Civita in the west part of Tarquinia has yielded eight skeletons and fragments of skeletons, all oriented with their head to the east, without or with very few personal belongings.[54] This is remarkable as humans were usually buried in cemeteries, and sometimes under the floors of huts.[55] The skeleton of a ca. eight years-old boy in Pian di Civita, dated to the end of the ninth century BCE, buried next to the central rock cavity,[56] seems to have been epileptic but he died in a natural way. His illness may have

been interpreted as a *morbus sacer*.[57] Skeletons of newborn babies or fetuses were buried in the seventh century BCE. One was buried under the temple-like building (building bèta) with a rectangular enclosing stone wall built in Phoenician style, probably as a foundation sacrifice. The skeleton of a ten-years-old boy, whose feet were buried under a wall, was found without head (fig. 4.14).[58]

The head was cut from the body, which, again, is an indication of human sacrifice made during a foundation.[59] Further, the skeleton of an adult man was found, buried with the sherd of an Euboean geometric pot dated to ca. 750-725 BCE. His skull shows a healing sword-wound and a more recent fatal one caused by an axe. It has been conjectured that the man was a captive Greek seaman (a pirate?) from Euboea, which had two colonies in Italy, Cumae and Pithecusae. He may have been executed for expiatory reasons. However, we cannot be sure that the sherd proves the man's origin from Euboea. In addition, why was he first cared for and sacrificed or killed later on? From the fourth to the second century BCE there is evidence for symbolic ritual killing. A pair of inscribed lead statuettes (18 and 16 cm high), dated to the third century BCE, show a nude man, called Zer[t]u[r] Cecnas, and a nude woman, called Velia Satnea, both with their hands bound

53 Bonghi Jovino, 'Tarquinia'. Types, 9-10, 13.

54 Bonghi Jovino, 'Tarquinia', 33-37. Donati, 'Sacrifici', 139, nos. 11-14. It is, however, extremely difficult to find material traces of epilepsy in a skeleton.

55 Di Fazio, 'Sacrifici umani', 484-486.

56 The cavity, centre of the complex, may have received blood from sacrificial animals slaughtered in Building beta in the seventh century BCE.

57 Leven, *Antike Medizin*, 260-261, s.v. 'Epilepsie'.

58 Bonghi Jovino, *Tarquinia Project*, 167, fig. 5.

59 For parallels in the Greek world, see Bonghi Jovino, *Tarquinia*, 35.

Figure 4.14 Skeleton in Pian di Civita, Tarquinia. Courtesy Maria Bonghi Jovino.

on their backs, was found in an older, seventh or sixth century BCE tomb in Sovana.[60] Perhaps it symbolises the imaginary punishment of adulterous persons by wishing them dead. In addition, graffito-like inscriptions on small lead tablets, found in tombs at Monte Pitti near Populonia and at Volterra, list the names of cursed persons who were wanted dead by an anonymous person. The words '…thapicun thapintas…' probably mean 'I curse, having cursed…'.[61] The magic ritual, however, is not typically Etruscan. The Greeks called curse inscriptions *katadesmoi*, and the Romans *defixiones*, words which mean binding down, enchantment, bringing persons under a magic spell. Finally, for completeness' sake, it should be mentioned that in the second century BCE *haruspices* (seers) ordered that hermaphrodites (*androgyni, semimares*) had to be killed[62] or closed in a chest and thrown into the sea as they were seen as negative omens.[63] The interpretation of livers, lightning and monstra belonged to the competency of these Etruscan priests. The act of casting out was not a human sacrifice but a slow ritual killing.

4.5. Conclusion

Although the evidence is not abundant, I conclude, mainly on the base of archaeological data, that the Etruscans practiced human sacrifice incidentally, during the founding of a sacred building, and during funerals, in the latter case probably because the dead were supposed to need blood. Ritual killings of captives took place after a battle, probably as an act of vengeance. After ca. 510 Phersu lost his cruel, bloodthirsty character, and after ca. 350 BCE mythological depictions may have replaced real killings of war captives.[64] Indirect slow killings were burying alive, and throwing hermaphrodites into the sea. Curse texts express symbolic, wishful ritual killings. Some Etruscan rites like live burials may have been repeated in the Roman period.

4.6. Acknowledgments

My warm thanks go to Laura Michetti and especially to Jean MacIntosh Turfa.

60   Massarelli, *Testi*, 214-217; Ambrosini, 'Nuovi dati', pl. VId. Massarelli holds that the statuettes have the same meaning as tabellae defixionum (curse tablets).
61   Massarelli, *Testi*, 177-214, 217-220.
62   Livy 39.22.5; Obsequens (IV AD) 3 (on 186 BCE).
63   Livy 27.37. 5-6; 31.12.6-8; Obsequens 22 (on 142 BCE); 36 (on 117 BCE). Orosius (ca. 400 CE) 5.4.8. For the passages not mentioning haruspices, see Obsequens 27-28, 32, 34-37, 47-48, 50.

64   The Achilles and Troilos scene in the Tomba dei Tori (ca. 540 BCE) mentioned above, however, may have been a far earlier example of replacement.

4.7. References

Ambrosini, L, 'Nuovi dati sul tema dell'adligatus in Etruria e il cratere del Funnel Group dalla tomba 33 di Aléria', in Paoletti, O., ed., *La Corsica e Populonia. Atti del XXVIII Convegno di Studi Etruschi ed Italici. Bastia.Aléria. Piombino.Populonia, 25-29 ottobre 2011* (Roma, 2015), 177-195.

Belelli Marchesini, B., M.C. Biella, and L.M. Michetti, *Il santuario di Montetosto sulla via Caere-Pyrgi* (Roma, 2015).

Bernardini, P, P.G. Spanu, and R. Zucca, eds, *Machè. La battaglia del Mare sardonio. Studi e ricerche* (Cinisello Balsamo, 2000).

Bonfante, L., 'Human sacrifice. Etruscan rituals for death and for life', in C. Chiaramonte Treré, G. Bagnasco Gianni, and F. Chiesa, eds, *Interpretando l'antico. Scritti di archeologia offerti a Maria Bonghi Jovino I, Quaderni di Acme* 134, 1 (2012), 67-82.

Bonghi Jovino, M., 'Tarquinia. Types of Offerings, Etruscan Divinities and Attributes in the Archaeological Record', in L.B. van der Meer, ed., *Material Aspects of Etruscan Religion. Proceedings of the International Colloquium Leiden, May 229 and 30, 2008* (Leuven, Paris, Walpole, MA, 2010), 5-16.

Bonghi Jovino, M., *Tarquinia etrusca. Tarconte e il primato della città* (Roma, 2008).

Bonghi Jovino, M., 'The Tarquinia Project: A Summary of 25 Years of Excavation', *American Journal of Archaeology* 114 (2010), 161-180.

Bonnechere, P., *Le sacrifice humain en Grèce ancienne. Kernos, Supplément* 3 (Athens, Liège, 1994).

Bonnechere, P., 'Le sacrifice humain à la croisée des a priori: quelques remarques méthodologiques', in À. A. Nagy and F. Presecendi, eds, *Sacrifices humains. Dossiers, discours, comparaisons. Actes du colloque tenu à l'Université de Genève, 19-20 mai 2011* (Turnhout, 2013), 21-37.

Brelich, A., *Presupposti del sacrificio umano* (Roma, 1966).

Bremmer, Jan N., 'Myth and Ritual in Greek Human Sacrifice: Lykaion, Polyxena and the Case of the Rhodian Criminal', in Jan Bremmer, ed., *The Strange World of Human Sacrifice*, (Leuven, Paris, Dudley, MA, 2007), 55-79.

Briquel, D., 'Sur un épisode sanglant des relations entre Rome et les cités étrusques: les massacres de prisonniers au cours de la guerre de 358/351', in *La Rome des premiers siècles, légende et histoire. Table ronde en l'honneur de M. Pallottino, Paris, mai 1990*, Biblioteca di Studi Etruschi 24 (Firenze, 1992), 37-46.

Briquel, D., 'Le sacrifice humain attribué à Octave lors du siege de Pérouse', in G. Bonamente, ed., *Augusta Perusia. Studi storici e archeologici sull'epoca del bellum Perusinum* (Perugia, 2012), 39-63.

Briquel, D., 'Le sacrifice des prisonniers faisait-il partie du rituel étrusque de la victoire?', in C. Chiaramonte Treré, G. Bagnasco Gianni, and F. Chiesa, eds, *Interpretando l'antico. Scritti di archeologia offerti a Maria Bonghi Jovino I Quaderni di Acme* 134 (2012) 83-109.

Camporeale, G., 'Achle', in *Lexicon Iconographicum Mythologiae Classicae* I, (Zürich, München, Düsseldorf, 1981), 200-214.

Camporeale, G., 'The Deified Deceased in Etruscan Culture', in S. Bell and H. Nagy, eds, *New Perspectives on Etruria and Early Rome: In Honor of Richard Daniel De Puma* (Madison, 2009), 220-250.

Colonna, G., 'Apollon, les Étrusques et Lipari', *Mélanges de l'école français de Rome, Antiquité* 96 (1984), 557-578.

Cristofani, M., 'Achille e Troilo', in M.A. Rizzo, ed., *Un artista etrusco e il suo mondo. Il Pittore di Micali* (Roma, 1988), 101-102.

Di Fazio, M., 'Sacrifici umani e uccisioni rituali nel mondo etrusco', *Rendiconti della Accademia Nazionale dei Lincei. Classe di scienze morali, storiche e filologiche*, serie 9, 3, volume 12, 3 (2001), 437-505.

Di Fazio, M., 'Callimachus and the Etruscans: human sacrifice between, myth, history, and historiography', *Histos* 7 (2013), 48-69.

Donati, L., 'Il sacrificio umano', in *Thesaurus Cultus Rituum Antiquorum* 1 (Chicago, 2004), 136-139, 150.

Emmanuel-Rebuffat, D., 'Le jeu du Phersu à Tarquinia: une nouvelle interprétation', *Comptes rendus des scéances de l'Académie des Inscriptions et de Belles-Lettres*, 127 (1983), 421-438.

Furtwängler, A. and K. Reichhold, *Griechische Vasenmalerei* (München, 1904).

Giglioli, G. Q., *L'Arte etrusca* (Milan, 1935).

Grummond, N. de, 'The cult of Lur: Prophecy and human sacrifice', *Mediterranea* 11 (2014), 307-318.

Herodotus, *The History of Herodotus*, Translation by G.C. Macauley (London,New York, 1890).

Heurgon, J., *Die Etrusker* (Stuttgart, 1971).

Hughes, D.D., *Human Sacrifice in Ancient Greece* (London, 1991).

Körte, Gustav and Heinrich von Brunn, *I rilievi delle urne etrusche* (Berlin, 1890).

Laurens, A.-F., 'Busiris', in *Lexicon Iconographicum Mythologiae Classicae* III (Zurich, München, Düsseldorf, 1986), 147-152.

Leven, K.-H., *Antike Medizin. Ein Lexikon* (München, 2005).

MacIntosh Turfa, J. and A. Harrison, 'The Plague of Caere (c. 535 BCE): airborne botulism?', *Medical Research Archives* 3 (2015), 1-14.

Maggiani, A., 'Agoni funebri 'hellenikois nomois' per Vel Kaiknas', *Ocnus* 5 (1997), 123-135.

Massarelli, R., *I testi etruschi su piombo* (Pisa, Roma, 2014).

Meer, L.B. van der, 'Greek and local elements in a sporting scene by the Micali Painter', in E. Swaddling, ed., *Italian Iron Age Artefacts in the British Museum. Papers of the Sixth British Museum Classical Colloquium* (London, 1986), 439-446.

Meer, L.B. van der, *Myths and more on Etruscan Stone Sarcophagi* (Louvain, Dudley, 2004).

Meer, L.B. van der, *Liber Linteus Zagrabiensis. The Linen Book of Zagreb. A Comment on the Longest Etruscan Text* (Louvain, Dudley, 2007).

Meer, L.B. van der, *Etrusco ritu. Case studies in Etruscan ritual behavior* (Louvain, Walpole, MA, 2011).

Monumenti Antichi (Reale Accademia Nazionale dei Lincei). XXIV (Milan, 1916).

Nielsen, M. and A. Rathje, 'Artumes in Etruria – The borrowed goddess', in T. Fischer-Hansen and B. Poulsen, eds, *From Artemis to Diana. The Goddess of Man and Beast*, Danish Studies in Classical Archaeology, Acta Hyperborea 12 (Copenhagen, 2009), 261-301.

Prayon, F., 'The Tomb as Altar', in L.B. van der Meer, ed., *Material Aspects of Etruscan Religion. Proceedings of the International Colloquium Leiden*, May 29 and 30, 2008 (Leuven, Paris, Walpole, MA, 2010), 75-82.

Sassatelli, G., 'Riflessioni sulla 'stele della nave' di Bologna', in S. Bruni, ed., *Etruria e Italia preromana. Studi in onore di G. Camporeale II* (Pisa, Roma, 2009), 833-840.

Sassatelli, G. and Govi, E., 'Ideologia funeraria e celebrazione del defunto nelle stele etrusche di Bologna', *Studi Etruschi* 63 (2007 [2009]), 67-92.

Schwenn, F., *Die Menschenopfer bei den Griechen und den Römern* (Giessen, 1915).

Steuernagel, D., *Menschenopfer und Mord am Altar. Griechische Mythen in etruskischen Gräber*, Palilia 3 (Wiesbaden, 1998).

Torelli, M., 'Delitto religioso. Qualche indizio sulla situazione in Etruria', in *Le délit religieux dans la cité antique. Actes de la table ronde de Rome (6-7 avril 1978)*, Collection de l'École française de Rome 48 (Rome, 1981), 1-7.

Thuillier, J.-P., *Les jeux athlétiques dans la civilisation étrusque* (Rome, 1985).

Várhelyi, Z., 'The Specters of Roman Imperialism: The Live Burial of Gauls and Greeks at Rome', *Classical Antiquity* 26 (2007), 277-304.

Warden, P.G., 'The Blood of Animals: Predation and Transformation in Etruscan Funerary Representation', in S. Bell and H. Nagy, eds, *New Perspectives on Etruria and Early Rome: In Honor of Richard Daniel De Puma* (Madison, 2009), 198-219.

Weber, K.-W., *Geschichte der Etrusker* (Stuttgart, 1979).

Chapter 5

Phoenician synthesis

Patterns of human sacrifice and problems
with ritual killing

Brien Garnand*

5.1. Introduction[1]

The study of that type of sacrificial infanticide allegedly practiced by the ancient Phoenicians
faces formidable obstacles. Such research demands specialist knowledge across a range
of varied disciplines – classical philology (Greek, Latin), biblical philology (Hebrew) and
Northwest Semitic epigraphy (Phoenician, Punic, Neo-Punic), ancient history, archaeology
and osteology, history of religions, etc., a range that makes holistic interpretation difficult.
We have many textual references, but they are tendentious and lack detail; numerous
inscriptions, but tantalizingly brief and enigmatic; thousands upon thousands of artifacts,
but nearly all unscientifically extracted with no record of their context. Even the history
of scholarship of the Phoenician rites remains fraught with peril, since it was born in
an environment of Orientalism and has since devolved into a seemingly inexhaustible,
polarising debate about whether their practices should be categorized as human sacrifice or
ritual killing, or dismissed entirely, and about whether the cremated infant remains found
in so-called *tophet* precincts were the product of natural distribution or artificial selection.
Here our focus rests less upon resolving these debates and more upon methodology, upon
how we can best reduce uncertainty when working with incomplete data. In other words,
how we can best distinguish the signal from the noise.

5.2. Orientalist use of "human sacrifice" and redemption through "ritual killing"

In scholarship during the eighteenth to mid-nineteenth century, learned commentators
recognised the significant role played by Phoenicians in their varied cultural contacts and
interactions across the Mediterranean.[2] Those clever merchants mentioned in Homer, had
preceded the Greeks in westward expansion – they brought the alphabet, founded cities, and

---

1   The symposium "Rituele Mensdoding en Mensenoffers," corresponded with the Rijksmuseum van
     Oudheden exhibition *Carthago*, so it is particularly fitting to record here the four stelae exported by
     Humbert in 1817 (fig. 4), which formed an early kernel of the museum's collection. A previous version of
     this paper was presented at the conference *Santuari mediterranei tra Oriente e Occidente* (Civitavecchia/
     Rome, 18-22 June 2014).
2   Winterer, 'Model Empire'.

*Howard University,
Washington DC

Figure 5.1 The Italians in Tripoli – Italy Draws the Sword of Old Rome. After: Matania, 'Italians in Tripoli'.

established trade networks. By the latter 1800s, however, Philophoenicianism had given way to Philhellenism, where the role of Greek cultural contacts and interactions and those of their Roman successors was elevated, while the Phoenician role was denigrated, arguing that they brought only their limited syllabary, founded mere trading posts and their commerce barely penetrated inland. This demotion stemmed in part from ready credulity of inimical and tendentious ancient sources, focusing only upon certain allegations of ritual infanticide that marked Phoenicians and their religion as raw and savage.

Contemporary nineteenth century racial theories that legitimised colonialism and imperialism also contributed to this demotion. Scientific racism and nationalist history established a foundation for research into the Phoenicians,[3] undertaken both by scholars of the Near East[4] and by "historical" novelists.[5] Edward Said labelled this specific form of essentialist thought "Orientalism" – on the one hand, an imaginative designation of Levantine peoples and their mentality; on the other hand, a discursive designation that describes a "Western style for dominating, restructuring, and having authority over the Orient."[6]

Narratives about superior Romans defeating ancient Phoenicians, in particular, provided a discursive paradigm to legitimise how their Indo-European descendants (i.e., the French) should extend dominion over modern Phoenicians in the Maghreb (i.e., the Arabs of Algeria and Tunisia). These same narratives continued to have salience into the twentieth century, as the French extended their control into the Levant (Lebanon and Syria). Italians could also readily imagine themselves as Romans returning to reclaim Libya (fig. 5.1), as in the film *Cabiria*, with intertitles written by the irredentist D'Annunzio.[7] Its Roman heroes save the eponymous young maiden from depraved Semitic rites of child sacrifice, while distracted Phoenicians bow before Moloch in a crude parody of Islamic prayer (fig. 5.2).

Some had resisted these tendencies and had tried to rehabilitate the Phoenicians, first in response to Flaubert's *Salammbô*,[8] then as a general response to over-reliance upon inimical and tendentious Greek, Latin, and Hebrew sources,[9] or in specific response to presumably misguided excavations at Motya and Carthage that had seemed to confirm Phoenician ritual infanticide.[10] The most significant shift toward rehabilitation, however, came in the wake of the so-called "reflexive turn" in anthropology, which itself followed on the literary critique of Said, when Martin Bernal (*Black Athena* 1987) sought to demonstrate how scholars of Greece and Rome had systematically ignored or distorted Phoenician contributions to Mediterranean civilization.

At the same time, within the nascent field of Phoenician Studies, two key rehabilitative works appeared, quite independent of Bernal and of each other – one by Moscati (*I Fenici*, 1988) and the other by Gras, Rouillard and Texidor (*L'Univers phénicien*, 1989). This paradigm shift had begun in the mid-1980s, after Bénichou-Safar had argued that, since infants were absent from other cemeteries, the *tophet* should be considered a cemetery for children who had died prematurely;[11] after Simonetti had discarded the classical sources as unreliable and irrelevant;[12] and after Fedele suggested that the majority of the bones from the Tharros *tophet* belonged to perinatal infants. These all necessitated a "drastic" or "global" reframing of Phoenician ritual activities.[13] The call for a *ridimensionamento* reached its

3   E.g. Michelet, *Histoire romain*, 125, 177-78; Gobineau, *L'inégalité des races*, 371-372, 396.
4   E.g. Renan, *Histoire générale*; *Mission de Phénicie*.
5   E.g. Flaubert, *Salammbô*.

6   Said, *Orientalism* 2-3; cf. Bernal *Black Athena*, 233-237.
7   Bertetto and Rondolino, *Cabiria e il suo Tempo*; Musso, *Cabiria*.
8   E.g. Frœhner, 'La roman archéologique'; Sainte-Beuve *Salammbô*; cf. Gras, Rouillard, and Teixidor, *L'Univers phénicien*, 151.
9   E.g. Bérard, *Les Phéniciens et l'Odyssée*.
10   E.g. Saumagne, 'Notes sur les découvertes'.
11   Bénichou-Safar, 'À propos des ossements' and 'Sur l'incinération'; cf. Schaeffer, 'Communication', Weinfeld, 'Worship of Moloch'.
12   Simonetti, 'Sacrifici umani'.
13   *Drastico ridimensionamento*, Fedele, 'Anthropology of the *tophet*'; *riconsiderazione globale*, Ribichini, *Il tofet*, 120.

Figure 5.2 *Sacrificio a Baal* (*i.e.* Moloch), with Fulvius Auxilla, Maciste, and Croessa in the foreground. Courtesy Collezione Museo nazionale del cinema, used with permission.

tipping point at 1986 conferences in Sardinia[14] and Rome,[15] after which this reframing garnered wide support.[16]

Angelo Brelich's distinction between ritual killing and human sacrifice provided the key theoretical groundwork for rehabilitation, allowing Phoenicians to plead guilty of a lesser charge. Instead of frequent sanguinary offerings of infants made to a divinity (*riti cultuali*), scholars of the *ridimensionamento* only allowed for infrequent offerings of older victims with no divine recipient (*riti autonomi*).[17] While primitive cultures might often employ human sacrifice to sustain a divinity, higher civilizations might employ ritual killing only in exceedingly rare circumstances to avert a disaster. Since classical and biblical sources speak of rare crises and

older victims (specifically war prisoners), this allowed an attractive solution for the Phoenicians, who could join the higher civilizations that were said to follow such practices, in contrast to the regular sacrificial infanticide that had uniquely adhered to them. The acceptance or denial of cultic sacrifice / ritual killing dichotomy has become a definitional feature of the ensuing debate.[18] Yet such a dichotomy was never maintained in antiquity – we find little to no semantic distinction maintained between "human sacrifice" and "ritual killing" in classical (or biblical) terminology.[19] Furthermore, scholars who apply this distinction for the sake of rehabilitation have failed to note two key points identified by Paolo Xella – first, whenever victims (like war prisoners) were offered to a divinity, Brelich himself might very well have categorized those situations as cultic sacrifice; second, he did in fact mention Phoenician sacrifice, which he categorized as

14   Moscati, 'L'olocausto dei fanciulli'; Ribichini, 'Il sacrificio di fanciulli'.

15   Moscati, 'Il sacrificio punico'.

16   Cf. Moscati, 'L'olocausto'; idem, *Gli adoratori di Moloch*; Ribichini 'Il sacrificio' 'La questione del "tophet"; Moscati and Ribichini, 'Il sacrificio dei bambini'; Ribichini, 'La questione del "tophet"'; Bénichou-Safar, *Le tophet de Salammbô*; Bernardini, 'Per una rilettura'; Buttitta, 'Tophet'.

17   Brelich, *Presupposti*; Idem, *Introduzione*, 32ff.

18   D'Andrea, *Bambini nel "limbo"*, 67-98, 169; cf. 44-45; Mosca has offered a third option, a sort of transformation through fire ('The Tophet', 119-136).

19   Hughes, *Human Sacrifice*, 1-12.

regular, primitive, and tied to cult.[20] According to Brelich's own arguments, the charges of cultic human sacrifice would stand, not replaced by autonomous ritual killing.

Whereas some traditionalists had painted a literary-positivist picture of Oriental excess (evoking the odor of burnt flesh), serving to advance the thesis that the Phoenicians practiced ritual infanticide,[21] the *ridimensionamento* rehabilitation offers a detached and more scientific reconstruction of burial ritual (describing the calcination of bones).[22] The traditional *thesis*, that they practiced cultic sacrifice, has been supplanted by its *antithesis*, that they did not. After dismissing all of the classical and biblical sources as overtly hostile, the remaining archaeological and epigraphic evidence provides explanations both disjointed and inconsistent, some combination of funerary and votive offerings that would serve as some sort of ritual purification or communal integration. Recent work suggests that the tide may perhaps be turning once again to a holistic interpretation – not back to an extreme positivist/imperialist narrative of depravity, not back to an ideologically-charged and stagnant debate about whether or not the Phoenician sacrificed infants, but instead a new and modest *synthesis* that demonstrates how the textual and material evidence remains consistent and coherent.[23]

Besides misapplying Brelich's theory, scholars of the *ridimensionamento* have amplified the significance of variations and gaps in our evidence. After disassembling various categories of evidence that previously had been conjoined, they then analyse and dismiss each category in isolation, finding only confusion and contradiction concerning the age of the victims, the meaning and function of the rites, the intended recipient, etc. This process seems an inversion of the Indian parable of the six blind men and the elephant, which cautions against compartmentalized assessment of the unknown from limited data. In our case, most scholars had at one time agreed that they were holding on to a comprehensive "elephant" (infant sacrifice). A revisionist then approached each individual category of evidence and suggested, "That leg could be a tree!" or "That trunk could be a snake!" etc. In this case, giving priority to disconnected parts instead of the whole results in a chimera, a multi-use facility for votive / burial / purfiication / (pre)enfranchisement with attendant animal sacrifice and rare human sacrifice, but this hardly seems more accurate, plausible or coherent than comprehensive assessment.

Here we will follow this compartmentalization method, to a certain extent, in that we look at each category of evidence separately but, in contrast, we examine how the sacrificial syntax, or "signal," within each category of evidence remains consistent. We start with a brief survey of the tendentious classical sources and test them for consistency, next the biblical sources, then the inscriptions and the archaeological evidence from the precincts themselves. These votive precincts remain the best-attested components of Phoenician religion, particularly those precincts found in the central Mediterranean that were dedicated to Baʻal (and Tinnit), where we find the cremated remains of infants in urns buried beneath stone memorials. We have yet to find such precincts either in the far West (in Iberia or Morocco) or in the East (although Amathus on Cyprus, and both Tyre and Achziv in the Levant have provided weak contenders). We have dozens of classical and biblical texts describing Phoenician ritual infanticide that have adhered to these sites, the vast majority of the Phoenician-Punic epigraphic corpus consists of dedications from these sites, and the standard typologies of Phoenician artifacts – urns, amulets, sculpture – derive from these sites.

5.3. The signal and the noise
Repetition within the literary sources, the rigid formulae of the inscriptions, and the limited repertoire of the material remains argue for consistency. The redundancy of this system and the enormity of the data set (comparatively large for antiquity) allow for comprehension even when individual objects have no context, when individual inscriptions have letters or words missing, or when individual urns are fragmentary. In the same way that brief silence and static do not prevent comprehension during electronic communications over radio waves and transmission lines, singular gaps and errors within this votive sacrificial system create background interference but, in terms of information theory, the redundancy within a system allows basic information ("signal") to overcome distortion ("noise"). In our case, redundancy allows the continuity of evidence to persist despite its apparent heterogeneity.

The use of "signal" and "noise" in information theory derives from electrical engineering.[24] First, an information source produces a message (e.g. text, speech, image) that a transmitter then converts into a "signal" (e.g. sound pressure converted into electrical current), carried by a channel (e.g. cable) to a receiver that reconstructs the message for its final destination (e.g. the intended recipient).

20 Brelich, *Presupposti*, 131-132; cf. Xella, 'Del "buon uso,"'; Idem, 'Sacrifices humains'.

21 Février, 'Essai de reconsitution' 183; cf. Picard and Picard, 'La vie quotidienne', 253.

22 Bénichou-Safar, 'Sur l'incineration', 66-67; cf. Lancel, 'Questions sur le *tophet*', 254-265, Ribichini, 'Histoires de Moloch', 224 n.50.

23 Xella, *The* tophet *in the Phoenician Mediterranean*.

24 Shannon, 'A mathematical theory'; cf. Shannon and Weaver, *Mathematical Theory*.

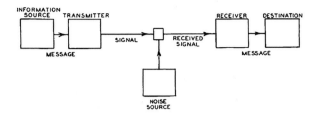

Figure 5.3 Schematic Diagram of a General Communication System. After: Shannon 'A mathematical theory', 381.

Anything in the transmission channel that makes the output unpredictable, anything that can distort or perturb the received message (e.g. static), is "noise" (fig. 5.3).

Shannon's mathematical theorems sought to minimize uncertainty, to minimize the "noise," with information ideally transferred through the channel so successfully that input at the source would very nearly match output at its destination. Redundancy at the source produces no new information, thus can be compressed, while redundancy in the communication channel (e.g. repeating the message) combats "noise" and minimizes uncertainty. His theorems proved influential in electrical engineering, but the concept of removing uncertainty from a message found application in a variety of disciplines, among them social sciences,[25] communications,[26] and recently to the science of political polling.[27]

In the case of the Phoenicians, their communication system (the alphabet) provided a revolutionary compression of redundancy at the source. Instead of a syllabary, as deployed in Akkadian cuneiform and related languages, with their hundreds of vowel-consonant clusters, the limited characters used in the consonantal scripts of Ugarit, then Phoenicia, greatly reduced the number of signs needed to encode a message by requiring the recipient to readily supply missing vowels (modern Semitic languages continue to accommodate the absence of vowel marking). Latin employed the same principle when using a limited set of abbreviations, whether to encode praenomena, funerary monuments, or a votive inscriptions (e.g. Q[*uod*] B[*onum*] F[*austum*] F[*eliciter*] F[*actum*] S[*it*]).[28] One can also find this type of encoding in yesterday's personal ads (SWF–"single white female"), automobile ads (4WD), or classified ads (2BDR–"two bedroom"), and in today's text messages (*lol*, *omg*). Information theory recognizes how, for the sake of efficiency, these methods limit redundancy at the point of transmission.

Nate Silver used the metaphor of "signal" and "noise" to explain how one might predict outcomes – from the turn of a playing card to location and magnitude of earthquakes, from climate change to political polls – based upon reliable models. His near perfect success in predicting precise state-by-state results for the US presidential elections of 2008 and 2012 (*pace* 2016), and the utility of his blog (fivethirtyeight.com), made his book a non-fiction bestseller and increased popular awareness of the "signal" and the "noise." In his view, predictions fail when one starts to find patterns in random "noise," when one overfits limited data into predictive models that mistake correlation for causation. Silver describes how "systems with noisy data and underdeveloped theory" follow a certain pattern:

> First, people start to mistake noise for signal. Second this noise starts to pollute journals, blogs, and news accounts with false alarms, undermining good science and setting back our ability to understand how the system really works.[29]

When uncertainty is amplified, one misses context and misreads the underlying structure.

Information theory applies to Phoenician Studies not only in relation to the encoding of a message in antiquity but also to the uncertainty inherent during its transmission to recipients at its modern destination. On the one hand, the Phoenician votive inscriptions model the suppression of redundancy during encoding in that they omit not only vowels but also key terms that can readily be supplied by context. The same holds for the classical and biblical sources, where omissions can be resupplied from context provided by more complete narratives. On the other hand, formulaic repetition in the inscriptions, for example, adds redundancy to the signal, as do tendentious ethnographic stereotypes in the literary sources. Suppression during encoding at transmission and redundancy of the signal both serve to reduce the uncertainty of the message.[30] Whereas ancient recipients could readily supply missing vowels or context, modern recipients struggle to fill these gaps.

5.4. Classical sources

Starting with sources chronologically and ethnographically remote from Phoenicia, scholars of the *ridimensionamento* have noted deficiencies in the ancient Greek and Latin sources, such as the reticence of the narratives and inconsistencies of terms, particularly those used for the recipient, the victim, or

---

25   Garfinkel, *Towards a Sociological Theory.*

26   Pierce, *Symbols, Signals, and Noise*; Hawes, *Pragmatics of Analoguing.*

27   Silver, *Signal and Noise.*

28   E.g. *Corpus Inscriptiorum Latinarum* 18.630 (N'gaous 4), mentioned below.

29   Silver, *Signal and Noise*, 162.

30   Cf. Shannon and Weaver, *Mathematical Theory* 13, 22, 75; Malaspina, *Epistemolgy*, 51-60.

the mode of sacrifice.[31] As for the recipient, where one might expect Zeus (Lat. Jupiter), since the precincts are dedicated to the chief god of the pantheon, one finds instead Cronus (Lat. Saturn). A single author might refer to an unnamed recipient generically, both as an ignoble deity (*daemon* or *daemonium*) and as a noble god (*theos*, Euseb. *Praep.evang.*4.16-17); while others might specifically name Saturn but only as a *daemon* (e.g. Diod. 20.14, Dion.Hal.1.38). The accounts may mention a temple and/or an altar (e.g. Drac. 5.148-50) and/or a statue, but most omit the location of the ritual. The sanctified victim could be an infant, an older child, a prisoner, or even an elder. The parents as sacrificants might regularly make offerings, in the course of vows, or irregularly, either at age grade transitions or in response to disaster. The perceived gaps and inconsistencies within this category of evidence present apparent heterogeneity that threatens to distort the message.

Nevertheless, due to repetition, little confusion exists within the classical sources since more complete passages allow gaps in the evidence to be filled. Our earliest fragment referring to ritual infanticide comes from Sophocles' *Andromeda* (F126) and employs a unique neuter diminutive *kourion/korion*, corresponding to a rare Latin diminutive *puellus* (Ennius, in Festus, *s.v.*). In both of these cases, the term refers to an age-indefinite "youngster." These and subsequent sources call attention to the tender age of the victims and their relationship to those offering sacrifice, but with little precision, e.g. by using neuter terms that do not specify gender (*paidion, brephos, teknon, kourion/korion*), or terms that could refer to either gender (*pais, proles, impubes, infans, liber*), or masculine (diminutive) terms with collective, gender-inclusive plurals (*puelli, filii, parvi nati*), or gender-specific but not age-specific terms (*huios, puer*).[32] Cleitarchus of Alexandria (*FGrHist* 137), often cited or paraphrased by later authors, described the victims both generically as children and specifically as infants, small enough to have been roasted in the hands of a bronze statue:

Cleitarchus says that the Phoenicians and especially the Carthaginians, in order to honor Cronus whenever they want to succeed at something important (*megalon*), they make a vow (*eukhesthai*) concerning one of their children (*paides*). If they should succeed in the things they wanted, they immolate this child to the god (*theos*). With their brazen Cronus set up among them, hands extended palms upward (*hyptiai*) over a bronze brazier (*kribanos*), they incinerate their own little baby (*paidion*). When the flame attacks the exposed body, the limbs draw in while the mouth

appears to grimace, very much like a laugh, until the child has contracted and has slipped into the brazier. Grimacing laughter, then, is called 'sardanian' since the victims die laughing. 'Grimacing' is the mouth drawing wide and gaping open.

(*FGrHist* 137 F9 – Schol.Plat. *Rep.*337a, *codices* T and W)

Another *codex* (A) within the same *scholia* provides a context of important feasts (*megalai euōkhiai*) rather than important vows (*megalai eukhai*, cf. *Suda* Σ 124), a transmission error that employs an ethnographic motif depicting *barbaroi* as cannibals (cf. Aristot.*Eth.Nic.*7, 1148b-1149a).

The historic-ethnographic etymology of "sardonic grimace" in Cleitarchus (infanticide) was repeatedly preserved in commentaries and paroemiographies, *i.e.* collections of colloquial expressions, set alongside competing interpretations (Appendix II). For example, Demon of Athens (*FGrHist* 327 F18), Timaeus of Taormina (*FGrHist* 566 F64) and Aeschylus of Alexandria (*FGrHist* 488) attributed to the Sardinians the killing of elders (senicide) and/or killing of prisoners (hosticide), with each ritual regarded as type of sacrifice:

Those settling Sardinia, since they are from Carthage, carry on a certain barbaric custom that diverges greatly from the Greek. They sacrifice (*thuein*) to Cronus, on certain fixed days, not only the finest among their war captives but also those among their elders who have reached the age of seventy. For those being sacrificed (*thuomenoi*), not only does it seem a shameful and cowardly thing to cry, but conversely it seems a fine and manly pretense to laugh and embrace death. Hence they also say that feigned laughter in the face of evil is called 'Sardonian' (from the *History* of Demon).

(*FGrHist* 327 F18a – Schol.Hom.*Od.*20.302)

Each source offers a different origin for "sardonic laughter," a grimace masking pain in the face of death, derived either from "Sardinia" (*Sardon-*) or from "grimacing" (*sardan-*), or from both (Appendix II). A certain Philoxenus of Alexandria[33] allowed noise from these other historians to distort the message of Cleitarchus, claiming that newborns (*brephē*) on the island of Sardinia laughed at death while roasting in the hands of Cronus (Philoxenus F591). Nevertheless, together these etymologies marked Phoenician customs as non-normative, and non-Greek (cf. Plat.*Min.*315b-c). In these narratives, instead of parents

---

31   A nearly complete list was first compiled by Mayer, 'Kronos'; see also. Leglay, *Saturne africain*, 314-320; Garnand, *Phoenician Human Sacrifice*, 446-587; Xella, 'Sacrifici di bambini'.

32   See Garnand et al., 'Infants as Offerings', 195-196.

33   *Die Fragmente*, 214-217.

caring for their infants, or children caring for their elders, parricidal Sardinians offer them in sacrifice.

Besides this cluster of etymologies, brief accounts of Phoenician infanticide find their way onto multiple lists of culturally relative ethnographic practices, sometimes philosophical (e.g. Sex.Emp.1.145-155, 3.197-213), polemical and apologetic (e.g. Porph.4.21). Normally four groups, at four geographic axes, represented any one of four modes of human sacrifice:

> How many groups – like the Taurians on the Euxine, king Busiris of Egypt, the Celts, the Phoenicians – think that immolating human beings is both pious and most pleasing to the immortal gods!
>
> (Cic.Rep.3.15)

To the NE, Scythians practiced *senicide* and the Taurians *xenocide* (*i.e.* killing of foreigners), and both of these ethnographic motifs transferred to the Phoenicians (above, cf. Eratosth. in Strab 17.1.19 [C802]). To the NW, the Celts practiced *hosticide*, which also transferred to the Phoenicians (above, cf. Hdt.7.180, Diod.20.65). To the SE, the Egyptians practiced *xenocide* and the Indians *senicide*. To the SW, the Phoenicians of Carthage alone practiced *infanticide*, as this motif did not transfer to others. Foreign Phoenician rituals fit into patterns of diametrical opposition (*i.e.* barbarian vs. Greco-Roman) and of symmetrical balance with radical practices of other groups.[34]

Returning to Cleitarchus' Sardonic etymology, the siege of Tyre provides its most probable context. Diodorus Siculus (17.40-47), Curtius Rufus (4.2-3) and Pompeius Trogus (in Justin 11.10.10-14) provide parallel accounts of the Tyrian campaign of Alexander the Great, each derived from Cleitarchus.[35] This signal, either created or recorded by Cleitarchus, served as the basis for most later repetitions, which taken together allow for recovery of the full narrative. At the point when Alexander had proposed to make an offering at the temple of Heracles (*i.e.* Melqart) during the god's annual festival in 332 BCE, the Tyrians refused and found their city besieged. In Curtius' account (4.3.19-23), the besieged then discovered that they had little hope of reinforcement from their colonists since the Syracusans had coincidentally besieged Carthage. Cleitarchus had likely digressed at this moment in the narrative and inserted the sardonic etymology, his only known reference to events in the far West, forging a false synchronism between the siege of Alexander at Tyre and that of Agathocles at Carthage. However, this does damage to both the historicity and the logic of the narrative since, on the one hand, he had Tyrians implausibly send refugees to a besieged city and, on the other, the Syracusans did not besiege Carthage until 310 BCE. For his part, Diodorus Siculus solves this dilemma with a rare editorial intervention, inserting the episode into its proper context (20.14), a departure from his normal reliance "upon his best standard author" over extensive portions of his text.[36] He begins his inserted passage with an account of Carthaginians transferring their statues and other movable wealth to the metropolitan temples, which runs roughly parallel to the account of the Tyrian siege by Curtius. The besieged Tyrians, filled with irrational anxiety, considered reinstituting their traditional rite of sacrificing a noble child (*ingenuus puer*, Curt.4.3.23), but they did not. At that very same moment, the Carthaginians, likewise filled with irrational anxiety, actually did sacrifice their noblest children, an ancestral honor (*patrioi timai* Diod.20.14.5) that they had learned from the Tyrians:

> They also alleged that Cronus had turned against them. In former times the most powerful (*kratistoi*) used to sacrifice their children (*huieis*) to this god, but more recently, they had secretly bought and raised children (*paides*) and had sent these as sacrifices (*thusia*). Having held an investigation, the Carthaginians discovered that some of those consecrated as victims (*kathierourgēmenoi*) had been secretly substituted in this way…In their zeal to make amends for their blunder, they selected 200 of the noblest children (*epiphanestatoi paides*) and sacrificed them publicly; and others who were under suspicion sacrificed themselves voluntarily, no less than 300 in number. There was among them a bronze statue of Cronus, extending its hands, palms upward (*hyptiai*) but sloping down to the ground, so that when one of their children (*pais*) was set upon (the hands), it would roll down and hurl into a certain pit (*chasma*) full of fire.

> Euripides probably drew upon this for the myth found in his account of the sacrifice (*thusia*) among the Taurians where Iphigeneia is asked by Orestes:

> But what sort of tomb shall receive me when I die?
> A sacred fire within and earth's broad chasm

> The myth passed down by the Greeks, an ancient tradition describing how Cronus eliminated his own children (*paides*), seems to have been upheld by the Carthaginians through this custom (*nomimon*).
>
> (Cleitarchus (?), in Diod.20.14.4-7)

---

34 Garnand, *Use of Phoenician Human Sacrifice*, 224-331.
35 Heckel, 'Notes'; Hamilton, 'Cleitarchus and Diodorus'.
36 Hammond, 'The Sources', 149.

As in his sardonic etymology, the 200 must be very small children, small enough to fit into the statues upturned palms extending over a firepit, called a *kribanos* ("brazier") in his etymology but *chasma* ("pit") here, for comparison to the xenocide cited from Euripides (*IT* 625-26). The use of similar distinctive terms and contexts (e.g. bronze statue, up-turned palms, noble child, holocaust offering) indicate that, despite not being cited himself, Cleitarchus served here as the source for Diodorus.

The 300 would have been older, at least the age of reason and capable of giving their willing assent, but they must have been consecrated and secretly substituted at an earlier age. Whether or not derived from Cleitarchus, these generic terms for children would not exclude infants, particularly regarding the 200 new victims. In addition, this immediate sacrifice, a desperate reaction to extreme anxiety, does not exclude an initial normative consecration for the other 300 at a tender age. Moreover, the Carthaginian response here allegedly followed an ordinary practice (*nomimon*) rather than an extraordinary divine command (e.g. an oracle), thus their dire superstition and their overzealous response marked the Phoenicians as *barbaroi*, as did the staggering number of their child victims.

Phoenicians themselves referred to the ritual sacrifice of firstborn sons. Eusebius of Caesarea and Porphyry of Tyre both drew upon the *Phoenician History* by Herennius Philo of Byblos (*FGrHist* 790 F1-3), who himself had relied upon a certain ethereal Phoenician, Sanchuniathon. According to Philo, the god Elos (El or Cronus, Euseb. *Praep.evang.*1.10.16) had a first and only-begotten son (*monogenēs* 4.16.11), either named Jeoud (Heb. *yāḥid* "only-begotten," Gen. 22:12.) or named Sadidus (perhaps Heb. *yədîd* "beloved," Deut. 32:12), whom he killed by sword (Euseb.*Praep.evang.*1.10 21) and/or sacrificed in wartime (4.16.11) and/or immolated during crisis – famine, plague or drought – as the victim chosen by lot (1.10.33, cf. Porph.2.56). Silius Italicus, a near contemporary of Philo, must have drawn from similar sources as he poetically described how the sortition fell upon the first and only-begotten child (*unica proles*) of Hannibal Barca and his distraught wife Himilce. She tore at her cheeks and hair in anticipation of the annual and unspeakable rite that set little children (*parvi nati*) upon fiery altars (*Punica* 4.763-796; cf. Plut.*Mor.*171B-E, Min.Fel.30.3).

Although Silius Italicus named no specific deity as recipient, Philo labelled the recipient as El/Cronus (Lat. Saturn) due to parallel generational struggles, both having killed their own children and having castrated their fathers (in Euseb *Praep.evang.*1.10.16-17). Philo had criticized the Greco-Roman habit of translating the names of Phoenician deities due to inherent ambiguity (1.10.7-8, cf. *interpretatio Romana*, Tac.*Ger.*.43.4). Yet at the same time Philo himself increased ambiguity by noting how Phoenicians appealed to both Ba'al/Zeus and El/Cronus

during droughts, as well as by positing a brother for Ba'al named Cronus, son of Cronus (1.10.26). One might conclude that the manifestation of Ba'al in Carthage, as Ba'al Ḥammon (*b*ʿ*l ḥmn*), would resolve as Zeus/Jupiter, yet the *interpretatio* consistently renders Cronus/Saturn, who had killed his own children (cf. Diod.20.14.7).

The classical sources may be tendentious and sensationalistic, but their message is clear: the Carthaginians carried out their traditional practices, in their city or on Sardinia, as had been done in metropolitan Phoenicia; the recipient was Cronus/Saturn; the victims very young children; the ordinary context either votive or annual/seasonal or both; and the rite was a slaughter and a sacrifice (*sphagia* and *thusia* – more likely stages in a singular ritual rather than distinct practices). The rite could also occur under conditions of extreme anxiety (e.g. drought, plague, war). Nevertheless, the signal remains consistent, with the message that the exaggerated rites (mass sacrifices, brazen idols, grimacing infants, wailing mothers) of these *barbaroi* stood in contrast to normative Greco-Roman practice, legitimizing the conquest of Phoenician territories. Classical sources imagined that Phoenician child sacrifice had three distinctive components – geographic location (Phoenicia, Libya/Africa, Sardinia), age of the victim (child, specifically infant), and divine recipient (Cronus/Saturn) – such that any two of these elements in the signal suffice to indicate a Phoenician rite, even though some Romans and Athenians were said to sacrifice older children (but not to Cronus/Saturn), and some Rhodians and Cretans were said to sacrifice humans to Cronus (but not children). As for the status of the victim, the signal held that the Phoenicians sacrificed children as opposed to adults (e.g. Varro in Aug. *Civ.*7.19), parents offered either their own sons and daughters or substitutes (e.g. Plut.*Mor.*171B-E), and the tender age of the victims inspired pity (e.g. Pomp.Trog. in Just.18.6.12). Nothing in these repeated and consistent signals excludes infants.

5.5. Biblical sources

While the biblical sources were written by those chronologically and ethnographically proximate to the Canaanites (*i.e.* Phoenicians), scholars have again noted deficiencies in the ancient Hebrew texts, the reticence of the narratives and inconsistencies of terms, particularly those used for the recipient, the victim, or the mode of sacrifice.[37] As for the recipient, the texts at times name Ba'al (*ba*ʿ*al*) or the ba'als (*ba*ʿ*ālîm*, e.g. 2 Chron. 28.3), at others Molech (*mōlek*, e.g. Lev. 20.2-5), sometimes both (Jer. 32.5), and sometimes they name generic (ʾ*elōhîm*, Deut. 12:31) or idolatrous deities (*ṣelem*, e.g. Ezek. 16:17; ʿ*aṣabbîm*, e.g. Ps. 106:36; *gillûlîm*, e.g.

---

37   See Mosca, *Child Sacrifice*; Heider, *The Cult of Molek*; Day, *Molech*; Levenson, *Death and Resurrection*; Garnand, *The Use of Phoenician Human Sacrifice* 417-445; Noort, 'Child sacrifice'; Xella, *The* tophet.

Ezek. 16:36). Among the Canaanites, the sanctified victim could be a son or a daughter (e.g. Deut. 18:10), perhaps the first-born, with age unspecified. Parents might sanctifiy their children in the course of vows and, then, either sacrifice (Judg. 11) or redeem them (e.g. Lev. 22:18-19; Num. 18:15-16); they might occasionally do the same at age-grade transitions of eight days (e.g. Ex 22: 29-30) or one month (e.g. Num. 18:16); or they might periodically do so in annual celebration of first fruits (e.g. Ex. 34:19-26). The perceived inconsistencies in this category of evidence present an apparent heterogeneity that can distort the message.

Nevertheless, due to repetition, little confusion exists within the biblical sources, with more complete passages allowing gaps in the evidence to be filled. Narratives of the chronologically remote past ("back then"–Abraham, Jephtha) and of the ethnically remote present ("over there"–Mesha) affirmed Israelite normative ritual practice (in the here and now). In the former instance, perhaps the most famous account of (averted) child sacrifice (Gen. 22: 7-14), YHWH demanded that Abraham offer Isaac, his son (*bēn*) and only-begotten child (*yāḥîd*) with Sarah, a child whom he should slaughter (*šḥṭ*) and offer as a holocaust (*ʿōlāh*). Isaac was also designated a "little youngster" (*naʿar*), a generic rather than age-specific term that can apply to a fetus (Judg. 13.5-8), a neonate (e.g. 1 Sam. 4:21), an infant (e.g. Ex. 2:6), either weaned or not (e.g. 1 Sam. 1:22-27), or an older child (e.g. Gen. 37:2). In this case, Isaac spoke with Abraham, so he would not have been *infans* (*i.e.* "speechless"). A high point on the Temple Mount in Jerusalem, Mt. Moriah (Gen. 22:2; cf. 2 Chron. 3:1) provided the locale for Abraham's offering. There he constructed an *ad hoc* altar, brought a knife for the slaughter and wood to fuel the sacrificial pyre, and found a ram which he substituted for his son at the last moment. Due to the provision of the ram, Abraham named the locale "LORD-will-Provide" (YHWH-*yirʾeh*, 22:8, 14). Similar to this etymology, in the months before the judge, Jephthah, sacrificed his daughter in fulfillment of a vow, she wandered the hills to bewail her unspoiled virginity and thus provided the etiology for an annual pre-marital ritual (Judg. 11:29-30). Here, again, the only-begotten child (*yāḥîd*) is older, at least of marriageable age.[38]

The victims were generically designated as children or offspring (*yəlādîm*, e.g. Isa. 57:5; *zeraʿ* "seed," e.g. Lev. 18:21), more specifically and more commonly as "sons and daughters" (*bānîm/bānōt*, e.g. Deut. 12:31) or simply as "sons" (either as a gender inclusive plural or as a synecdoche, Jer. 19:5), but in all of these cases emphasizing familial relations, rather than age grade, and the role of the parent as sacrificant. A second type of designation was as only-born, *yāḥîd* (as above) or first-*born*, either *peṭer reḥem* (e.g. Ezek. 20:26) or *bəkōr* (e.g. 1 Kings 16:34), or both

(e.g. Num. 3:12-13, 8:17-18, 18:11-19), again not age specific but commonly found in reference to sanctification before redemption. The first (or only) born would be sanctified on their eighth day, then redeemed after their thirtieth day by the offering of a substitute and a payment of a ransom of 5 *šeqel* (Num. 18:16), the same ransom paid for a child devoted in the course of a vow (Lev. 27:1-7).

Thus far we have been discussing Israelite depictions of sacrifices averted (or performed) in their own distant past, otherwise of sacrifices averted through substitution and redemption in their contemporary practice. At the same time depictions of sacrifices performed among their culturally distant neighbors marked foreign rituals as non-normative. Mesha, king of the Moabites, offered his first-born son in a holocaust, an effective sacrifice that diverted Israelite invaders (e.g. 2 Kings 3:27); Sepharvaites offered their sons in holocaust to Adrammelech and Anammelech (e.g. 2 Kings 17:31); and those peoples (*gōyīm*, cf. *babaroi*) inhabiting the land before, namely the Canaanites/Phoenicians, burned (*śrp*) their children in fire to Baʿal (e.g. Deut. 12:31), or caused them to pass through (*ʿbr*) fire (e.g. Deut. 18:10). Like the classical sources, the biblical sources include this sacrificial ritual on lists of culturally absolute, negative ethnographic practices:

When you come into the land that the Lord your God is giving you, you must not learn to imitate the abhorrent practices of those nations (*gōyīm*). No one shall be found among you who makes a son (*bēn*) or daughter (*bat*) pass through (*ʿbr*) fire (*ʾēš*), or who practices divination, or is a soothsayer, or an augur, or a sorcerer, or one who casts spells, or who consults ghosts or spirits, or who seeks oracles from the dead. For whoever does these things is abhorrent to the LORD; it is because of such abhorrent practices that the LORD your God is driving them out before you.

(Deut. 18:9-13)

On the one hand, the Israelites are commanded to reject Phoenician/Canaanite practice in order to avoid being seduced (*znh* "whoring after") by these sacrifices (*zbh*, e.g. Ex. 34:13-17), and to shun setting up their high places (*bamōt*), altars (*mizbəḥōt*), pillars (*maṣṣēbōt*), sacred poles (*ʾăšērôt*), and graven images (*massēkāh* and *pesel*, *ʾēpôd* and *tərāpîm*, cf. Jdg 18:14). On the other hand, the Israelites ignore these very same specific and repeated divine mandates and imitate foreign practices, with such apostasy leading directly to the fall of both the northern (Hoshea: 2 Kings 17:7-17) and southern kingdoms (Manasseh: 2 Kings 21:2-7, cf.24:3, 2 Chron. 33; Josh. 23:4-15, 19-24;).[39]

---

38   Cf. Marcus, *Jephthah and his Vow.*

39   Stavrakopoulou, *King Manasseh.*

Beyond the historical texts, the prophets blamed apostasy for disaster, both due to generic devotion to foreign idols (*gillûlîm* e.g. Ezek. 16:36, 20:24) and to specific devotion to Ba'al at the high place (or places) in Tophet, located in the valley west and south of Jerusalem, where their children were "burned in" (*śrp*) or "passed through" (*ᶜbr*) fire:

> They built the high places (*bāmôt*) of Ba'al in the Valley of Ben-Hinnom, to pass their sons (*bānîm*) and daughters (*bānôt*) over to Molech (*lmlk*), though I did not command them, nor did it enter my mind that they should do this abomination, causing Judah to sin. Now therefore thus says the LORD, the God of Israel, concerning this city of which you say, "It is being given into the hand of the king of Babylon by the sword, by famine, and by pestilence."

(Jer. 32:35-36)

In modern times the proper name of Tophet ("place of burning" Jer. 7:31-32, cf. 19:4-6) has lent its name to any of the generic Central Mediterranean sites (*tophet*), where votive stelae mark the interred remains of cremated infants.

Together with Ba'al, Jeremiah names Molech as recipient, considered either a distinct deity (e.g. Isa. 57:9) or perhaps two aspects of the same deity (*i.e.* Ba'al-Melek, cf. 2 Kings 17: 31).[40] In any case, his name remains problematic since one would expect consistent vocalization as Melek (from *malk* "king," √*mlk* "rule"). Ingenious scholars first resolved this vocalization by proposing a dysphemism, whereby the so-named Ammonite deity (1 Kings 11:7) had been intentionally mis-vocalized on analogy to *bōšet* ("shame").[41] A more definitive resolution followed upon the discovery of votive stelae from Nicivibus (mod. N'gaous), with the Phoenician-Punic *mlk ᵓmr* resolving as *molcholmor* or *morchormor* in Latin transcription (*CIL* 18.630).[42] This discovery led Eissfeldt to interpret *mlk* as a causative participle (√*hlk* or √*ylk* "to go forth")[43] meaning that *lmlk* would refer to the sacrifice ("as an offering," lit. "as a causing to go forth") rather than to a deity ("to Molech").[44] In this case, noise has distorted the signal, whether intentionally (through mis-vocalization) or unintentionally (through confusion with the deity), away from an original message that referred to *mlk* as a type of sacrifice.

The biblical sources may be tendentious and inimical, but their message is clear: the Israelites carried out rituals at high-places in Tophet, adjacent to Jerusalem, in imitation of certain *goyim* who were in the land previously (*i.e.* Canaanites/Phoenicians); offerings were made generically to foreign and idolatrous deities, specifically to Ba'al, as a *mlk*-offering; the context could be votive (cf. Jephthah's daughter) or could be either occasional (at an age-grade transition) or annual/seasonal (or both), but in any case served as a mode of first-fruits offering, with children donated by their parents; the rite was a slaughter (*šḥṭ*), a sacrifice (*zbh*), and a holocaust (*ᶜlh*, *śrp b'ēš*, *ᶜbr b'ēš*), not necessarily distinct rites but more likely stages in a singular ritual. And the sacrifice could also occur under conditions of extreme anxiety (e.g. drought, plague, war – Jer 32:36, 2 Kings 3). The signal remains consistent, with a message that the exotic rites of these *goyim* stood in contrast to normative Israelite practice, legitimizing the conquest of Canaan. Following on the assumption that proper Israelite rituals had become distorted in times of apostasy, the victims would have been children at age-grade transitions, very young and firstborn, who would have been sanctified after their first week and then sacrificed.

5.6. Phoenician-Punic sources

As for the archaeological and inscriptional evidence, modern scholars are at a distinct disadvantage. Although this evidence has the most immediate chronological and ethnographical proximity, produced by the Phoenicians/Canaanites themselves, little has been recovered from properly recorded contexts, nearly all of which remain unpublished. Despite over a century of archaeological exploration, no final report has appeared for any Central Mediterranean *tophet* precinct. Without these records, we cannot reconstruct relationships between specific votive stelae and adjacent urns. In addition to lost contexts, more than 2000 stelae were themselves obliterated when their transport ship, the ironclad *Magenta*, exploded in the port of Toulon on Halloween of 1875.[45] The site of Carthage provides the overwhelming majority of Phoencian-Punic material remains, but the upper strata of artifacts were either removed and displaced by the Romans in antiquity or were divorced from their context in modern times by clandestine and amateur extraction. Add to these gaps and losses the reticence of the Phoenician-Punic inscriptional texts, which tend not to describe or even name the votive offerings.[46]

---

40 Frendo, 'Burning Issues'.
41 Geiger, Urschrift, 301; for Ashtart >Ashtōreth, see Day, 'Ashtoreth', 492; for Ashtart >Ashtōreth, and *tephet > tōphet*, see Noort, 'Child sacrifice', 114-115.
42 Alquier *et al.*, 'Communications'.
43 Cf. Alt, 'Karatepe', 284, S IV 2-6.
44 Eissfeldt, *Molk als Opferbegriff*.

45 *CIS* I, tome 1.1, 279; Lancel, 'La fouille de l'épave'.
46 E.g. Dussaud, 'Précisions épigraphiques'; Février, 'Molchomor'; Idem, 'Essai de reconstitution'; Mosca, *Child Sacrifice*; Amadasi Guzzo, 'La documentazione'; Idem, *Scavi a Mozia*,; Idem,'Per una classificazione'; Idem. 'Il tofet'; Garnand, *The Use of Phoenician Human Sacrifice*, 390-416; Amadasi Guzzo and Zamora, 'Epigraphy of the Tophet'.

As for the recipient, the texts generally name Baʿal, normally manifest as Baʿal Hammon (*bʿl ḥmn*), quite rarely manifest as Baʿal Addir (*bʿl ʾdr*) or Baʿal Shamem (*bʿl šmm*), with Tinnit (*tnt*) as his consort.[47] Nearly all inscriptions name a single dedicant, normally the presumed father, less commonly just the presumed mother,[48] sometimes both presumed parents (e.g. *CIS* I.382-3, 386), but in certain very rare cases we find two women (*CIS* I.385), a brother and a sister (e.g. *CIS* I.4596), a father and a daughter (e.g. *CIS* I.5702), as well as dedications made on behalf of others (*CIS* I.198, 5939).[49]

Lacking published contexts, scholars cannot reconstruct precise relations between stelae and urns, thus leading some to claim that no relationship existed. In Carthage, tens of thousands of burials were marked by aniconic fieldstones, tens of thousands by iconographic but anepigraphic rough, sandstone *cippi*, and some ten thousand by iconographic and epigraphic limestone stelae. Any changes in material, form, style, or iconography, and any variation in the number of stelae in relation to urns has been taken to demonstrate a diversity of ritual within the votive precinct.[50] The urns contain the remains of very young children, most near one month old, some up to three months old, but a very few contain even older children. While the stelae relate to votive dedications, without clear association with the urns the burials might then be distinctly funerary and the precinct might be multi-purpose, given that infants are almost entirely absent from adult cemeteries despite high mortality rates within that age grade.[51] Again, perceived inconsistencies in this category of evidence present an apparent heterogeneity that can distort the message.

Yet more than any other category of our evidence, repetition within the vast numbers of inscriptions (given their limited range of formulae), combined with the vast number of artifacts and osteological remains (given their similar limited range), all together provide a consistent message. In addition, more complete formulae and contexts allow for gaps in the evidence to be filled, such that one votive inscription can readily serve as an example of the entire category. The very first small group of inscriptions were extracted from Tunisia in 1817 by J. E. Humbert, member of the Dutch diplomatic mission to the *bey* of Tunis. Humbert reported that four of the stelae, which he misidentified as funerary, were found at the quarter of Douar el-Chott in Carthage and, although *ex situ*, he claimed to have seen the cavities from which

they had been removed.[52] He later transferred them to the Rijksmuseum van Oudheden in Leiden. Three of the four are inscribed and they provide examples of the reticent but rigid formulae (fig. 5.4 a-b):

H1

¹LRBT LTNT PN ²BᶜL WL³DN LB³ᶜL ḤMN	For the Mistress, for Tinnit Visage of Baʿal, and for the Lord, for Baʿal Ḥammon,
	[is a votive]
⁴Š ND³R GRᶜŠTRT ³HSPR BN ᶜBDMLQRT	which Gerashtart the scribe vowed, son of Abdimelqart
	[because the deity heard his voice and blessed him]

H2

¹[L]RBT LTNT PN BᶜL ²[W]L³DN LBᶜL ḤMN	For the Mistress, for Tinnit Visage of Baʿal, and for the Lord, for Baʿal Ḥammon,
	[is a votive]
³[ʾ]Š NDR ᶜBD³ŠM ⁴[N] BN BD³ŠTRT BN ⁵[ᶜ]BD³ŠMN	which Abdešmun vowed, son of Bodaštart, son of Abdešmun
	[because the deity heard his voice and blessed him]

H3

¹[LRBT LTNT] P[N BᶜL] WL³DN LB²[ᶜL] ḤMN	For the Mistress, for Tinnit Visage of Baʿal, and for the Lord, for Baʿal Ḥammon,
	[is a votive]
⁴Š NDR ᶜBDMLQRT ³[BN] ḤMKT BN [ᶜ]BD³ŠMN	which Abdimelqart vowed, son of Hamilcar, son of Abdibaʿal
	[because the deity heard his voice and blessed him]

Votive dedications fall into one of two formulaic patterns that remain remarkably consistent over a vast span of time and space – from the earliest time to the Roman Period, in the Phoenician, Punic and Neo-Punic scripts, from Ḥammon (mod. Umm el-ʿAmed) to Citum (mod. Larnaka), from Motya (mod. Mozia) to Sulcis (mod. Sant'Antioco), from Malta to Mactar; from Hadrumetum (mod. Sousse) to Althiburus (mod. Abbah Quṣūr), from Calama (mod. Guelma) to Cirta (mod. Constantine). While such formulae apply to all votive dedications, the single *tophet* at Carthage provides the overwhelming majority of the Phoenician-Punic corpus, more than three-quarters of all surviving inscriptions.

The patterns nearly always include a prepositional phrase ("to the deities") and a relative clause ("which someone dedicated") but, besides omitting vowels, as we noted above, inscriptional reticence often omits a causal blessing ("because they heard his voice") and nearly always omits the main clause, a nominal phrase ("this is a votive dedication"). Suppression of redundancy during encoding here requires the reader to supply the main clause, thus the key syntax for nearly all of these votive dedications must be

---

47 E.g. Berthier and Charlier, *el-Hofra*, nos. 3-4; CIS I.3778.

48 E.g. *CIS* I.302, 307; *KAI* 109.

49 Amadasi Guzzo and Zamora, 'Epigraphy of the Tophet,' 170n.

50 E.g. Bartoloni, 'Studi sul tofet,' 163.

51 E.g. Bénichou-Safar, 'À propos des ossements'; Schwartz *et al.*, 'Skeletal Remains'.

---

52 Humbert, 'Notice sur quattre cippes'; Halbertsma, *Scholars*.

Figure 5.4a-b Four Stelae Brought from Tunisia to Leiden by Humbert (1817), photos (a) and drawings (b), scale 1:8, left to right – photos courtesy of the Rijksmuseum van Oudheden / National Museum of Antiquities, Leiden; drawings adapted from Humbert 1821: RMO H1, CAa1 (*CIS* I.240); RMO H2, CAa2 (*CIS* I.187); RMO H3, CAa3 (*CIS* I.186); RMO H4, CBa2 (uninscribed).

Table 1a Primary Pattern of Distributions for Formulaic/Semantic Cola.

I	II	III	IVa / IVb	V
PREPOSITIONAL PHRASE	NOMINAL PHRASE	RELATIVE CLAUSE	NOMINAL PHRASE / TEMPORAL CLAUSE	CAUSAL BLESSING
L + *DN*	subject	ꜣŠ + *verb* + *PN*	subject / date	K + ŠMᶜ QL BRK
For (the deity/deities)	[this is an offering]	which (*name*) son of (*name*) offered	[this is an offering] / [in the month of and in the reign of (*name*)]	because (the deities) heard my/his voice and blessed me/him.

Table 1b Secondary Pattern of Distributions for Formulaic/Semantic Cola.

I	II	III	IVa / IVb	V
NOMINAL PHRASE	RELATIVE CLAUSE	PREPOSITIONAL PHRASE	NOMINAL PHRASE / TEMPORAL CLAUSE	CAUSAL BLESSING
subject	ꜣŠ + *verb* + *PN*	L + *DN*	subject / date	K + ŠMᶜ QL BRK
[This is an offering]	which (*name*) son of (*name*) offered	for (the deity/ deities)	[this is an offering] / [in the month of and in the reign of (*name*)]	because (the deities) heard my/his voice and blessed me/him.

understood without being expressed. Taken to an extreme, certain perfectly preserved stelae had just a few letters or even a single letter inscribed, requiring that the reader furnish the entire dedication.[53] In those few cases where they did inscribe the main nominal phrase, it normally shared the same root as the relative clause (e.g. *ndr ꜣš ndr* "a votive which he vowed");[54] in other cases, it paralleled the relative clause (*mtnt ꜣš ndr* "a gift which he vowed").[55] In rare cases, the nominal phrase repeated (*ndr...mlkt ndr š* "a votive...this votive is a *mlk*-offering"),[56] or provided a poetic parallel (*ndr...bšrm* "a votive...of his own flesh (?)").[57] In the latter case, the term *bšrm* remains enigmatic and yet, due to the rigid formulae and limited semantic range, it must parallel the better known *ndr* and *mtnt*. The components of votive expressions each have a semantic unity, and by themselves can be called formulae, or at least the building blocks of formulae. These elemental blocks can move to other parts of the dedication just so long as they maintain their function, but they regularly fall into certain cola. Because these formulae repeat so regularly, the sense of any omitted phrase or missing fragment can readily restored (see table 1a-b, with common omissions in gray).

Of the thousands of votive inscriptions from *tophet* precincts, nearly all omit the main clause (a nominal phrase), although from the verb alone we can presume that a "votive" was "devoted," that a "gift" was "given," etc. in a few cases, the dedication was "made" (*pᶜl*), "placed" (*šym*), "raised" (*tnꜣ* or *nšꜣ*), or "sacrificed" (*zbḥ*), each verb recording an act within the ritual. In similarly rare cases, the dedication was "a stone" (*ꜣbn*), "something raised up" (*nšꜣ* or *nṣb*), or "a sacrifice" (*zbḥ*), most likely specifying the various components of the votive process rather than distinct ritual artifacts. Certain quite uncommon but even

more enigmatic terms, rarely attested outside the *tophet*, must also fit into this formulaic-semantic system – the dedication was an "offering" (*mlk* or *mlkt*) or, as a syntagm in construct, an "offering of a sheep" (*mlk ꜣmr*), "offering of a commoner (?)" (*mlk ꜣdm*), or "offering of a noble (?)" (*mlk bᶜl*); possibly "bodily intact (?)" (*bšrm btm*); possibly "male/female cut short (?)" (*ꜣzrm ꜣš / ꜣšt*).[58] In any case these uncommon terms, no matter how enigmatic, must be understood as having the same basic semantic function, since they serve as the main nominal phrase or in a parallel noun clause, each describing the object dedicated.

One should assume that the inscribed votive stelae, and the even more numerous iconographic and aniconic orthostats, even fieldstones, relate to immediately adjacent urns containing infant remains, but these tens of thousands of burial markers were removed before recording their precise associations. Nevertheless, the *Corpus Inscriptionum Semiticarum* (*CIS*) does include photographic evidence of stelae *in situ*. Finds in the 1880s were imprecisely located near the Douar el-Chott and Dermech tram stations, during the campaigns of É. De Sainte-Marie, of S. Reinach and E. Babelon, and of A. L. Delattre. A French municipal tax collector, F. Icard, discovered the precise location at the propriété Regulus-Salammbô (1921), having followed a clandestine excavator to the site (fig. 5.5).

He was joined in his amateur excavation by the local police inspector, P. Gielly, and together they bought the property, arousing the interest of L. Poissot and R. Lantier of the Direction des Antiquités (1922). Soon afterward a swashbuckling adventurer with claims to nobility, Byron Kuhn de Prorok (1924), bought their property and the adjacent Villa Narhavas with the financial backing of his father-in-law, William F. Kenny. He then enlisted J. B. Chabot (who was preparing the *CIS*) and Francis W. Kelsey from the University of Michigan,

---

53   E.g. *CIS*.I.3807-3821, Kenny 70-78.

54   E.g. *CIS*.I.3800-01, Kenny 65-66.

55   E.g. *CIS*.I.3712, Kenny 6; *CIS*.I.3714; Berthier and Charlier, *el-Hofra*, no. 120.

56   E.g. Berthier and Charlier, *el-Hofra*, no. 43.

57   E.g. *CIS*.I.3745, Kenny 29; see Amadasi Guzzo and Zamora, 'Epigraphy of the Tophet', 174-175.

58   This coherent pattern of *mlk*-offering syntagms, as stages of substitution, has been suggested Mosca, *Child Sacrifice* 77; for the range of possible interpretations, see Amadasi Guzzo and Zamora, 'Epigraphy of the Tophet', 169-171.

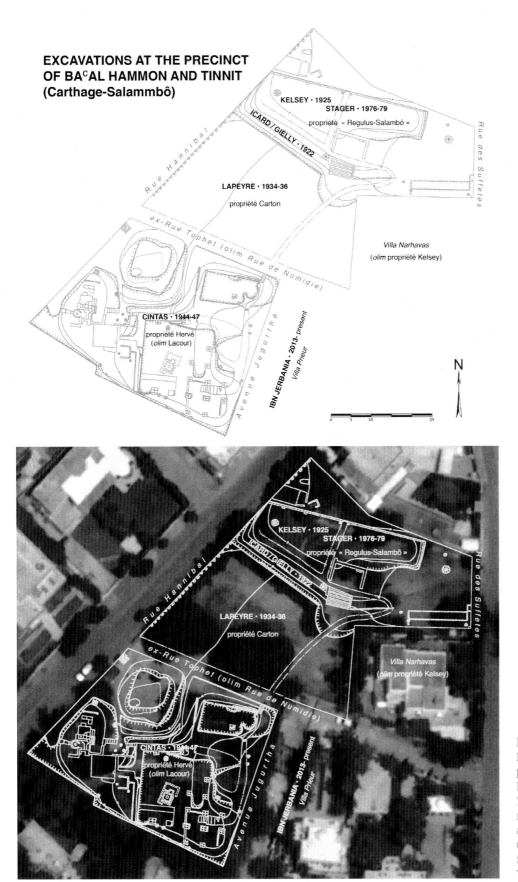

Figure 5.5 Carthage tophet Precinct Excavations, 1920-present. Modified from Benichou-Safar, *Le Tophet de Salammbo*, 5, 7 n.9, with labels (above) and superimposed on GoogleEarth (below). Sanctuary of Ba'al and Tinnit (*tophet*), Carthage.

both of whom added legitimacy to his endeavors (1925). Despite scandals that revealed Prorok as not a Count but a fraud, and despite the untimely death of Kelsey (with no final report forthcoming), the stelae that they had uncovered were eventually published by Chabot, some under Kenny's name, without their contexts but with a good number photographed *in situ* (*CIS* I.3709-3905). There followed the largely unrecorded excavations of G. G. Lapyere on the adjacent propriété Carton (1934-36, *CIS* I.3922-5275), producing more artifacts but recording no contexts, and then those of P. Cintas and G. C. Picard on the propriété Lacour/Hervé (Direction des Antiquités, 1944-47, *CIS* I.5684-5940), the final publication of which was abandoned with the French withdrawal from Tunisia (fig. 5.5). This wretched tale of extended and often amateur excavation, then artifact extraction with no final publication of contexts, has been repeated at every *tophet* site across the central Mediterranean.

During UNESCO's "Campagne internationale de sauvegarde de Carthage," L. E. Stager of the University of Chicago directed the A.S.O.R. Punic Project excavations, which were reopened in the same terrain as the University of Michigan (1976-1979, fig. 5.5) where Prorok and Kelsey had already removed nearly all of the inscribed stelae. Most of the inscriptions that Stager did recover were found in disturbed secondary contexts (e.g. in the fill of the adjacent commercial harbor); only a select few were found in stratigraphic contexts that had direct relationships to stelae, including the following hold-over from the Kelsey excavations still *in situ* (fig. 5.7):[59]

619 V0068¶

[1]LRBTN LTNT PN^ɔ B^cL [2]WL^ɔDN LB^cL ḤMN	For our Mistress, for Tinnit Visage of Ba'al, and for the Lord, for Ba'al Ḥammon,
	[is a votive]
[3]^ɔŠ [3]NDR ^ɔŠMNḤLṢ BN YT[4]NMLK BN B^cL^cMS [5]BN MLKYTN BN ḤMY [6]BN B^cLḤN	which Eshmunḥilleṣ vowed, son of Yatonmilk son of Ba'al'amas son of Milkyaton son of Ḥamay son of Ba'alḥanno.
YŠM^ɔ QL^{c?ɔ} YBRKY^ɔ	May they hear his voice and bless him!

This nearly unique case, with a known contextual association, can still be used to extrapolate unknown contexts. One can hope that current excavations by Imed ben Jerbania at the Villa Prieur (Institut national du patrimoine, 2013-present, fig. 5.5) may have better success in finding and recording inscribed stelae in secure stratigraphic relationships.

Even in preliminary reports from various sites (e.g. Carthage, Hadrumetum, Motya, Sulcis), one sees how open-air *tophet* precincts were used, back-filled, and re-used again, with multiple stratigraphic contexts superimposed in layers and with little regard for previous phases (see fig. 5.6, for Carthage).

The earliest phases had fine painted urns marked by fieldstones and roughly hewn sandstone *cippi*, while the later phases had crudely-made urns with finely carved limestone stelae, indicating a shift in resources rather than a change in ritual (e.g. figs. 5.6-8).

In Carthage, the markers were imported from a distance and at no small expense – both fine limestone from a quarry near Nepheris (south of Tunis) and rough sandstone from Ghar el-Kebir (at the tip of Cap Bon) – yet once valuable markers from earlier phases could be employed as wedges supporting later stelae. Over half of the urns contained at least one artifact (e.g. flecks of gold foil), with a few superabundant deposits with numerous beads and Egyptianizing amulets (fig. 5.8).

The foil, beads of varied materials and seals of varied forms, once strung together with linen, were set atop urn contents. After having a spell cast over them, such artifacts together would have served an amuletic function (as in this parallel Middle Egyptian version against poison):

It is a protective amulet. One should speak this spell over the flattened (piece) of gold, the bead of garnet (or carnelian?), the seal of a crocodile and a hand, strung upon the finest linen cord, made as an amulet, placed at the throat of a child. Good (or, It is finished).

pBerlin 3027, spell P, [15] verso 2.2-7[60]

Within or alongside the urns one also finds the occasional miniature toy vessel or *biberon* (*i.e.* sippy cup). Deposits such as these belong to those interred, while the votive inscriptions above the urns name only those making the dedications. In all periods of the site's use, conspicuous consumption distinguished these infant burials, with unparalleled energy and wealth expended on fine ceramics, precious amulets, carved burial markers, etc.

Also unparalleled are the cremated infant remains. Despite high infant mortality, very young infants are nearly invisible in the archaeological record across the ancient Mediterranean. Although paleo-demographic models would predict the greatest number of infant deaths in the first weeks after birth, we find a vast underrepresentation if not an invisibility of neonates in multi-generational cemeteries, a Mediterranean-wide and cross-cultural indiscernibility of infant death.[61] In contrast we find a significant number of Phoenician settlements in the Central Mediterranean with *tophet* precincts set aside for the exclusive commemoration of these marginal members of the society. We might imagine

---

59   **619 V0068**: *CIS* I.3709, Kenny, 3.

60   Cahail, 'New Look', 237.

61   Cf. Orsingher, 'Forever Young'.

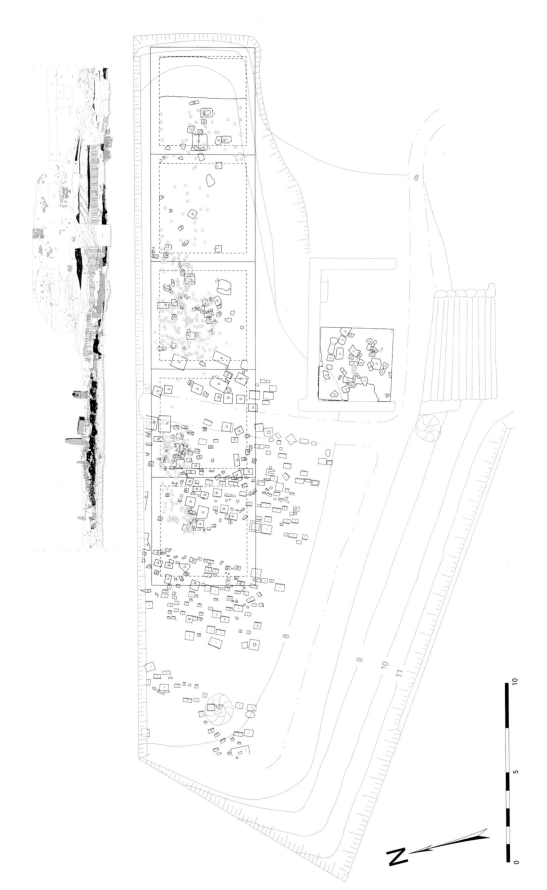

Figure 5.6 "Precinct of Tanit" (tophet), American Schools of Oriental Research (ASOR) Punic Project, Stager Excavations (1976-1979), C. Sevara plan (a) and F. Gignac section (b). Courtesy ASOR Punic Project, used with permission.

Figure 5.7 Sample Stelae and Urns, in situ – inscribed limestone stela **619** V0068 (*CIS* I.3709) above urn 6031 (right); iconographic stela **616** V0065 above urn 6030 (not visible) and **618** V0067 adjacent to urns 6027 and 6029 (middle), with rough sandstone base **617** V0066 above urns 6026 and 6028 (left), photo PN0945A (above) with annotations (below). Courtesy ASOR Punic Project, used with permission.

J0984 - *Homo*: 4 deciduous germs, 3 months; *Ovis/Capra*: none

220 X0792 - **gold foil sheet**	**227** X0799 - **glass ring bead**
221 X0793 - **three silver earrings**	X0800 - **faience pendant**
222 X0794 - **silver double axe bead**	**228** X0801 - **faience *wɪdyt* eye pendant**
223 X0795 - **silver suspension hoop**	**229** X0802 - **faience barrel bead**
224 X0796 - **silver pendant**	**230A** X0803A - **bone conical bead**
225 X0797 - **six silver annular beads**	**230B** X0803B - **stone fox pendant**
226 X0798 - **24 glass spherical beads**	X0807 - **unidentified faience**

5826
78.1.121
II.4
infant (3 mo.)

Figure 5.8 Urn 5826 (stratigraphic unit: CT78.1.121; phase: II.4)–counterclockwise from top left: urn drawing (B. Garnand Ai5826UC) and photo (PN0831E), 1:5 scale; field photo of urn mouth with contents (PN0752), detail of amulets (PN0753), 1:1 scale; laboratory photo of contents (PN0847B), 1:1 scale. Courtesy ASOR Punic Project, used with permission.

that Phoenicians, like the Israelites, sanctified infants after their first week and sacrificed (or redeemed) them after their first month, and that this precinct somehow commemorated this rite of passage. Two teams have analyzed the very same osteological samples from the ASOR Punic Project excavations and have reached two incompatible conclusions, based upon interpretations of tooth and bone shrinkage and of microstructures on tooth enamel.[62] The one led by Jeffrey Schwartz determined that the majority of infants were prenatal and perinatal, thus likely stillborn and unsuitable for sacrifice, with the precinct commemorating those who had not yet been recognized as full members of

---

62   Garnand et al., 'Infants as Offerings', 211-214.

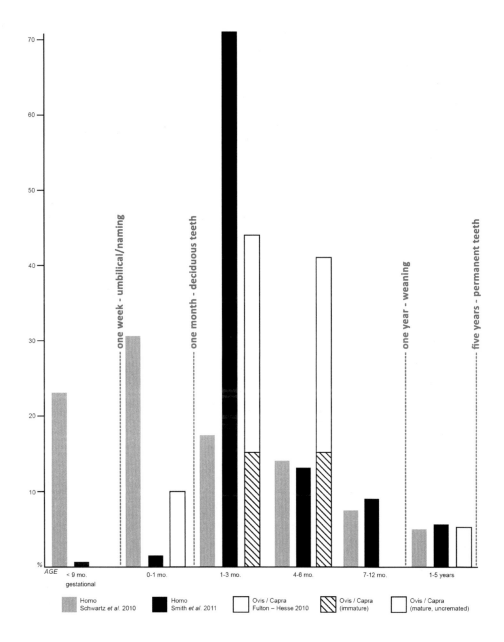

Figure 5.9 Distribution of Infants and Juvenile Ovicaprids (adapted from Garnand et al. 'Infants as Offerings', fig. 3), with age-grade transitions and attendant rites of passage.

society.[63] The one led by Patricia Smith determined that the infants were viable and suitable, with the precinct commemorating those who had been devoted and sacrificed.[64] In both cases, the majority of infants fall between the first week and the third month, an age distribution that indicates artificial selection rather than natural mortality (fig. 5.9).

The selected infants seem to have passed the first-week survival threshold and fall between the social-developmental thresholds of the eruption of deciduous teeth (i.e. teething) and their replacement by permanent teeth, with some corresponding public rite of passage commemorated at the precinct. While we might expect that infants' burials would differ from older children and adults in multi-generational cemeteries, we would not expect distinct and public commemoration with conspicuous displays of wealth.

Epigraphic and archaeological evidence may be reticent, fragmentary and poorly recorded, but stelae in the precinct describe a votive offering, not a funerary ritual. The markers record votive offerings to Baʻal (and his consort Tinnit) that were "vowed" (ndr) or "given" (ytn) or as a "votive" (ndr), "gift" (mtnt) or "offering" (mlk), because the deity had (or will) give their blessing. While preliminary data from Schwartz suggested that neonates were co-interred with older children, the analysis of

---

63   Schwartz et al., 'Skeletal Remains'; Idem, 'Bones, Teeth, and Estimating Age'; Idem, 'Two Tales of One City'.

64   Smith et al., 'Aging Cremated Infants'; Idem, 'Age Estimations'.

Smith, demonstrates that those co-interred were not born at the same time (e.g. twins) but were commonly separated by less than nine months, thus not born of the same mother. We also find cremated remains of juvenile *Ovis/Capra* interred together with or separately from the infants, and the faunal age distribution indicates a similar deliberate selection of juvenile sheep and goat (fig. 5.9). Votive offerings, co-interment with unrelated individuals, co-interment with age-specific cremated ovicaprids, and the separate burial but equal treatment of those ovicaprids, do not support interpretation of the precinct as a cemetery.

5.7. Conclusion

Modern scholarship about the Levant was born in an environment of scientific racism and Orientalism, with allegations of human sacrifice proving useful for essentialist depictions of Semitic excess. The *thesis*, that Canaanites/Phoenicians regularly practiced human sacrifice, has now found its *antithesis*, that they did not. The complete reimagining (*ridimensionamento*) of their practice did allow for occasional ritual killing, in rare moments of crisis, but focused upon on heterogeneity and inconsistency within the evidence in order to dismiss traditional interpretations. As for the archaeological evidence, inimical ancient sources and imaginative modern scholars had so corrupted research that new excavations were needed to produce uncorrupted discoveries in support of these new hypotheses.

Our attempt at a new *synthesis* here focuses instead on homogeneity and consistency across the literary, inscriptional and archaeological record. Instead of calling upon others to find uncorrupted evidence, we use the metaphor of "signal" and "noise" to interpret the vast amount of evidence, however limited, that we already have at our disposal, since we have more classical and biblical evidence for sacrificial infanticide than for any other Phoenician/Canaanite cultural practice. While granting that these tendentious sources used foreign rituals to stereotype other groups in order to define their own rituals as normative, the narratives remain remarkably consistent across linguistic and cultural boundaries, although not necessarily precise or valid. The repetitive nature of these stereotypical depictions allow gaps in the narratives to be filled – the victims were sanctified as infants, devoted to Ba'al (Cronus/Saturn), and sacrificed. Minor variations in terminology may enter the transmission as "noise," but these variations do not affect the "signal." The inscriptions from *tophet* precincts commemorate votive offerings, having been placed above urn burials of cremated infants, and the age grade of these infants suggests artificial selection rather than a natural distribution, with preference given to infants between one and three-months old in a unique display of conspicuous consumption. Any hypothesis must accommodate rather than deny the consistent ritual patterns and rigid inscriptional syntax. Rather than uncertainty, the redundancy within and the correlation across categories of evidence argue for the certainty of these messages – not their truth, just the reliability of their transmission.

5.8. References

CIS I

Renan, E., ed., *Corpus inscriptionum semiticarum, Pars prima: Inscriptiones phoenicias continens, Tomus I*, nᵒˢ 1-437 (Paris, 1881-1887).

Renan, E., P. Berger, and J.-B. Chabot, eds,. *CIS I: Inscriptiones phoenicias continens, Tomus II*, nᵒˢ 438-3251 (Paris, 1890-1911).

Chabot, J.-B. and J.-G. Février, eds., *CIS I: Inscriptiones phoenicias continens, Tomus III*, nᵒˢ 3252-6068 (Paris, 1925-1962).

FGrHist

Jacoby, F., *Die Fragmente der griechischen Historiker, I (1-63): Genealogie und Mythographie* (Berlin, 1923).

Jacoby, F., *FGrHist, II: volume A-D (64-261): Zeitgeschichte.* (Berlin, 1926-1930)

Jacoby, F., *FGrHist, III: volume A-B, commentary a-b, supplement b (261-607): Geschichte von staedten und voelkern, horographie und ethnographie.* (Leiden 1940-1964).

Cf. *Brill's New Jacoby* (https://referenceworks.brillonline.com/browse/brill-s-new-jacoby)

KAI

Donner, H. and W. Röllig, *Kanaanäische und aramäische Inschriften, I: Texte*, 5th ed. (Wiesbaden, 2006).

Donner, H. and W. Röllig, *KAI, II: Kommentar.* 3rd ed. (Wiesbaden, 1976).

Donner, H. and W. Röllig, *KAI, III: Glossare und Indices, Tafeln*, 3rd ed. (Wiesbaden, 1973).

Alquier, J., P. Alquier, J.-B. Chabot, and S. Gsell, 'Communication: Stèles votives à Saturne découvertes près de N'gaous (Algérie)', *Comptes rendus, Académie des inscriptions & belles-lettres*, ser. 4 (1931), 21-27.

Alt, A., 'Die phönikischen Inschriften von Karatepe', *Die Welt des Orients* 1.4 (1950), 272-287.

Amadasi Guzzo, M.G., 'La documentazione epigrafica dal tofet di Mozia e il problema del sacrificio *molk*', in C. Bonnet, E. Lipiński, and P. Marchetti, eds, *Religio Phoenicia, Acta Colloqui Namurcensis habiti diebus 14 et 15 mensis Decembris anni 1984.* Studia Phoenicia 4 / Collection d'études classiques 1 (Namur, 1986), 187-204.

Amadasi Guzzo, M.G., *Scavi a Mozia: Le iscrizioni, Collezione di studi fenici* 22 (Rome, 1986).

Amadasi Guzzo, M.G., 'Per una classificazione delle iscrizioni fenicie di dono', in G. Bartoloni, G. Colonna, and C. Grottanelli, eds, *Anathema. Scienza dell'Antichita* 3-4 (1989-1990), 831-844.

Amadasi Guzzo, M.G., 'Il tofet: Osservazioni di un'epigrafista', in G. Bartoloni and M. G. Benedettini, eds, *Sepolti tra i vivi / Buried among the Living. Scienza dell'Antichita* 14 (2007-2008), 347-362.

Amadasi Guzzo, M.G. and J.-Á. Zamora López, 'The Epigraphy of the Tophet', *Studi epigrafici e linguistici sul Vicino Oriente antico* 29-30 (2013), 159-192.

Bartoloni, P., 'Studi sul tofet', *Rivista di studi fenici* 43 (2015), 161-167.

Bénichou-Safar, H., 'À propos des ossements humains du *tophet* de Carthage', *Rivista di studi fenici* 9 (1981), 5-9.

Bénichou-Safar, H., 'Sur l'incinération des enfants aux *tophet*s de Carthage et de Sousse', *Revue de l'histoire des religions* 205 (1988), 57-68.

Bénichou-Safar, H., *Le tophet de Salammbô à Carthage: essai de reconstitution* (Rome, 2004).

Bernal, M., *Black Athena: The Afroasiatic Roots of Classical Civilization, I: The Fabrication of Ancient Greece, 1785-1985* (New Brunswick, NJ, 1987).

Bernardini, P., 'Per una rilettura del sanctuario tofet – I: Il caso di Mozia', *Sardinia, Corsica et Baleares antiquae: An International Journal of Archaeology* 3 (2005), 55-70.

Bérard, V., *Les Phéniciens et l'Odyssée* (Paris, 1902-1903).

Bertetto, P. and G. Rondolino, *Cabiria e il suo tempo* (Turin, 1998).

Berthier, A. and F. Charlier, *Le sanctuaire punique d'el-Hofra à Constantine, II: Planches* (Paris, 1952).

Berthier, A. and F. Charlier, *Le sanctuaire punique d'el-Hofra à Constantine, I: Texte* (Paris, 1955).

Brelich, A., *Introduzione alla storia delle religioni*, (Rome 1964).

Brelich, A., *Presupposti del sacrificio umano.* (Rome, 1967).

Buttitta, I.E., 'Tophet o dell'ambiguo statuto mortale degli infanti', *Thalassa: genti e cultura del Mediterraneo antico* 2 (2005), 87-99.

Cahail, K.M., 'A New Look at the *pds.t-n.t-nbw* of Zaubersprüche für Mutter und Kind, Spell P', *Journal of the American Research Center in Egypt* 52 (2016), 231-253.

D'Andrea, B., *Bambini nel «limbo»: Dati e proposte interpretative sui tofet fenici e punici.* (Rome, 2018).

Day, J., *Molech: A God of Human Sacrifice in the Old Testament*, University of Cambridge Oriental Publications 41 (Cambridge, 1989).

Day, J., 'Ashtoreth', in D.N. Freedman, ed., *Anchor Bible Dictionary, I: A-C.* (New York, 1992), 491-492.

Dussaud, R., 'Précisions épigraphiques touchant les sacrifices puniques d'enfants', *Comptes rendus des séances de l'Académie des Inscriptions et Belles-Lettres* 90.3 (1946), 371-387.

Février, J.-G., 'Molchomor', *Revue de l'histoire des religions* 143.1 (1953), 8-18.

Février, J.-G., 'Essai de reconstitution du sacrifice *molek*', *Journal asiatique* 248 (1960), 167-187.

Eissfeldt, O., *Molk als opferbegriff im punischen und hebräischen, und das ende des gottes Moloch*, Beiträge zur Religionsgeschichte des Altertums 3 (Halle, 1935).

Fedele, F.G., 'Tharros: Anthropology of the *tophet* and paleoecology of a Punic town', in P. Bartoloni et al., eds, *Atti del I Congresso Internazionale di Studi Fenici e Punici* vol. 3 (Rome, 1983), 635-650.

Flaubert, G., *Salammbô* (Paris, 1862).

Frendo, A.J., 'Burning Issues: *mlk* Revisited', *Journal of Semitic Studies* 61.2 (2016), 347-364.

Frœhner, G., 'La roman archéologique en France', *La Revue contemporaine* (31 Dec 1862), 853-870.

Garfinkel, H., *Toward a Sociological Theory of Information* (Boulder, CO, 2008).

Garnand, B.K., *The Use of Phoenician Human Sacrifice in the Formation of Ethnic Identities*, PhD dissertation, University of Chicago, 2006.

Garnand, B.K., Stager, L.E., and Greene, J.A., 'Infants as Offerings: Palaeodemographic Patterns and Tophet Burial', *Studi epigrafici e linguistici sul Vicino Oriente antico* 29-30 (2013), 193-222.

Geiger, A.. *Urschrift und Übersetzungen der Bibel in ihrer Abhängigkeit von der inneren Entwicklung des Judenthums* (Breslau, 1857).

Gobineau, J.-A. comte de, *Essai sur l'inégalité des races humaines* (Paris, 1853-1855).

Gras, M., P. Rouillard, and J. Teixidor, *L'Univers phénicien* (Paris, 1989).

Gras, M., P. Rouillard, and J. Teixidor, 'The Phoenicians and Death', *Berytus* 39 (1991), 127-176.

Halbertsma, R.B., *Scholars, Travellers, and Trade: The Pioneer Years of the National Museum of Antiquities in Leiden, 1818-1840* (London, 2003).

Hamilton, R., 'Cleitarchus and Diodorus 17', in Konrad H. Kinzl, ed., *Greece and the Eastern Mediterranean in Ancient History and Prehistory: Studies Presented to Fritz Schachermeyr on the Occasion of his Eightieth Birthday* (Berlin, 1977), 126-146.

Hammond, N.G.L., 'The Sources of Diodorus Siculus XVI, 2: The Sicilian Narrative', *Classical Quarterly* 32.3/4 (1938), 137-151.

Hawes, L.C., *Pragmatics of Analoguing: Theory and Model Construction in Communication* (Reading, MA, 1975).

Heckel, W., 'Notes on Q. Curtius Rufus' "History of Alexander"', *Acta Classica* 37 (1994), 67-58.

Heider, C., *The Cult of Molek: A Reassessment*, JSOT Supplement Series 43 (Sheffield, 1985).

Hughes, D.D., *Human Sacrifice in Ancient Greece* (London, 1991).

Humbert, J.E., *Notice sur quatre cippes sépulcraux et deux fragments, découverts en 1817, sur le sol de l'ancienne Carthage* (The Hague, 1821).

Lancel, S., 'Questions sur le *tophet* de Carthage', *La Tunisie: Carrefour du monde antique. Les dossiers d'archéologie* 200 (1995), 40-47.

Lancel, S., 'La fouille de l'épave du Magenta et le sauvetage de sa cargaison archéologique', *Comptes rendus des séances de l'Académie des Inscriptions et Belles-Lettres* 139.3 (1995), 813-816.

Leglay, Marcel, *Saturne Africain: Monuments*, I-II, (Paris, 1961-1966).

Leglay, Marcel, *Saturne Africain: Histoire*, Bibliothèque des Écoles françaises d'Athènes et de Rome 205 (Paris, 1966).

Levenson, J.D., *The Death and Resurrection of the Beloved Son: The Transformation of Child Sacrifice in Judaism and Christianity* (New Haven, 1993).

Malaspina, C., *An Epistemology of Noise* (London, 2018).

Marcus, D., *Jephthah and his Vow* (Lubbock, 1986).

Matania, E., 'The Italians in Tripoli – Italy Draws the Sword of Old Rome', *The Sphere: An Illustrated Newspaper for the Home* 47.616 (1911), 101.

Mayer, M., 'Kronos, VII: Der orientalische Kronos, 2. Der sogenannte Moloch', in W.H. Roscher, ed., *Ausführliches Lexikon der griechischen und römischen Mythologie, II* (Leipzig, 1890-94), 1501-1507.

Michelet, J., *Histoire romain, I: République* (Paris, 1831).

Mosca, P.G., *Child Sacrifice in Canaanite and Israelite Religion: A Study in mulk and מלך*, PhD dissertation, Harvard University, Cambridge, MA. 1975.

Mosca, P.G. 'The Tofet: A Place of Infant Sacrifice?', *Studi epigrafici e linguistici sul Vicino Oriente antico* 29-30 (2013), 119-136.

Moscati, S., *Il sacrificio punico dei fanciulli: Realtà o invenzione?*, Problemi attuali di scienza e di cultura 261 (Rome, 1987).

Moscati, S., ed. *I Fenici* (Milan,1988).

Moscati, S., 'L'olocausto dei fanciulli', in *Riti funerari e di olocausto nella Sardegna fenicia e punica*, Quaderni di archeologia 6/1989 Supplemento (Cagliari, 1990), 7-12.

Moscati, S., *Gli adoratori di Moloch: Indagine su un celebre rito cartaginese* (Milan, 1991).

Moscati, S., and S. Ribichini, *Il sacrificio dei bambini: Un aggiornamento* (Rome, 1991).

Musso, L., *Cabiria: I Cento anni del mito* (Turin, 2014).

Noort, E., 'Child Sacrifice in Ancient Israel: The *status quaestionis*.', in J.N. Bremmer, ed., *The Strange World of Human Sacrifice* (Leuven, 2007), 103-125.

Orsingher, A., 'Forever Young: Rethinking Infancy and Childhood at Motya.', in J. Tabolli, ed., *From Invisible to Visible. New Methods and Data for the Archaeology of Infant and Child Burials in Pre-Roman Italy and Beyond*, Studies in Mediterranean Archaeology CLIX, (Nicosia, 2018), 197-206.

Picard, G.-C., and C. Picard.. *La vie quotidienne à Carthage au temps d'Hannibal IIIe siècle avant Jésus-Christ* (Paris, 1958).

Pierce, J.R., *Symbols, Signals, and Noise: The Nature and Process of Communication* (New York, 1961).

Renan, E., *Histoire générale et système comparé des langues sémitiques, 1: Histoire générale des langues sémitique*s (Paris, 1855).

Renan, E., *Mission de Phénicie*. (Paris, 1864).

Ribichini, Sergio, *Il tofet e il sacrificio dei fanciulli* (Sassari, 1987).

Ribichini, Sergio, 'Il sacrificio di fanciulli nel mondo punico: Testimonianze e problem', in *Riti funerari e di olocausto nella Sardegna fenicia e punica*, Quaderni di archeologia 6/1989 Supplemento (Cagliari, 1990), 45-66.

Ribichini, Sergio, 'La questione del «tophet» punico', in S. Verger, ed., *Rites et espaces en pays celte et méditerranéen. Étude comparée à partir du village d'Acy-Romance (Ardennes/France). Actes du Colloque international (Roma, École Française, 18-19 aprile 1997)* (Rome, 2000), 293-304.

Ribichini, Sergio, 'Histoires de Moloch, le roi effroyable', in A.A. Nagy and F. Prescendi, eds, *Sacrifices humains: Dossiers, discours, comparaisons*, Bibliothèque de l'École des hautes études, Section des sciences 160 (Turnhout, 2013), 209-213.

Schaeffer, C.F.-A., 'Communication', *Comptes rendus, Académie des inscriptions & belles-lettres* ser. 4 (1956), 67.

Schneider, J. 'Les commentaires du « rire sardonique »: grammaire et parœmiographie.' in A. Garcea, M.-K. Lhommé, and D. Vallat, eds, *Polyphonia Romana: Hommages à Frédérique Biville* (Hildesheim, 2013), 843-854.

Schwartz, J.H., F.E. Houghton, L. Bondioli, and R. Macchiarelli, 'Skeletal Remains from Punic Carthage do not Support Systematic Sacrifice of Infants', *PLoS One* 5.2, 1-12 (www.plosone.org/article/info%3A-doi%2F10.1371%2Fjournal.pone.0009177).

Schwartz, J.H., F.E. Houghton, L. Bondioli, and R. Macchiarelli, 'Bones, Teeth, and Estimating Age of Perinates: Carthaginian Infant Sacrifice Revisited', *Antiquity* 86 (2012), 738-745.

Schwartz, J.H., F.E. Houghton, L. Bondioli, and R. Macchiarelli, 'Two Tales of One City: Data, Inference and Carthaginian Infant Sacrifice', *Antiquity* 91 (2017), 442-454.

Shannon, C.E., 'A Mathematical Theory of Communication', *Bell System Technical Journal* 27 (1948), 379-423, 623-656.

Shannon, C.E. and Weaver, W., *The Mathematical Theory of Communication* (Urbana, IL 1949).

Silver, N., *The Signal and the Noise: Why So Many Predictions Fail – But Some Don't* (New York, 2012).

Simonetti, A., 'Sacrifici umani e uccisioni rituali nel mondo fenicio-punico: Il contributo delle fonti letterarie', *Rivista di studi fenici* 11 (1983), 91-111.

Smith, P., G. Avishai, J.A. Greene, and L.E. Stager, 'Aging Cremated Infants: The Problem of Sacrifice at the Tophet of Carthage', *Antiquity* 85 (2011), 859-874.

Smith, P., G. Avishai, J.A. Greene, and L.E. Stager, 'Age Estimations Attest to the Practice of Infant Sacrifice at the Carthage Tophet', *Antiquity* 87 (2013), 1191-1207.

Stavrakopoulou, F., *King Manasseh and Child Sacrifice: Biblical Distortions of Historical Realities* (Berlin, 2004).

Tabolli, J., *From Invisible to Visible: New Methods and Data for the Archaeology of Infant and Child Burials in Pre-Roman Italy and Beyond*, Studies in Mediterranean Archaeology, 149 (Nicosia, 2018).

Weinfeld, M., 'The Worship of Molech and of the Queen of Heaven and its Background', *Ugarit-Forschungen* 4 (1972), 133-154.

Winterer, C., 'Model Empire, Lost City: Ancient Carthage and the Science of Politics in Revolutionary America', *William and Mary Quarterly* 67.1 (2010), 3-30.

Xella, P., 'Sacrifici di bambini nel mondo fenicio e punico nelle testimonianze in lingua greca e latina – I', *Studi epigrafici e linguistici sul Vicino Oriente antico* 26 (2009), 59-100.

Xella, P., 'Del "buon uso" di Angelo Brelich: Sacrifici umani e uccisioni rituali.', in I. Baglioni, ed., *Storia delle religioni e archeologia: Discipline a confronto* (Rome, 2010), 305-311.

Xella, P., ed., *The* tophet *in the Phoenician Mediterranean*, Studi epigrafici e linguistici sul Vicino Oriente antico 29-30 (Verona, 2013).

Xella, P., 'Sacrifices humains et meurtres rituels au Proche-Orient ancien', *Pasiphae: Rivista di filologia e antichità Egee* 9 (2015), 181-191.

5.9. Appendix I: Classical Abbreviations

Greek texts derive from the digital editions of the *Thesaurus Linguae Graecae* (TLG), Latin from the Packard Humanities Institute (LAT), with exceptions noted below. Transcriptions and abbreviations follow the *Brill's New Pauly* standard. Infelicities in translation remain the responsibility of the author.

Aeschylus	Aeschylus of Alexandria (3rd BCE), TLG0321.001 F 455 – Zenob.5.85; *FGrHist* 588; cf. Hesych. *Σ* 204
Aristot.*Eth.Nic.*	Aristotle of Stagira, *Nichomachean Ethics* (4th BCE), TLG0086.010
Aug.*Civ.*	Aurelius Augustinus, *City of God* (4th/5th CE), Dombart ed. 1877
Cic.*Rep.*	M. Tullius Cicero, *Republic* (1st BCE), LAT0474.043
Cleitarchus	Cleitarchus of Alexandria (4th/3rd BCE), TLG1279.002 *FGrHist* 137 F9 – Schol.Plat.*Rep.*337a; Phot. *s.v.* Σαρδόνιος γέλως; *Suda Σ* 124
Curt.	Curtius Rufus, *History of Alexander the Great* (1st CE), LAT0860.001
Demon	Demon of Athens (4th/3rd BCE), TLG1307.002 *FGrHist* 327 F18a – Schol.Hom.*Od.*20.302; F18b – Phot. *s.v.* Σαρδόνιος γέλως
Didymus	Didymus of Alexandria, *Proverbs* (1st BCE / 1st CE) epitomized by Zenobius, TLG0098.001
Diod.	Didorus of Sicily, *Library of History* (1st BCE), TLG0060.001
Dion.Hal.	Dionysius of Halicarnasus, *Roman Antiquities* (1st BCE), TLG0081.001
Drac.	Blossius Aemilius Dracontius, *Romulea* (5th CE), von Duhn ed. 1873
Ennius	Q. Ennius, *Annales* (2nd/1st BCE), LAT0043.001 quoted by Festus s.v. *puelli*, and Nonius s.v. *puellos*
Eratosth.	Eratosthenes of Cyrene, *Geography* (3rd BCE), Berger 1880 ed. F1 B.9 – Strab.17.1.19 [C802], cf. *FGrHist* 241, TLG0222
Eur.*I.T.*	Euripides of Athens, *Iphigenia in Tauris* (5th BCE), TLG0006.013
Euseb.*Praep. evang.*	Eusebius of Caesarea, *Preparation for the Gospel* (4th CE), TLG2018.001 cf. *Life of Constantine* 36, TLG2018.020; *In Praise of Constantine* 13, TLG2018.022
Eust.*Com.Od.*	Eustathius of Thessalonica, *Commentary on Homer* (12th CE), TLG4083.003
Festus	Sex. Pompeius Festus, *On the Meaning of Words* (2nd CE), LAT0043.001
Hdt.	Herodotus of Halicarnassus, *History* (5th BCE), TLG0016.001
Hesych.	Hesychius of Alexandria, *Lexicon* (5th/6th CE), TLG4085.002
Just.*Epit.*	M. Junianus Justinus, *Epitome of the Philippic History* (3rd CE), LAT0984.002
Lactant.*Div. Inst.*	L. Caelius Firmianus Lactantius, *Divine Instructions* (3rd/4th CE), LAT1236.001
Lucillus	Lucillus of Tarrha, *Proverbs* (1st CE) quoted in Schol.Plat.*Rep.*337a; epitomized by Zenobius, TLG0098.001
Min.Fel.	M. Municius Felix, *Octavius* (3rd CE), Kytzler ed. 1992
Nonius	Nonius Marcellus, *Doctrinal Compendium* (4th/5th CE), Lindsay and Onions ed. 1903
Paus.	Pausanias the Periegete, *Description of Greece* (2nd CE), TLG0525.001
Pausanias	Pausanias of Athens, *Collection of Attic Words* (2nd CE), TLG1569.001

pBerlin	Berlin Papyrus 3027 ("Mutter und Kind"), Spell P, [15] verso 2.2-7, Erman ed. 1901
Pescennius	Pescennius Festus, *History through Satire* (2nd CE) known from a single quotation in Lactant.*Div.Inst.*1.21.13, LAT1236.001
Philo	Herennius Philo of Byblos, *Phoenician History* (1st/2nd CE), TLG1416.006 *FGrHist* 790 F1 – Euseb.*Praep.Evang.*1.9.19-29; F2 – Euseb.*Praep. Evang.*1.9.30-10.42; F3 – Porph.2.56; Euseb.*Praep.Evang.*4.16.11
Philoxenus	Philoxenus of Alexandria (1st BCE), TLG1602.001 F591 – Zenob.1.68, *recensio Athoa*
Phot.	Photius of Constantinople, *Lexicon* (9th CE), TLG4040.030
Plat.*Min.*	Plato of Athens, *Minos* (4th BCE), TLG0086.010
Plut.*Mor.*	Plutarchus of Chaeronea, *Moralia* (1st/2nd CE) *On Superstition* 164E-171F, TLG0007.080
Pomp.Trog.	Pompeius Trogus, *Phillipic History* (1st BCE) epitomized by Just.*Epit.*, LAT0984.002
Porph.	Porphyrius of Tyre, *On Abstinence from Eating Meat* (3rd CE), TLG2034.003 cf. Euseb.*Praep.Evang.*4.16
Schol.Hom.*Od.*	Scholia on Homer *Odyssey*, TLG5026.007
Schol.Plat.*Rep.*	Scholia on Plato *Republic*, codices T &W, TLG5035.001, *codex* A, Pearson ed. 1987
Sex.Emp.	Sextus Empiricus, *Outline of Pyrrhonianism* (4th BCE), TLG0544.001
Sil.*Pun.*	Tib. Catius Asconius Silius Italicus, *Punica* (1st CE), LAT1345.001
Silenus	Silenus of Caleacte, *On the Syracusans* (3rd BCE), TLG1970.003 *FGrHist* 175 F5 – Phot. *s.v.* Σαρδόνιος γέλως; Suda *Σ* 124 cf. Hesych. *Σ* 202; Schol.Plat.*Rep.*337a
Soph.	Sophocles of Athens, *Andromeda* (5th BCE) F126 – Hesych. *K* 3859, TLG4085.002; NB *kourion / korion*, Musurus ed. 1521
Strab.	Strabo of Amaseia, *Geography* (1st BCE/1st CE), TLG0099.001
Suda	*The Suda*, or *Suidas* (10th CE), TLG9010.001
Tac.*Ger.*	Cornelius Tacitus, *Germany* (1st CE), LAT1351.002
Timaeus	Timaeus of Taormina, *History* (4th/3rd BCE), TLG1733.002 *FGrHist* 566 F64 – Schol.Plat.*Rep.*337a; cf. Zenob.5.85; Phot. *s.v.* Σαρδόνιος γέλως; *Suda Σ* 124; Schol.Hom.*Od.*20.302; Eust.*Com. Od.*20.302; Tzetz.Lycophr.796
Tzetz.Lycophr.	Johannes Tzetzes, *Scholia in Lycophronem* (12th CE), TLG5030.001
Varro	M. Terentius Varro, *Antiquity of Things Human and Divine* (1st BCE), LAT0684.004 quoted in Aug.*Civ.*7.19
Zenob.	Zenobius Grammaticus, *Epitome of Proverbs from Didymus and the Tarrhaean* (2nd CE), TLG0098.001 also *Epitome (recensio Athoa)*, Miller ed. 1868

5.10 Appendix II: Sardonian Grimace[65]

sinister smile of triumph which bodes pain on others

Homer *Odyssey* 20.302	8th BCE	Odysseus regarding the suitors
Plato *Republic* 337a	4th BCE	Thrasymachus toward Socrates

smile of compliance disguising the victim's own pain in (the face of) death
Minos (on Sardinia)

Simonides of Ceos	6th/5th BCE	Talos
Sophocles of Athens	5th BCE	

Carthaginians (on Sardinia)

Clitarchus of Alexandria	3rd BCE	infanticide
Philoxenus of Alexandria	1st BCE	

Sardinians (Carthaginian colonists)

Timaeus of Taormina	3rd BCE	senicide (and hosticide)
Demon of Athens	3rd BCE	
Aeschylus of Alexandria	3rd BCE	

poisonous Sardinian parsley

Silenus of Caleacte	3rd/2nd BCE	*Ranunculus sardous*
Lucillus of Tarrha	2nd BCE	

	Sardinian prisoners/elders	Sardinian elders	Carthaginian infants	Talos' victims	parsley eaters
Schol.Plat.*Rep* 337a, *codices* T&W		Timaeus	Cleitarchus	Simonides /Sophocles	Lucillus [Silenus]
Schol.Plat.*Rep* 337a, *codex* A	ὅτι	ἡ ὅτι	οἱ δέ ὅτι	ἄλλοι δέ	οἱ δέ ὅτι
Pausanias; Photius; *The Suda*	Demon	Timaeus	Cleitarchus	Simonides	Silenus
Michael Apostolius	Demon				–
Schol.Hom.*Od*.20.302	Demon	Timaeus		φασί	ἔνιοι
Eust.Com.*Od*.20.302		Timaeus		φασί	φασί
Hesych.	[Aeschylus]				τινές
Zenob.5.85	Aeschylus	Timaeus		Simonides	τινές
Zenob.1.68 *recensio Athoa*			Philoxenus		λέγουσι
Tzetz.Schol.Hes.*Op*.59		ἄλλοι			–
Tzetz.Schol.Lycoph.796		Timaeus			–
Paus.10.17.13					–

---

65   Adapted from *FGrHist, III* (supplement), 214-217, cf. Schneider,
     'Les commentaires'.

Chapter 6

Human sacrifice from ancient Israel to early Christianity

Karel C. Innemée*

6.1. Introduction

The term 'human sacrifice' may evoke in the first place images of horror, belonging to civilisations of a remote past or far away. It may not be associated with Christianity to the casual eye, but the connection exists and in a simplified manner of speaking one could even say that human sacrifice is at the heart of Christian belief. In the Old Testament, sacrificing the first-born, both human and animal, to God is a basic requirement, even if the child could be substituted by a sacrificial animal. According to Christian doctrine, as a reversal of this obligation God manifested himself in human form in order to sacrifice this god-man for the redemption of hereditary sin. This sacrifice is the basis of the Christian ritual, where flesh and blood, be it in their essence and by no means strictly symbolical, are consumed by the believers. In the first centuries of the Christian era countless martyrs have sought a death by choice, sacrificing themselves in what appears almost as a sacred suicide. Therefore, it seems perfectly justified to have a closer look at the phenomenon of human sacrifice, its origin, its meaning, and its iconography in Christian tradition.

Human sacrifice and ritual killing are phenomena that no longer have a place in either Judaism or Christianity, at least not in the literal sense. The practice of animal sacrifice as part of the Jewish cult was brought to an end by the destruction of the temple and the rest of Jerusalem, and the dispersion of the city's inhabitants in 70 CE.

Christianity, on the other hand, has abolished the sacrificial practice with the argument that the death of Christ has replaced the sacrifices that were made for the atonement for the sins of Israel. Nevertheless, in Christian writings and in iconography the metaphors of sacrifices, both of animals and humans, have persisted until the present day. The term 'Lamb of God' (the sacrifial Paschal lamb) has been coined as an epitheton for Christ, and 'bloodless sacrifice', a term also used in the late antique cult of Cybele, has become a designation for the Eucharist.[1] Sacrifice, be it in a symbolised form, has remained central in Christian theology and liturgy, and its symbolism was apparently not always well understood by outsiders.[2] It may have been a sometimes explicit use of metaphors that led to blood libels against Christians in the first three centuries; in turn, Christians in later periods used similar false accusations against heterodox believers and Jews.[3] At the same time, Christian iconography, folk-tales, and legends used explicit images of small

*University of Amsterdam, University of Divinity, Melbourne

---

1   Eckhardt, 'Bloodless Sacrifice'.
2   Pongratz-Leisten, 'Ritual Killing', 4.
3   Lanzilotta, 'The Early Christians and Human Sacrifice', 81-102.

children (representing Christ) being slaughtered in order to convince the (un)believers of the consubstantiality of the Eucharist with the flesh and blood of Christ, an image known in iconography as the *Melismos*.[4] In other words, Christianity has a complex and not always unambiguous relationship with the phenomenon of human sacrifice.

In Christian iconography, especially in the decoration of the sanctuary of a number of churches, the sacrifices of Abraham and Jephthah -Old Testament narratives in which a father sacrifices or is at the point of sacrificing his offspring- are depicted as prefigurations of the death of Christ, also sacrificed by his father. Both stories appear in patristic writings as parallels for the crucifixion, which shows that in Christian thought there is continuum between the old and new covenants between God and mankind, the old covenant and the Old Testament being seen as the forerunner and foreshadowing of the coming and death of Christ and the lifting of hereditary sin.

A religion is usually a conglomerate of undisputed axioms and values with a divine origin. A deity stands above time and space, and religious dogmas are meant to be of timeless significance. Human society, on the other hand, is subject to change, and social conventions and civil law can vary according to time and place. This, in two simplified sentences, is the background of the friction between the fundamentalist approach of religion and the approach of a liberal society. Nowadays, many of the norms and regulations that were the standard in a Near Eastern society three thousand years ago cannot be applied to the letter anymore.

The idea that there is a divine plan that starts with the creation of Adam and has a continuation until the present may exist in the thoughts of church fathers and theologians. The historical reality, however, is far more complex and full of discontinuity and question marks. The use of the term 'Judeo-Christian tradition' invoked from time to time, especially in (American) conservative political circles, seems to suggest that there is a continuity from Old Testament times into the history of Christianity, with a set of values and morality which have not basically changed since the bestowal of the Ten Commandments. It almost goes without saying that the use of this term has been questioned numerous times.[5] One need only look at certain examples of morally justified institutions and behaviour in the Old Testament that would be considered crimes against humanity nowadays, such as and ethnic cleansing and slavery.[6]

Christianity has its roots in the religion of ancient Israel, but contemporary (western) society has hardly anything in common with societies in the Near East of 3000 years ago. Not only in modern history, but also at earlier moments in the course of this stretch of time, attitudes must have changed. Religious views and convictions in Israel of the Iron Age were no longer the same during and after the Babylonian exile, when many of the books of the Old Testament were edited and probably adapted to the then prevailing views, while at the very beginning of the Christian era, when Second Temple Judaism still flourished side by side with the emerging new religion, we find again an entirely different mindset.

The attitude to life and death in early Christianity was different from our views. During the first three centuries of the Christian era martyrdom, or voluntary death with characteristics of human sacrifice, stood in high esteem, even to such an extent that certain Chrisitian believers reported themselves to the authorities, hoping to 'receive the crown of martyrdom', an attitude that has disappeared with the legalisation of the Church.[7] This means that what we call now the Christian tradition has gone through various stages and has preserved a religious inheritance of more than three millennia that at some points is difficult to fit into modern society in which human sacrifice has no longer a place. The way that individuals and religious authorities have dealt with this uncomfortable inheritance of a past that accepted human sacrifice, and the transformation that must have been the result of this, deserve closer examination.

6.2. Human sacrifice in the ancient Near East and Israel

6.2.1. The wider context of Hebrew biblical cult

Much has been written about the question of the historicity of human sacrifice, especially child sacrifice, in the Tanakh.[8] There are strong indications for ritual killing and human sacrifice in the ancient Near East and it is very likely to have been practiced in ancient Israel as well. It is, however, difficult to find evidence in the strict sense of the word, evidence that would stand in court, so

---

4   For a discussion of this theme, see below, 6.3.5.
5   For instance by Cohen, *The Myth of the Judeo-Christian Tradition* and by Nathan and Topolski, *Is there a Judeo-Christian Tradition?*
6   In Deut. 20:10-16, for instance, God decrees to kill the male population of opponent states and to take women and children as slaves. Exodus 21 mentions various regulations for (sexual) slavery.

7   The belief was that martyrs would be exempted from the *refrigerium interim* and were assured of a place in heaven. Ignatius of Antioch, for instance, condemned to fight beasts in the year 107, asked especially not to be saved from martyrdom: 'Pray, then, do not seek to confer any greater favour upon me than that I be sacrificed to God while the altar is still prepared'. Ignatius, *Epistle to the Romans* 2, Roberts, Donaldson, and Cleveland Coxe, *Ante-Nicene Fathers* 1.
8   For instance Sales, 'Human Sacrifice in Biblical Thought'; Day, *Molech: a God of Human Sacrifice*; Stavrakopoulou, *King Manasseh and Child Sacrifice*; Lange, 'They Burn Their Sons and Daughters'; Dewrell, *Child Sacrifice in Ancient Israel*; Noort, 'Child Sacrifice'.

to speak. The circumstantial evidence that is available consists entirely of texts, most of which are biblical texts. The use of such texts, however, is debated, or, as Francesca Stavrokopoulou formulates:

> Underlying this discussion is the continuing debate concerning the use of the Hebrew Bible within historical reconstructions of ancient Israelite and Judahite societies and their religious beliefs and practices. The perceived historical reliabilty of the Hebrew Bible remains in a state of flux: though the tension of historical memory and literary fiction within the biblical texts is widely acknowledged, a consensus concerning the extent to which the Hebrew Bible preserves reliable historical information about the people, practices and events it describes has not emerged – nor is it likely to.[9]

The most important books in the Bible that contain information which is relevant for the discussion, such as Genesis and Exodus, describe events that have an almost mythological character, such as the lives and deeds of the archfathers Abraham, Isaac, and Jacob, and the story of the Exodus from Egypt and the divine legislation. The other three books of the Pentateuch, especially Leviticus, contain instructions and rules concerning sacrifices and other ritual acts. Without going into the details of the extremely complicated textual history, we can say that Genesis in the redaction that we know dates back to the late sixth century BCE, possibly from during the Persian period after the Babylonian exile. The Pentateuch as a whole took its final shape probably not earlier than 400 BCE.[10] This means that the passages such as the ones that refer to the sacrifice of the firstborn could have been adapted to the prevailing views of that time. Most of the passages that mention the sacrifice of children do so in a negative way, forbidding it in the strongest of terms (for instance Lev. 18:21, 20:2-5). This in itself can be seen as evidence that such sacrifices were indeed practiced, since one does not forbid things that do not occur in the first place.

There can be hardly any doubt that ritual killing and human sacrifice, including child sacrifice, were practiced in the ancient Near East, especially in the Phoenician-Punic reach. The archaeological evidence consists of *tophets*, places of worship and child sacrifice.[11] In the Syro-Palestine region and Mesopotamia the evidence is less overwhelming and does not point in the direction of such a practice on a systematic scale. Ritual killing, in various forms, can be attested mainly on the basis of textual sources, with the exception of retainer sacrifice, for which archeological evidence exists.[12] Archaeological remains of numerous places of worship dating back to the Bronze and Iron Ages show that the Hebrew cult practice did not differ much from those of other populations in Canaan and contemporary neighbouring states. Although several prophets fulminated against the religions of neighbouring Canaanite peoples, the tablets that were found at Ras Shamra (ancient Ugarit) in 1929 show that Israel's religious beliefs and rituals had considerable overlap with those of these adversaries.[13] Places of worship consisted of altars in the open air, many of them on elevated places, meant for holocaust-sacrifices.[14] In some of such excavated sites clear evidence for sacrifices in the form of animal remains was found, and in two cases there are reasons to believe that human sacrifices were made as well. The high place of worship at Gezer (central Israel, ca. 1600 BCE) was excavated by R.A.C. Macalister between 1902 and 1909 and contained numerous burials of newborn children, believed to have been victims of sacrifice.[15] In 1955 John Basil Hennessy excavated a Late Bronze Age (thirteenth century BCE) building near the airport in Amman, which he identified as a temple. The numerous remains of burnt human bones seem to indicate that human sacrifices were made there.[16] Human sacrifice was condemned by biblical writers, and there are no reasons to believe that it was institutionalised in the cult of YHWH, but it must have been practiced from time to time, be it in times of crisis or under the influence of the cults of neighbouring peoples.[17]

6.2.2. Hebrew sacrifice before Exodus

The Hebrew pre-Mosaic cultic practices are almost unknown, apart from the mentions of altars and sacrifices on elevated places and mountains, and the veneration of large erect stones (Bethel, *Bet-El, baitylos*) that were associated with the presence of God. Such practices are known from other Near Eastern religions as well.[18] Only very few passages in Genesis and Exodus mention cultic activities. Gen. 4:4 states "Abel also brought of the firstborn

---

9   Stavrakopoulou, *King Manasseh and Child Sacrifice*, 1.
10 McEntire, *Struggling with God*, 8.
11 Mosca, *Child Sacrifice in Canaanite and Israelite Religion*; For a more elaborate study on the Punic tradition, see Garnand in this volume; Green, *The Role of Human Sacrifice*, 149-200 deals with child sacrifice in Hebrew religion.

12 See Krispijn in this volume.
13 Robinson, 'The God of the Patriarchs'.
14 Waszkowiak, 'Pre-Israelite and Israelite Burnt Offering Altars'.
15 Macalister, *Excavations at Gezer II*, 401-402, 431-435. Green, *The Role of Human sacrifice*, 152-153.
16 Hennessey, 'Thirteenth Century B.C. Temple of Human Sacrifice'; Shanks, 'First Person'. Waszkowiak, 'Pre-Israelite and Israelite Burnt Offering Altars', 59-60.
17 Sales, 'Human Sacrifice in Biblical Thought', 112-113.
18 Gen. 28: 10-19; 31:10-13; 35:1-7, 14-15, where Jacob has a vision of God, erects a stone which he anoints, and comes back later to build an altar. In the apocryphal Book of Jubilees Jacob even attempts to build a temple at Bethel. Schwartz, 'Jubilees, Bethel and the Temple of Jacob'.

of his flock and of their fat. And the Lord respected Abel and his offering", a passage which suggests that sacrificing the firstborn was a custom from long before the Mosaic laws were codified. Long before Jacob had his dream and named the place where it happened Bethel, Abram sacrificed on an altar near a place also called Bethel, possibly a cult site where a sacred stone was venerated (Gen. 12:8, 13:3). When God gave Abraham the instructions to sacrifice his son Isaac, the latter travelled to the mountain of Moria in order to perform the sacrifice (Gen. 22:1-19). Jacob, fleeing from his brother Esau, had a dream in which he saw the heavens opening, and after waking up, took the stone on which he had slept, anointed it, and called it Bethel (House of God), apparently a second place with this name.[19]

After departing from his father-in-law Laban, "Jacob offered a sacrifice on the mountain, and called his brethren to eat bread. And they ate bread and stayed all night on the mountain." (Gen. 31:54-55). As an old man, on his way to Egypt, Jacob "... took his journey with all that he had, and came to Beersheba, and offered sacrifices to the God of his father Isaac." (Gen. 46:1). The way that the people of Israel worshipped their god during their stay in Egypt remains equally obscure. Only when Moses asks for permission for the people to leave, on the pretext of going to the desert to sacrifice, a hint is given that such worship took place in the open air, possibly on mountaintops.[20] Although these texts cannot be taken as historical documents, the authors apparently wanted to show that since the time of the creation God was worshipped by the archfathers. This cult, as far as the scarce allusions reveal, could take place on mountaintops or other places where God had manifested himself, and it could involve anointing stones, or sacrificing (firstborn) animals, possibly even human firstborns. These elements do not differ basically from what we know of other religions in the Near East of the Bronze and Iron Ages.

How does the story of the sacrifice of Abraham fit in this image? As said, we cannot read the passage in Genesis (22:1-19) as a historical document, given the redaction it has undergone and the long span between the moment when the events it describes presumably happened and the moment when it was written down. On one hand, the narrative does not mention astonishment or objection on the side of Abraham, which could be interpreted as a sign that sacrificing a child was not uncommon. On the other hand Abraham, until the very last moment, tries to hide the fact that Isaac will be the victim from his servants and the child himself, which shows his extremely uncomfortable feelings about it. In the end, at the climax of the story, the child is spared and redeemed by the sacrifice of a ram.

This redemption can be seen as a foreshadowing of the way in which the firstborn son would be redeemed in the Mosaic laws, or rather, as a way in which the author of Abraham's story wants to show that the Mosaic law had its antecedents in the time of Abraham.

6.2.3. The firstborn and his redemption
It appears that the sacrifice of the firstborn was of crucial importance in the Hebrew cultic practice. Even before the Ten Commandments were given, immediately after the people of Israel had left Egypt, Moses and Aaron received the decree: "Consecrate to Me all the firstborn, whatever opens the womb among the children of Israel, *both* of man and beast; it is Mine." (Ex. 13:1). Only later in the same chapter (Ex. 13:11-15) the possibility of redemption is given:

> And it shall be, when the Lord brings you into the land of the Canaanites, as He swore to you and your fathers, and gives it to you, that you shall set apart to the Lord all that open the womb, that is, every firstborn that comes from an animal which you have; the males shall be the Lord's. But every firstborn of a donkey you shall redeem with a lamb; and if you will not redeem it, then you shall break its neck. And all the firstborn of man among your sons you shall redeem. So it shall be, when your son asks you in time to come, saying, 'What is this?' that you shall say to him, 'By strength of hand the Lord brought us out of Egypt, out of the house of bondage. And it came to pass, when Pharaoh was stubborn about letting us go, that the Lord killed all the firstborn in the land of Egypt, both the firstborn of man and the firstborn of beast. Therefore I sacrifice to the Lord all males that open the womb, but all the firstborn of my sons I redeem.

Here the explicit connection is made between the death of all the firstborn of the Egyptians and the sacrifice of the firstborn in Israel. The death of all the firstborn in Egypt, as a punishment for the stubbornness of the pharaoh, is contrasted to the redemption that the sons of Israel receive. In spite of this, there are enough indications that show that children were sacrificed to YHWH in the monarchic period of Israel. In the post-exilic period, when the final redaction of Exodus was achieved, however, this time was past and it would have been out of the question to suggest that YHWH would condone human sacrifice in any way.

6.2.4. The death of the firstborn as a punishment
The Israelite rituals distinguish between five diferent kinds of sacrifices, which are specified in the first six chapters of Leviticus. On one hand there are the offerings that should be brought regularly or annually (the ten percent of the harvest, specified in Deut. 13:22-23); on the other hand there are sacrifices that have the goal to restore a disrupted

---

19   Little is known about the status of this place of worship until a temple, rivalling the temple in Jerusalem, was established here by king Jeroboam I in the late tenth century BCE (1 Kings 12:28-33).
20   Ex. 5:3, 8, 17; 8:8, 25-27.

relation with God, namely the purification and guilt offerings. No mention is made of children being sacrificed. However, in two cases mentioned in the Old Testament it is clear that the death of a firstborn is a punishment for a transgression. The most conspicuous example is of course the above-mentioned death of all the firstborn, animal and human, among the Egyptians. A second case where a firstborn dies as the consequence of a transgression is when king David commits adultery with Bathsheba, with whom he conceives a child and whose husband he causes to get killed in battle. The prophet Nathan is sent by God to David to reprimand him.

> So David said to Nathan, "I have sinned against the Lord." And Nathan said to David, "The Lord also has put away your sin; you shall not die. However, because by this deed you have given great occasion to the enemies of the Lord to blaspheme, the child also who is born to you shall surely die. (2 Sam. 12:13-14)

In neither of the two cases, the pharaoh's and David's, the death of the firstborn can be called a sacrifice in the strict sense, but rather a retribution for opposing the will of God. In both cases it is a king that is punished, not by a death sentence, but by killing his potential successor. The punishment affects directly an innocent person and not the transgressor himself, and the father is redeemed by the death of his son. This brings to mind the exclamation of the prophet Micah:

> Will the Lord be pleased with thousands of rams, ten thousand rivers of oil? Shall I give my firstborn for my transgression, the fruit of my body for the sin of my soul? (Micah 6:7)

The eldest son represents the continuity of the bloodline and having to lose him can be seen as a more severe punishment than giving one's own life, especially in a society where the family as a whole is more important than the individuals that it is composed of. Micah's text probably dates back to the second half of the eighth century BCE and one may wonder if in those days it was more than a just a metaphor or a hyperbole in which the prophet expresses his despair. In any case, it hints at the possibility that in extreme circumstances a firstborn could be sacrificed. According to 2 Kings, approximately a century earlier king Mesha of Moab sacrificed his eldest son to prevent his city from being taken by the king Jehoram of Israel:

> So when they came to the camp of Israel, Israel rose up and attacked the Moabites, so that they fled before them; and they entered their land, killing the Moabites. Then they destroyed the cities, and each man threw a stone on every good piece of land and filled it; and they stopped up all the springs of water and cut down all the good trees. But they left the stones of Kir Haraseth intact. However the slingers surrounded and attacked it. And when the king of Moab saw that the battle was too fierce for him, he took with him seven hundred men who drew swords, to break through to the king of Edom, but they could not. Then he took his eldest son who would have reigned in his place, and offered him as a burnt offering upon the wall; and there was great indignation against Israel. So they departed from him and returned to their own land. (2 Kings 3:24-27)

The passage shows that such a sacrife was an extraordinary measure, and that it was effective, even though the last sentence leaves open the question of what exactly happened. Did the Israelites leave in fear of an intervention by the god to whom the sacrifice was made? Again, instead of reading this passage as a historically reliable source, we should rather consider it as an illustration of the attitude of the author towards human sacrifice and its effects.

6.2.5. The mlk sacrifice

A name that has become proverbial for something that requires horrific sacrifices is that of Moloch. In many translations of the Old Testament the name is used as that of a god to whom children are sacrificed and whose cult is despised by the prophets. Gruesome images of his cult are sketched by John Milton in *Paradise Lost* and by Gustave Flaubert in *Salammbô*. The figure of Moloch and his cult, however, are based on a misinterpretation of the term *mlk*, which is used in Hebrew and Punic.[21] Already in 1935 Otto Eissfeldt showed that the term, which is derived from the word for 'king', is used for a specific kind of sacrifice, which can involve either a child or an animal in its place. In spite of the fact that other scholars after Eissfeldt have confirmed his interpretation, the misunderstanding has not been eradicated yet and some insist that the term does refer to a god.[22] The New King James Version (1982), an authoritative translation of the Bible, still uses the term Molech as a proper name. The term is used a number of times, mostly in connection with sacrifices of children, which are condemned unconditionally:

> And you shall not let any of your descendants pass through the fire to Molech, nor shall you profane the name of your God: I am the Lord.' (Lev. 18:21)

---

21 The first use of the term Moloch as a proper name for a pagan god can already be found in Acts 7:43. The New King James Version uses the spelling 'Molech', which will be used here only in quotes.

22 Eissfeldt, *Molk als Opferbegriff*; Mosca, *Child Sacrifice*; Reynolds, 'Molek: Dead or Alive?'. See also Stavrakopoulou, *King Manasseh and Child Sacrifice*, 207-297. An opponent of Eissfeldt's interpretation is for instance Day (*Molech: A God of Human Sacrifice*).

Then the Lord spoke to Moses, saying, "Again, you shall say to the children of Israel: 'Whoever of the children of Israel, or of the strangers who dwell in Israel, who gives any of his descendants to Molech, he shall surely be put to death. The people of the land shall stone him with stones. I will set My face against that man, and will cut him off from his people, because he has given some of his descendants to Molech, to defile My sanctuary and profane My holy name. And if the people of the land should in any way hide their eyes from the man, when he gives some of his descendants to Molech, and they do not kill him, then I will set My face against that man and against his family; and I will cut him off from his people, and all who prostitute themselves with him to commit harlotry with Molech." (Lev. 20:2-5)

The expression 'passing through the fire' is apparently used for a burnt offering. This is a practice that is mentioned elsewhere in connection with other gods; however, in the context of the passages from Leviticus no specific deity is mentioned. Neither do the passages imply that the expression concerns the sacrifice of the firstborn, only the practice of the *mlk*-sacrifice. The conclusion can therefore be drawn that this way of sacrificing children is condemned in the first place, regardless to which god it is made. It also shows that such sacrifices did take place, otherwise they would not be forbidden in such explicit terms.

The historical reality of the practice of sacrificing (firstborn) children to YHWH or other gods in the monarchic period is hidden behind a screen of the exilic and post-exilic redaction of a number of books, especially the Pentateuch. A passage in Ezekiel (20:25-26) suggests that it was God who deliberately provoked *mlk*-sacrifices, be it as a way to punish his people:

> Therefore I also gave them up to statutes that were not good, and judgments by which they could not live; and I pronounced them unclean because of their ritual gifts, in that they caused all their firstborn to pass through the fire, that I might make them desolate and that they might know that I am the Lord.

The book of the prophet Jeremiah contains a number of passages that describe the practice in question, and the site of the *mlk*-sacrifices in Judah. In the valley of Ben-Hinnom a *tophet*[23] was established where children were burnt either to YHWH or to Baal:

> 'And they have built the high places of Tophet, which is in the Valley of the Son of Hinnom, to burn their sons and their daughters in the fire, which I did not

command, nor did it come into My heart. Therefore behold, the days are coming,' says the Lord, 'when it will no more be called Tophet, or the Valley of the Son of Hinnom, but the Valley of Slaughter; for they will bury in Tophet until there is no room.' (Jer. 7:31-32)

and:

> 'And they built the high places of Baal which are in the Valley of the Son of Hinnom, to cause their sons and their daughters to pass through the fire to Molech, which I did not command them, nor did it come into My mind that they should do this abomination, to cause Judah to sin.' (Jer. 32:35)

These passages are from the so-called deuteronomistic redaction of Jeremiah, written in the end of the exilic period (586-539 BCE). During the Babylonian exile, authors and redactors reflected on the fate of Israel, the destruction of the Northern Kingdom, and the exile of Judah, and explained these events as a divine punishment for the abominations of Israel and its kings.[24] A series of kings of Judah and the Northern Kingdom are portrayed in the Book of Kings as godless rulers, and periods of decadence alternate with better times. 2 Kings 16:3 tells how king Ahaz "...made his son pass through the fire, according to the abominations of the nations whom the Lord had cast out from before the children of Israel." His son Hezekiah restored the proper wordship of YHWH, but his son and successor Manasseh (687-643 BCE) was portrayed in 2 Kings 21:1-6 as an evil king again:

> Manasseh was twelve years old when he became king, and he reigned fifty-five years in Jerusalem. His mother's name was Hephzibah. And he did evil in the sight of the Lord, according to the abominations of the nations whom the Lord had cast out before the children of Israel. For he rebuilt the high places which Hezekiah his father had destroyed; he raised up altars for Baal, and made a wooden image, as Ahab king of Israel had done; and he worshiped all the host of heaven and served them. He also built altars in the house of the Lord, of which the Lord had said, 'In Jerusalem I will put My name.' And he built altars for all the host of heaven in the two courts of the house of the Lord. Also he made his son pass through the fire, practiced soothsaying, used witchcraft, and consulted spiritists and mediums. He did much evil in the sight of the Lord, to provoke Him to anger.

According to Francesca Stavrakopoulou this illustrates how the practice of child sacrifice in pre-exilic Israel was

---

23   Place of sacrifice, cognate with Aramaic *tapya*, 'stove', 'fireplace'.

24   Lange, 'They Burn Their Sons and Daughters'.

distorted in retrospect during and after the Babylonian exile.[25] From that period onwards child sacrifice would be associated with polytheism and depicted as one of the most barbarian aberrations of God's law. Under king Josiah, Manasseh's grandson, monotheism was restored again and the tophet dismantled: "And he defiled Topheth, which is in the Valley of the Son of Hinnom, that no man might make his son or his daughter pass through the fire to Molech." (2 Kings 23:10), but the complaints of Jeremiah (see above) show that it was reinstalled again afterwards.

The history sketched in Kings is rather black-and-white: there were evil kings who dedicated themselves to polytheism and good kings who fostered only the cult of YHWH in Jerusalem. This ideologically biased image could be nuanced by archaeological finds, but unfortunately there are still many white spots on the map. From the Iron Age in Judah and Israel only two real temples are known, in Dan and Arad, which at least shows that the temple in Jerusalem did not have an absolute monopoly on cult activities.[26] Archaeological evidence for human sacrifices is scarce, and concerning the tophet in the valley of Ben Hinnom, of which not even the exact location is known, no physical evidence is available so far.[27] In Tyre and more recently in Achzib the presence of such places of sacrifice and incineration has been attested and it may just be a matter of time until the existence of the Ben Hinnom tophet can be confirmed.[28]

6.2.6. Jephtah and his daughter

Mentioned generally as one of the three examples of human sacrifice in the Old Testament, the story of Jephthah and his daughter is in fact a case on its own. It is not a sacrifice required by God, nor an extreme measure in extraordinary circumstances, but the result of an intiative by a man who does not realise the consequences of his reckless vow. The theme is not unique; in Greek mythology similar stories were known about Idomeneus of Crete, who promised to Neptune to sacrifice the first living being that would welcome him if he would survive the storm he was in (and had to sacrifice his son), and of a certain Maeander who made a similar vow for being victorious in battle, and had to sacrifice his wife, sister, and son.[29] As with other Old Testament stories, the historical reliability of the story of Jephthah is extremely doubtful. The question is therefore not whether it is a testimony of a case of human sacrifice, but what it tells about the attitude of the author and the redactor of the narrative.[30] The structure of the Book of Judges is a repeating pattern of events: Israel 'does evil in the sight of the Lord', mostly by worshipping other gods, and is punished by God by delivering them into the hands of enemies. Next a leader ('judge') stands up under the guidance of God and restores law and order. The sentence in Judges 17:6: "In those days there was no king in Israel; everyone did what was right in his own eyes.", which is repeated several times in the book, illustrates the view of the author/redactor, who was apparently writing from a monarchic point of view, on the situation in Israel.

The book was composed of a number of separate narratives, possibly written in the monarchic time (eighth to seventh centuries), and received a deuteronomistic redaction. One of the judges is Jephthah, and as a militia leader he takes the initiative to confront the Ammonites:

> Then the Spirit of the Lord came upon Jephthah, and he passed through Gilead and Manasseh, and passed through Mizpah of Gilead; and from Mizpah of Gilead he advanced toward the people of Ammon. And Jephthah made a vow to the Lord, and said, "If You will indeed deliver the people of Ammon into my hands, then it will be that whatever comes out of the doors of my house to meet me, when I return in peace from the people of Ammon, shall surely be the Lord's, and I will offer it up as a burnt offering. (Judg. 11:29-31)

After his victory he returns:

> When Jephthah came to his house at Mizpah, there was his daughter, coming out to meet him with timbrels and dancing; and she was his only child. Besides her he had neither son nor daughter. And it came to pass, when he saw her, that he tore his clothes, and said, "Alas, my daughter! You have brought me very low! You are among those who trouble me! For I have given my word to the Lord, and I cannot go back on it." So she said to him, "My father, if you have given your word to the Lord, do to me according to what has gone out of your mouth, because the Lord has avenged you of your enemies, the people of Ammon." Then she said to her father, "Let this thing be done for me: let me alone for two months, that I may go and wander on the mountains and bewail my virginity, my friends and I."... And it was so at the end of two months that she returned to her father, and he carried out his vow with her which he had vowed. She knew no man. (Judg. 11:34-39)

A remarkable formulation is that 'the Spirit of the Lord' is upon Jephthah when he makes his vow. Jephthah acts as a God-sent saviour and delivers his people under divine inspiration. This may be the reason why the narrator refrains from any negative comment on the decision of

---

25   Stavrakopoulou, *King Manasseh and Child Sacrifice*, 15-140.
26   Faust, 'Israelite Temples'.
27   Waszkowiak, 'Pre-Israelite and Israelite Burnt Offering Altars'.
28   Dearman, 'The Tophet in Jerusalem'.
29   Apollodorus, *Epitome* VI.10.
30   Thompson, *Early History of the Israelite People*, 96.

Jephthah that leads to the tragic outcome. The end of the chapter, "And it became a custom in Israel that the daughters of Israel went four days each year to lament the daughter of Jephthah the Gileadite." is where the author comes to the conclusion that it is a tragedy. The story is a tragedy, but the main actor is not blamed. It even seems for a moment that Jephthah blames his daughter for both for his and her own misfortune. The daughter, whose name is not even given, does not appear in the end of the story as a voiceless and will-less victim. To the contrary, she stands as a tragic heroine who does not even try to escape her fate, in the same way in which Iphigenia accepted her father's decision, but gives her life for the sake of the victory over Ammon.

Whereas the deuteronomistic redaction of other books has left a clear condemnation of the sacrifice of children, the story of Jephtah, which dates back to an earlier period, has apparently escaped the intervention of the redactors. This is probably due to the fact that the judges were seen as heroes of a period when anarchy lurked, whose deeds were inspired by God. Even in the New Testament the reputation of Jephthah remains untarnished, as the anonymous author of the Letter to the Hebrews writes: "And what more shall I say? For the time would fail me to tell of Gideon and Barak and Samson and Jephthah, also of David and Samuel and the prophets." (Heb. 11:32)

According to Avraham Faust,

> ... it appears as if biblical data and interpretations were influencing previous scholarship, and many scholars attempted to reconstruct a religion which was to a large extent expected on the basis of the interpretation of the texts.[31]

This remark concerns the archaeology of religious sites in Judah and Israel, but it can also be applied to the place of human sacrifice in Israelite religion. Biblical evidence for the actual sacrifice of firstborns or other children is mainly circumstantial in character. It is very likely that the practice in Israel in the Bronze and Iron Ages was not much different from that in other Canaanite religions, but the scale on which it took place can hardly be estimated so far in the absence of archaeological evidence.

6.3. Human sacrifice in Christianity

Countless books have been written on the subject of Christianity as a religion that is built on Judaism and the 'parting of the ways'; within the present context, however, the focus is on how human sacrifice in the Old Testament has been seen through Christian eyes and

how the phenomenon has survived in a transformed way within Christian doctrine and artistic culture. Human sacrifice, whether it once was a common practice or an exceptional deed, was eradicated in post-exilic Judaism, and the Old Testament writings were redacted so as to depict it as depraved and pagan. In Christianity, however, it made a comeback, both in a literal and a metaphorical way. The execution of Jesus was real and physical, and though at first it came as a disillusion to his followers, it had to be given a place and meaning in the teachings of his disciples. Looking to the past, it was seen as the fulfillment of Old Testament prophecies, and as the final and definite sacrifice of which the sacrifices of Abraham, Jepthah, and the Paschal lamb were the forerunners. Seen from the perspective of the first century CE, when the new teachings were directed not only at potential Jewish converts, the death of Jesus had to be given a meaning that would be acceptable for Roman and Greek converts as well. For them, the Jewish tradition had no meaning and the concept of a father sacrificing his child must have been utterly alien and reprehensible. In the Graeco-Roman tradition, however, the partly overlapping concepts of the 'noble death', self-sacrifice, and martyrdom were known and accepted phenomena, of which various historical and literary examples were known. Jan Willem van Henten has shown how these forms of self-sacrifice could be seen as heroic and beneficial.[32] From the non-Jewish point of view, the death of Jesus as a self-sacrifice and 'noble death' must have been more understandable and acceptable than a death as a son sacrificed by his father. The three effects of such a heroic death distinguished by Van Henten, namely that: 1. others are delivered or enabled to triumph; 2. others are saved from death; 3. one or more deities are appeased,[33] can, *mutatis mutandis*, be applied to the self-sacrifice of Jesus Christ.

The sacrificial death of Jesus has therefore two overlapping, but at the same time contradictory aspects: on one hand he is the passive victim, the lamb to the slaughter, sacrificed by his father, while on the other hand he is the one who sacrifices himself, being priest and victim at the same time (Heb. 7:26-27). This is, however, not the place to go deeper into the theological aspects of this matter, which are rooted in the problem of the divine and human natures of Jesus Christ and the question whether he suffered and died as a human being or as God.

The followers of Jesus, although being simply human, are invited to follow his example and lose their life in order to gain it; such a message is repeated in all four gospels (Matt. 10:39; Mark 8:35; Luke 9:24; John 12:25). According to these texts, from the believer's point of view it is not

---

31   Faust, 'Israelite Temples', 13.

32   Van Henten, 'Noble Death and Martyrdom'; Idem, 'Self-sacrifice and Substitution'.

33   Van Henten, 'Self-sacrifice and Substitution', 86-87.

the heroic death for the sake of others that constitutes the essence of giving up one's life, but saving one's own soul by detachment from the material world. The common aspect is the obedience to God and submission to his will. Especially in the first centuries of the Christian era, such *imitatio Christi* would lead martyrs to a self-chosen death. After the persecutions ceased and monasticism emerged, the mortification of the body was seen as another form of physical self-sacrifice, to such an extent that some anchorites died a premature death. Suicide has always been rejected by Christian morality, but in the case of voluntary martyrdom and extreme asceticism it seems as if the boundaries of what was morally acceptable were stretched to a critical point.

Although the accusations of cannibalism and child-sacrifice made against the believers in the first centuries of Christianity were unfounded, the reasons why they were made are not entirely fanciful, given the terminology that was and is used in the Eucharist.[34] Apart from the liturgical metaphors for the physical sacrifice of Jesus, certain legends and folk-tales, and even the officially sanctioned iconography of the *melismos* in post-Byzantine churches went to such an extreme that they depicted child-sacrifice in an almost realistic way. Such stories and imagery were meant to convince believers of the reality of the transubstantiation, but in their explicitness they also refer to child-sacrifice in its most basic form.[35]

6.3.1. Christ as the sacrificial lamb

The central and most important teaching of Christian doctrine is the death and resurrection of Jesus Christ. Jesus, God incarnate, is given over by his father to be killed as a sacrifice. A sacrifice of the 'only begotten son' by his father is nothing less than a human sacrifice, since Jesus suffers in a human body and dies like a human being.

In Christian theology the death of Christ is seen as a sacrifice with a dual character: on one hand a sacrifice for the forgiveness of sins and the lifting of the hereditary sin of Adam and Eve (Eph. 1:7; Rom. 5:8-18); on the other hand a renewal of the covenant with God and his people, or a repetition of the slaughter of the Passover lambs before the Exodus. At first, however, the shameful execution of Jesus was not understood as such by his followers and the stress was laid on his resurrection. The concept of the crucifixion as a sacrifice originates from the letters of Paul and cannot be found disclosed explicitly in earlier books of the New Testament.[36] The Gospel of John, written as the last one of the four gospels and later than the letters of Paul, also uses the metaphor of sacrifice for the death of Christ by referring to him as the Lamb of God. This term is first used by John the Baptist pointing at Jesus: 'The next day John saw Jesus coming toward him and said, "Look, the Lamb of God, who takes away the sin of the world!"' (John 1:29). The sacrificial lamb John refers to is the Paschal lamb that was slaughtered annually to commemorate Passover and the Exodus. During the night before the Exodus, the Israelites were ordered to sacrifice a lamb and smear some of its blood on the doorposts of their houses (Gen. 12:1-28). Only in the houses where God would find this mark would the firstborns be spared; in all houses of the Egyptians they would be killed as the tenth plague. Sacrifing a lamb therefore meant sparing the firstborn; therefore, if Christ is equalled with the Paschal lamb, it means that God as his father does not substitute an animal for his 'firstborn', but in fact does sacrifice his son, which is a reversal of what was required from the Israelites in Ex. 13:2. The sacrificial death of Christ seen in this way, however, is not a sacrifice of atonement, as has often been argued. Peter Lampe comes to the conclusion that Paul does not see Christ's death as such a sacrifice, even if in Rom. 3:23-25 he writes:

..., for all have sinned and fall short of the glory of God, being justified freely by His grace through the redemption that is in Christ Jesus, whom God set forth as a propitiation by His blood, through faith, to demonstrate His righteousness...[37]

One of the first references to the blood of Christ is in the words of institution of the Eucharist, as in the gospel of Mark: 'And he said to them, "This is my blood of the covenant, which is poured out for many."' (Mark 14:24). The term 'blood of the covenant' clearly refers to Jer. 31:31-34:

Behold, the days are coming, declares the Lord, when I will make a new covenant with the house of Israel and the house of Judah, not like the covenant that I made with their fathers on the day when I took them by the hand to bring them out of the land of Egypt, my covenant that they broke, though I was their husband, declares the Lord.

The term 'sacrifice' is not used at the Last Supper, but since it took place on the evening of Passover, it is clear that the term 'blood' cannot be anything else than an allusion to the blood of the Paschal lamb and the covenant that was instituted during the Exodus. In contrast to a sacrifice of atonement, where the animal (a ram) is partly burnt and partly eaten by priests, or burnt completely (Lev. 5:14-26, 6:17-23), the Paschal lamb is eaten by the community, and its blood effectuates the salvation of those who enter into a (new) covenant with God. This is also the basis for the

---

34   Lanzilotta, 'The Early Christians and Human Sacrifice'.
35   This will be discussed in paragraph 6.3.5 below.
36   Sales, 'Human Sacrifice in Biblical Thought'.

---

37   Lampe, 'Human Sacrifice', 192-194.

ritual of the Eucharist, where the body and blood of Christ are consumed, not burnt.

While, strictly speaking, the death of Christ is initially compared to the slaughter of the Paschal lamb, an additional meaning is attached to it seemingly soon afterwards, namely that of the sacrifice of atonement. The Letter to the Hebrews, long believed to be authored by Paul but now considered the product of an unknown author who wrote at the end of the first century, stresses the priesthood of Christ and at the same time calls his death a self-sacrifice, a sacrifice of atonement:

> For such a High Priest was fitting for us, who is holy, harmless, undefiled, separate from sinners, and has become higher than the heavens; who does not need daily, as those high priests, to offer up sacrifices, first for His own sins and then for the people's, for this He did once for all when He offered up Himself. (Heb. 7:26-27)

and:

> ...so Christ was offered once to bear the sins of many. To those who eagerly wait for Him He will appear a second time, apart from sin, for salvation. (Heb. 9:28)

The death of Christ as a sacrifice of atonement is also based on the Christian interpretation of Isa. 53, where a suffering servant of God is described as a scapegoat who carries the sins of many. He is not a priest, but a 'lamb to the slaughter'. Although innocent, he is killed as a human sacrifice. It is uncertain what is the precise original meaning of this piece of poetry; the text certainly does not refer to any Old Testament ritual of human sacrifice and in the Christian exegesis it has been interpreted as a prophecy of the burden of the Messiah. It is not unlikely that Paul in the Letter to the Romans also alludes to Isa. 53: "... who was delivered up because of our offenses, and was raised because of our justification" (Rom. 4:25).

The most explicit formulation referring to a sacrifice of atonement in the gospels is that of John 3:16:

> For God so loved the world that He gave His only begotten Son, that whoever believes in Him should not perish but have everlasting life.

It implies that the death of a beloved child can be an atonement for the guilt of others. It refers not only to the sacrifice of Abraham in Gen. 22:2, where Isaac is called Abraham's only son, but also to Jephthah's daughter, his "only begotten and beloved" (Judg. 11:34). However, since the sacrifices of Isaac and Jephthah's daughter were not meant as an atonement, the sacrifice of Christ, in its essence, may resemble more the death of David's and Bathsheba's firstborn child who had to die for the sin of its father (2 Sam. 12:13-14). In the gospel of John, however, the roles are significantly shifted, as it is the Father who willingly sacrifices his son for the trespasses of others.

6.3.2. A new view on the Old Testament: typology

The Christian Bible consist in eighty per cent of writings that antedate the birth of Jesus Christ, and, under the name of Tanakh, are in the first place the holy scriptures of Judaism. In other words, what is called the Old Testament is an example of literary appropriation, which is all the more remarkable if we consider that Christianity has gradually distanced itself from the religion and the culture that was its cradle, namely the Second Temple Judaism. The recognition of the Tanakh and its appropriation were logical consequences of the claim that Jesus offered the fulfilment of the prophecies that are contained in it, but for this purpose a new exegesis was necessary. At first it was restricted to certain prophecies such as the one of Isaiah concerning the servant of God, but over time more and more passages of non-prophetical character were interpreted as prefigurations of the events described in the New Testament. This way of looking at Old Testament events as prefigurations of the life and death of Christ starts in fact already in the apostolic era and continues in the following centuries. Not only church fathers and later patristic authors have dedicated writings to these parallels, also known under the term 'typology', but they also became a popular genre in the iconography of church decoration and illuminated manuscripts, such as the *Bible Moralisée* and the *Biblia Pauperum*.[38] Two prominent cases of (attempted or fulfilled) human sacrifice from the Old Testament, those of Abraham and Jephthah, have been given a place in Christian tradition and iconography as prefigurations of the death of Christ.

6.3.2.1. Abraham

A theme that has been mentioned by church fathers and theologians and depicted countless times in Christian art is Abraham's sacrifice of his son Isaac (Gen 22:1-19), also known as the *aqedah* (binding). It has not only been used as an image of unconditional obedience to God, but especially as a typology for the crucifixion of Christ. Allusions to a parallel between Isaac and Christ can already be found in the synoptic gospels, where after the baptism by John the Baptist the Holy Spirit descends in the form of a dove and

---

38 The Warburg Iconographic database contains a number of *Bible Moralisée* manuscripts: https://iconographic.warburg.sas.ac.uk/vpc/VPC_search/subcats.php?cat_1=14&cat_2=28&cat_3=2568&cat_4=5381. A fine example of an early fifteenth century *Biblia Pauperum* is Ms. King's 5 in the British Library: http://www.bl.uk/catalogues/illuminatedmanuscripts/record.asp?MSID=7880&CollID=19&NStart=5.

a voice is heard: "You are My beloved Son, in whom I am well pleased." (Mark 1:11, Matt. 3:17, Luke 3:22). It reminds clearly of Gen. 22:2 "Take now your son, your only son Isaac, whom you love...". The same epitheton "beloved son" is used in the Transfiguration, when a heavenly voice is heard again (Mark 9:7, Matt. 17:5, Luke 9:35). Possibly the earliest explicit typological mentioning of Abraham's sacrifice is that in Heb. 11:17-19:

> By faith Abraham, when he was tested, offered up Isaac, and he who had received the promises offered up his only begotten son, of whom it was said, "In Isaac your seed shall be called," concluding that God was able to raise him up, even from the dead, from which he also received him in a figurative sense.

This passage even compares the resurrection of Christ to the cancellation of the sacrifice of Isaac at the very last moment and suggests that even if Isaac had been killed, God would have been able to resuscitate him. Several church fathers and other early authors have commented on Gen. 22, comparing Christ to Isaac in various ways.[39]

6.3.2.2. Jephthah

The typological way of looking at the Tanakh is a distorting mirror. Minor events are put in the spotlight, while chapters with little or no potential prophetic characteristics in the Christian view remain unexposed. The story of Jephthah and his daughter is a good example of such an approach. The opinion about Jephthah in the Talmud is generally negative: he is seen as an insignificant and ignorant man and his vow as an irresponsible act. The Midrash Rabba even tells how God punished him by letting his limbs decompose slowly.[40] This is not surprising if we realise that human sacrifice is absolutely forbidden from a rabbinic point of view. In the Christian tradition opinions of Jephthah vary. The Epistle to the Hebrews mentions his name among the champions of faith:

> And what more shall I say? For the time would fail me to tell of Gideon and Barak and Samson and Jephthah, also of David and Samuel and the prophets. (Heb. 11:32)

The early church fathers generally display positive attitudes toward Jephthah and consider the sacrifice of his daughter as a typology of the death of Christ and of martyrdom, a phenomenon they were familiar with themselves. Origen, in his *Commentary on the Gospel of John* VI.36, writes:

> Jephthah's sacrifice of his daughter should receive attention; it was by vowing it that he conquered the children of Ammon, and the victim approved his vow, for when her father said, "I have opened my mouth unto the Lord against you", she answered, "If you have opened your mouth unto the Lord against me, do that which you have vowed." The story suggests that the being must be a very cruel one to whom such sacrifices are offered for the salvation of men; and we require some breadth of mind and some ability to solve the difficulties raised against Providence, to be able to account for such things and to see that they are mysteries and exceed our human nature.[41]

The Syrian author Aphrahat (ca. 280 – ca. 345) wrote a number of treatises called the *Demonstrations*. In the 21st treatise, *Of Persecution*, not only Jephthah's daughter, but also Jesus himself are presented as victims of persecution and martyrdom:

> Also Jephthah was persecuted, as Jesus was persecuted. Jephthah, his brethren drove out from the house of his father; and Jesus, His brethren drove out and lifted up and crucified. Jephthah though persecuted arose as leader to his people; Jesus though persecuted arose and became King of the Nations. Jephthah vowed a vow and offered up his firstborn daughter as a sacrifice; and Jesus was lifted up as a sacrifice to his Father for all the Gentiles.[42]

Martyrdom as a component of the *imitatio Christi* in the first three centuries, and the cult of the martyrs that coninued to play a role in the period immediately afterwards, must have influenced the way in which the early authors looked at human sacrifice in general, not only that of Jephthah's daughter. The later patristic sources tend to be more reserved about the story or downright condemn Jephthah's sacrifice.[43]

---

39   For the commentaries and typological comparisons by Origen, Clement of Alexandria, Ephrem the Syrian, Ambrose, and others, see Sheridan, *Ancient Christian Commentary on Scripture*, 101-116. Concerning the transformation of the *aqedah* into a Christian prefiguration of the death of Christ see Levenson, *The Death and Resurrection*.

40   Hirsch et al., 'Jephthah'.

41   Menzies, *Ante-Nicene Fathers*, Vol. 9. http://www.newadvent.org/fathers/101506.htm, (accessed 20-11-2020).

42   *Demonstration* 21.12; Schaff and Wace, *Nicene and Post-Nicene Fathers*, Second Series, Vol. 13, http://www.newadvent.org/fathers/370121.htm (accessed 20-1-2020).

43   For an elaborate discussion on the patristic comments on Jephthah, see Thompson, *Writing the Wrongs*, 111-138.

6.3.2.3. Abraham and Jephthah in iconography

The central part of the Christian ritual of worship consists of the sacral meal called Eucharist. This can be coinsidered a ritualised reenactment of the Last Supper, but has also characteristics of the *refrigerium*, or the commemorative meal for the dead as it was celebrated in antiquity. The Last Supper of Jesus and his disciples was in fact the annual Jewish Passover meal, but in the course of the meal the words of Jesus gave a second meaning to it. Knowing it would be the last meal before his death, he gave to the supper and its future reenactments also the significance and meaning of a *refrigerium* by saying "do this in remembrance of me".[44]

The terminologies used for the Christian altar and the Eucharist illustrate a gradual change for the meanings attached to them. Although nowadays the term 'altar' is customary for the place where in churches the Eucharist is consecrated, the most common designation in early Christianity was *mensa* or *trapeza* (dining table). This can also be explained by the fact that at first Christian liturgies took place at private homes, where altars were not present. The Latin term *altare* was initially reserved for places were sacrifices were offered to gods. In Christian thought, sacrifices of animals and other foodstuffs to God had become obsolete through the death and resurrection of Christ, which was the ultimate sacrifice (Heb. 10:4-10). In spite of the fact that the Eucharist is in the first place a ritual meal, the term 'bloodless sacrifice' became an expression for the Eucharist already at an early stage. The *Didache* (ca. 100 CE) calls the Eucharist a sacrifice (14:1):

> And on the Lord's own day gather yourselves together and break bread and give thanks, first confessing your transgressions, that your sacrifice may be pure.[45]

Ignatius of Antioch (died ca. 110) also expresses himself in explicit terms. The influence of the Gospel of John is evident in his work, but he seems unfamiliar with the other gospels. He does not focus on the aspect of the commemorative meal, but on the sacrifice, and in his letter to the congregation of Philadelphia he calls the Eucharist the flesh (*sarx*) of Christ and uses the term 'altar' (*thysiasterion*) instead of the more common *mensa* or *trapeza* for the table of the Eucharist.[46]

The term 'sacrifice' in the sense of offerings brought by the people may have its origins in pre-Constantinian times when ritual meals were held in private homes. Such meals were split into two parts in already an early stage: a non-liturgical meal (*agape*), and a ritualised and liturgical meal, the Eucharist.[47] The food required for these meals was brought by the members of the congregation and this practice must have continued in the period of Constantine and later.[48] Although the bread and wine consecrated and consumed during the Eucharist were strictly speaking bloodless, they were (and are) considered representations of the body and blood of Christ, and the fact that they are considered consubstantial means that there is more than a symbolical link with the physical crucified body of Christ. The Eucharist is not merely a ritualised reenactment of the Last Supper, it is the presence of the essence of a human sacrifice on a ritual dining table, which for that reason also takes the quality of a sacrificial altar. It is certainly not a coincidence that in the pre-Constantinian era, when the Eucharist was celebrated in the confinement of private homes and only accessible for baptised members of the congregation, rumours among non-Christians had it that cannibalism and child-sacrifice took place there.[49]

Church interiors are decorated with representations that have a meaning for what takes place within the walls of the building. Narrative images can adorn the nave, where the congregation can contemplate the illustrations of the scriptures, often with an additional references to the sacred topography and the liturgical calendar, while the eastern part of the church, where most rituals take place, is laden predominantly with symbolical imagery referring to the liturgy.[50] The subjects that can be used here to depict the prefigurations of the Eucharist are manifold. There are Old Testament stories that have a connotation with the sacral meal, such as the priest-king Melchizedek offering bread and wine to Abram (Gen. 14:18), or the hospitality of Abraham (Gen. 18:1-15), but a considerable number of typological images concern the theme of sacrifice. Here we see that the dual character of the Eucharist and the altar as dining table and place of sacrifice is underscored. Abraham's sacrifice of Isaac is one of the most frequently depicted stories in this context. Not only the concept of a father who is willing to sacrifice his only son, but also various details in the story are compared to the crucifixion of Christ, such as Isaac carrying the firewood for the burnt offering that was supposed to consist of himself, which is compared to Christ carrying his own cross.[51] Various

---

44 The first time this is quoted is in 1 Cor. 11:24; the gospel of Luke, where the same text is quoted (Luke 22:19), was written later.

45 Cody, 'The Didache', 3-14. For the Greek text, see Rordorf and Tuiller, *La doctrine des douze apôtres.*

46 *Philadelphians* 4; Schoedel, *Ignatius of Antioch*, 197-199.

47 For further reading, see Bradshaw, *Eucharistic Origins*, 43-115 and McGowan, 'Rethinking Eucharistic Origins'.

48 In the *Liber Pontificalis*, seven *altaria* are mentioned as part of the inventory of the cathedral of Rome, donated by Constantine the Great. These must have been offering tables where the faithful could bring their foodstuffs as donation for the community and the church. Klauser, 'Die konstantinischen Altäre'.

49 Roig Lanzilotta, 'The Early Christians and Human Sacrifice'.

50 For the schemes of Middle Byzantine church decoration, see Demus, *Byzantine Mosaic Decoration*, especially 1-36.

51 Lucchesi Palli, 'Abraham'.

Figure 6.1 The sacrifices of Abraham and Jephthah, gouache painting by Pierre Laferrière after the mural painting in the sanctuary of St Antony's monastery. After Van Moorsel, *Les peintures du monastère de Saint-Antoine*, pl. 10.

other Old Testament events and stories, some of them not immediately obvious to the eyes of modern viewers, were also considered prefigurations of the Eucharist, such as the visions of the prophets Isaiah (Isa. 6:6) and Ezekiel (Ezek. 3:1-2). In a number of Egyptian churches, the mural paintings in the sanctuary depict a variety of such typological scenes from the Old Testament.[52] In one church, in St Anthony's monastery near the Red Sea, the sacrifice of Jephthah is included in this decoration.[53]

Although unusual as an iconographical theme, the painting is not unique. In the church of St Catherine's monastery in Sinai the same subject has been illustrated in an encaustic painting to the right of the main altar.[54] In both churches the sacrifices of Jephthah and Abraham have been depicted as counterparts to each other, indicating that in the eyes of the people who commissioned them, the sacrifice of Jephthah had the same sacred prefigurative value as that of Abraham.[55] Aphrahat justified Jephthah's sacrifice[56] and Ephrem the Syrian sees its connection with the Eucharist when he writes:

Upright was the priest who sacrificed with blood of his own offspring, so that he may be an example of his Lord, who sacrificed with his own blood.[57]

Given the fact that Jephthah's sacrifice was controversial, it is not surprising that only two such paintings are known so far. The painting in St Catherine's monastery has been dated to the seventh century, while the one in St Anthony's dates back to the early thirteenth century. The considerable chronological gap shows that a positive evaluation of the subject in art was apparently not limited to the early Christian period, as was the case in patristic writings. A direct connection between the two monasteries cannot be presumed, as the former was Greek Orthodox and the latter Coptic. Notably, the monastic setting of the two depictions of Jephthah may be a key to understanding the appreciation for Jephthah's sacrifice. This is because monastic asceticism has been seen as a form of self-sacrifice, or a way of *imitatio Christi,* not only as a metaphor, but also in the physical sense.

6.3.3. Voluntary martyrdom and monastic askesis as self-sacrifice

A martyr, who is a person killed for his or her convictions, or for refusing to accept the religion or convictions of others, can be called a victim. The circumstances of martyrdom, however, do not make it automatically a form of ritual killing or human sacrifice. In most cases the interpretation depends on the perspective from which the killing is regarded. People who are seen as criminals or terrorists by their opponents can be regarded as role models or even saints by their own group. The lynching or execution of a martyr cannot be called a ritual, but certainly it is not a sacrifice either, since the person is not offered as a gift to a deity or a person in the hereafter.

---

52   Van Loon, *The Gate of Heaven.*

53   Van Moorsel, *Les peintures du monastère de Saint-Antoine*, 37-40.

54   Weitmann, 'The Jephthah Panel'; Van Moorsel, 'Jephthah?'.

55   In St Catherine's the epigraphic text even mentions 'Sainted Jephthah', Weitzmann, 'The Jephthah Panel', 344.

56   See note 329.

57   Weitzmann 'The Jephthah Panel', 352, cf. Ephrem, *Carmina Nisibena*, 216-217.

Nevertheless, martyrdom is often discussed within the context of human sacrifice, mainly in the cases of voluntary martyrdom. The degree to which martyrdom can be considered voluntary varies from case to case and can range from a cooperative attitude during arrest and interrogation by the authorities to reporting oneself unsolicited as a Christian in order to be martyred.[58] A certain degree of voluntariness seems intrinsic to the act of martyrdom: the true martyr does not deny his or her beliefs or try to resist or to escape death.

The question remains what are the motives for and the consequences of the martyr's death. The imitation of Christ can be considered one of the main motivations, if not the primary one. From the very beginning such *mimesis* was propagated, for instance by Paul in 1 Thess. 1:6-7; 2:14. This imitation or following of Christ as propagated and described by Paul can be interpreted in various ways. It does not just consist of leading a virtuous life, but also bearing persecution and suffering.[59] That such suffering leads to an inevitable death is not explicitly mentioned by Paul; however a martyr's death as the extreme consequence of discipleship can be concluded from the passage in Matt. 10:1-39, where the apostles receive instructions from Jesus for their mission. That still leaves open the question whether (voluntary) martyrdom is a form of sacrifice. If followers of Jesus Christ take their task so seriously that their life ends in the same way as Jesus', does their death has the same meaning and consequences? The death of Jesus Christ can be considered a sacrifice of atonement, but the same cannot be said of the death of a martyr, since it does not resolve anyone else's sins. Martyrs can be seen and venerated as heroes and role models, individuals who are rewarded with a special place in the hereafter from where they can intercede for the /ordinary believer.[60] The belief was that the reward for a martyr's death was the forgiveness of sins and admission straight to Paradise, without the need to await the Last Judgment in Hades.[61] It must have been this motivation of saving one's own soul that was the main incentive for many martyrs, especially the ones who reported themselves to the authorities in the hope of being executed and receiving the 'crown of martyrdom'. Many must have been that eager to do so; one of the most famous cases, described by Eusebius, is

Origen (ca. 184 – c. 253), who would have been martyred together with his father had it not been for his mother who had hidden his clothes, preventing him from going out.[62] Origen remained an advocate of martyrdom. However, while his *Exhortation to Martyrdom* glorifies martyrs in general, Origen's tutor Clement (ca. 150 – c. 215) displays a more balanced attitude. In his *Stromata*, Clement on one hand rejects the people who try to escape martyrdom in a cowardly way, while on the other hand he has no appreciation for those who merely report themselves, without any spiritual depth, to undergo physical martyrdom:

> If he who kills a man of God sins against God, he also who presents himself before the judgment-seat becomes guilty of his death. And such is also the case with him who does not avoid persecution, but out of daring presents himself for capture. Such a one, as far as in him lies, becomes an accomplice in the crime of the persecutor.[63]

The eagerness of a voluntary martyr who actively seeks execution seems to point in the first place to the desire to seek the salvation of his or her own soul rather than to follow the role model of Jesus.

The death of the individual martyr is not performed in a ritual, does not serve the well-being of others or save their lives, and therefore, strictly speaking, cannot be called a sacrifice. We can come to this conclusion based on our own definitions of sacrifice, but that does not mean that contemporary sources necessarily agree on this view. In the past, scholars may have explained the meaning of martyrdom for early Christianity too much from a sacrifial point of view, even where this was not justified, for instance in the case of the *Acta Martyrum*.[64] Nevertheless, there are certain texts that explicitly connect the meaning of martyrdom and sacrifice, such as the martyrdoms of Ignatius of Antioch and Polycarp of Smyrna.

Ignatius of Antioch was executed in the beginning of the second century. In his *Letter to the Romans*, written while he was being transported to Rome for execution, he shares his feelings and opinion about his approaching martyrdom.[65] He is prepared and looks forward to dying, and requests the readers of his letter not to make any effort to prevent his death:

---

58 De Ste. Croix, 'Voluntary Martyrdom'. For how the term was developed and applied, see Moss, 'The Discourse of Voluntary Martyrdom'.
59 Moss, *The Other Christs*, 45.
60 Moss, *The Other Christs*, 75-111.
61 Marinis, *Death and the Afterlife in Byzantium*, 24-27. The early Christian views on life after death were not consistent. Rather than being admitted to Paradise, the just could linger in *refrigerium interim*, which was the term used for the place or state in which they could await the second coming of Christ.

62 Eusebius, *Historia Ecclesiastica* 6.2, 240-241.
63 *Stromata* 4.10; *The Writings of Clement of Alexandria* II. *Miscellanies*, 173. See also Moss, 'The Discourse of Voluntary Martyrdom', 542-543.
64 Moss, *The Other Christs*, 83.
65 *Epistle to the Romans*. http://www.newadvent.org/fathers/0107. htm, accessed 10-12-2020. The letter of Ignatius is generally considered to be a genuine text.

For if you are silent concerning me, I shall become God's; but if you show your love to my flesh, I shall again have to run my race.[66]

Ignatius explicitly labels his death as a sacrifice (*thusia*), a term which is used for traditional animal sacrifices but also for Christ's death (Eph. 5:2):

Pray, then, do not seek to confer any greater favour upon me than that I be sacrificed to God while the altar is still prepared.[67]

Entreat Christ for me, that by these instruments I may be found a sacrifice.[68]

He even goes so far as to compare himself to wheat that will be turned into the pure bread of Christ, apparently alluding to the Eucharistic bread:

Allow me to become food for the wild beasts, through whose instrumentality it will be granted me to attain to God. I am the wheat of God, and let me be ground by the teeth of the wild beasts, that I may be found the pure bread of Christ.[69]

Here we see an inversion of symbolism: where the Eucharist represents the body of Christ offered to mankind, Ignatius sees his body as the bread to be offered to God.[70]

In other accounts of martyrdom, such as that of Polycarp of Smyrna, the martyr is also called a sacrifice: not only a *thusia*, but also a burnt offering (holocaust, *holokautoma*). In this case it is an understandable terminology, since the bishop was bound and burnt at a stake.[71] Because of this and other details in the narrative, Monika Pesthy-Simon sees parallels between the accounts of the martyrdom of Polycarp as described in the *Acta Martyrum* and the *aqedah* (lit. 'binding'), or the story of Isaac's sacrifice.[72]

There is a contradiction between the idea that the crucifixion of Jesus Christ was the ultimate sacrifice which was thought to be prefigured in the Old Testament and made all other sacrifices from that moment on superfluous, and the attitude towards martyrdom as an *imitatio Christi*, a replication of Christ's death as a personal sacrifice of his follower. Nevertheless, the latter concept has taken root, and after the Edict of Milan, when persecutions and executions

of Christians ceased, new forms of voluntary martyrdom and personal sacrifice had to be cultivated. It would be too simple to explain the rise of the monastic movement solely by this need of a new martyrdom. Monasticism emerged already in the third century in Egypt, where there were many who tried to escape from persecutions and possible death by withdrawing into the desert. Early monasticism was pluriform in its aspects, the motives for withdrawing from society, and the degree of seclusion and asceticism that individual anchorites and groups of hermits pursued. Nevertheless, there are some clear characteristics that link monasticism to human sacrifice and martyrdom. The ideal of the anchorite is to become 'dead to the world', which means not only cutting all ties with society and limiting food intake to the absolute minimum, but also extinguishing the emotional life, a potential source of temptation and sin, so as to make it like that of the dead.

This ideal is illustrated by an *apophthegma* about St Macarius. A young monk asks him how to act and Macarius sends him to the cemetery and orders him to abuse and insult the dead. After a while the young man comes back and, when asked how the dead reacted, he tells Macarius that they remained silent. The saint sends him back, this time to praise and flatter the dead. After coming back for a second time the young monk tells Macarius that their reaction was the same. Macarius' lesson to him is that he should become like the dead, indifferent to both scorn and praise, in order to avoid the sins of anger and pride, and to save his soul.[73] We find the same advice expressed elsewhere in different words, such as in an *apophthegma* of Abba Moses:

A brother questioned Abba Moses saying, 'I see something in front of me and I am not able to grasp it.' The old man said to him, 'If you do not become dead like those who are in the tomb, you are not able to grasp it'.[74]

The anchorite or monk who has severed all ties with his family and the world is physically still alive, but mentally has already passed the border between the material world and the hereafter. As a sign of this, some anchorites decided to live in tombs, in anticipation of the physical death to come.[75] Their asceticism brings them back to the divine origin of human life by renunciation of all passions.[76] The

---

66 *Epistle to the Romans*, 2.
67 Ibidem.
68 *Epistle to the Romans*, 4.
69 Ibidem.
70 Pesthy-Simon, *Isaac, Iphigenea, Ignatius*, 120.
71 *Martyrdom of Polycarp* 14, Musurillo, *The Acts of the Christian Martyrs*, 13-15.
72 Pesthy-Simon, *Isaac, Iphigenea, Ignatius*, 129-131.

73 Macarius 23, Ward, *The Desert Christian*, 132.
74 Moses 11, Ward, *The Desert Christian*, 140-141.
75 For the re-use of tombs by ascetics in the Theban west-bank area, see O'Connell, 'Transforming Monumental Landscapes'.
76 This crossing of a border between earth and heaven, a symbolical self-chosen death, is expressed until the present day in the ritual of the monastic profession, which, in both Eastern and Western Churches, has characteristics of a funeral service, with the monk lying prostrate on the floor of the church, covered with a funeral pall.

anchorite is a paragon of this attitude, but Athanasius (ca. 296-373) propagated an ascetic lifestyle for Christians in general, using the metaphor of a self-chosen death for renouncing the sinful world and undertaking a journey to the kingdom of God.[77] Mortification of the flesh, however, cannot be called a self-sacrifice in the litteral sense and remains a metaphor, since suicide, even for spiritual reasons, has always remained a taboo in Christianity.

Egyptian monasticism and asceticism have always been more moderate than their Syrian counterparts. The theologian and hymnographer Ephrem the Syrian (ca. 306-373) was probably never a monk, as later tradition teaches, but was nevertheless an advocate of asceticism. In some of his many hymns and sermons he praises anchorites who lead a life of strict abstinence, be it for reasons of repentance or simply with the goal of reaching heaven. It is noteworthy that in a number of passages he glorifies those who retreat into the desert with the goal of dying there. Here the metaphors have been exchanged for images of reality. In his first *Sermo*, in the part that deals with the motives of anchorites, he writes how some move into the desert in order to escape from temptation:

> Whoever flees and dies in order not to sin, his death is a sacrifice for God.[78]

These people, Ephrem claims, are comparable to martyrs:

> He who is tormented without sin shares in the sufferings of the martyrs.[79]

Some go to the desert to escape from temptation, others to do penance for their sins:

> Many women from our covenant have, just in order not to fall for men, bravely faced death in those times of persecution. Also have many saints who have sinned in different generations, improved their lives in the desert through faith and purity. And some have, in the ardour of their zeal, in faith in God, separated themselves from the people and have ended their lives in the desert.

> Some of them who fell became strong and some did so as not to fall, their minds made up to die, and they zealously rushed to meet terrible things. Others made themselves food for snakes and wild animals.[80]

A deliberate death is described as the goal of these anchorites, either as a self-inflicted death sentence for sins, or as an escape from a sinful world:

> Other people of rank endured an unusual death: through merciless, long-lasting hunger and terrible beatings by demons, their bodies were gradually tormented and worn out, and then the venerable departed by a courageous death in battle. Some of them died in their homes without anyone realising their death."[81]

Ephrem does not explicitly call the self-inflicted suffering a sacrifice, but clearly associates those who go to escape temptation with the martyrs and calls their death a sacrifice. A similar outspoken attitude is not found in the writings of other authors, but it shows that at least for some the escape into the desert was literally a matter of life and death.

6.3.4. Infanticide in a monastic context

Martyrdom and self-sacrifice, real or as metaphor, are associated with the individual who decides to sever ties with the world, but there is one more kind of sacrifice that is mentioned in connection with monasticism, and more specifically life in monastic community: child-sacrifice. Again, we have to distinguish between actual events and legendary narratives, but what counts most is the attitude that speaks from the stories under consideration. Two stories from the *Apophthegmata Patrum* relate how a father who wishes to join a monastic community is instructed to kill his child in order to be admitted. In the first one, from the alphabetic collection, Abba Sisoes receives a man from the Thebaid who wants to become a monk. Sisoes, after hearing that the man has a son, orders him to drown the child in the Nile and to come back. The man leaves, planning to do as he was told, but in the last moment Sisoes sends a messenger to prevent the killing. The *apophthegma* ends with "So he left his son and went to find the old man, and he became a monk, tested by obedience."[82] In the second *apophthegma*, from the anonymous collection, a brother who left his three children in the city and has lived as a monk for three years starts missing the children and asks the superior of the community (*abba*) for the permission to bring them to the monastery. He gets the permission, finds out that two of his children have died in the meantime and returns with the third child. The superior asks him if he loves the child, and after hearing an affirmative answer twice, orders the brother to throw the child into the furnace of the bakery. The brother obeys, "... but the flames became immediately

---

77   Brakke, *Athanasius and Asceticism*, 158-159.
78   *Sermo* I, 493, Beck, *Des heiligen Ephraem des Syrers Sermones IV*, 14; Translation from German by the author.
79   *Sermo* I, 497.
80   *Sermo* I, 549-573.

81   *Sermo* I, 597-605.
82   Sisoes 10, Ward, *The Desert Christian*, 214.

like the morning dew and he (the brother) gained esteem like the patriarch Abraham."[83]

Both apophthegmata contain a clear reference to the sacrifice of Isaac, the latter one even explicitly so, and the underscoring of the paternal love in the second story is apparently intended to stress the parallel with Gen. 22:2: "Take now your son, your only son Isaac, whom you love...". In both cases, however, it is also obvious that the children were not meant to be sacrificed to God, but simply murdered as a test of obedience, a virtue that is considered indispensable for a monk living in a community. Caroline Schroeder nevertheless describes the two stories as examples of child sacrifice, a claim which seems difficult to substantiate.[84] The children are innocent victims, and just like Isaac were rescued in the last moment, which explains the parallel with the *aqedah*, but the instruction to kill them comes from a monk, not from God. In both cases it is clear that the sacrifice that has to be made is not the life of the child, but the unconditional detachment from the world and from family and kin, of which the children are personifications. The *imitatio Christi* of the monk has to manifest itself in severing the ties with even the closest family members, as instructed in Matthew 8:22.

A second layer in the story of the child that was thrown into the furnace is an allusion to martyrdom. The innocent child is saved as "...the flames became immediately like the morning dew...", which must have been recognised by the readers as a clear allusion to the deuterocanonical passage in Daniel (3:49-50), which describes the deliverance of the three Hebrews in the furnace:

> But the angel of the Lord came down into the furnace to be with Azariah and his companions, and drove the fiery flame out of the furnace, and made the inside of the furnace as though a moist wind were whistling through it. The fire did not touch them at all and caused them no pain or distress.

The three men, convicted to death for their refusal to worship a statue, were considered prototypes of Christian martyrs, and this probably explains the popularity of the three Hebrews, both in iconography and in devotional graffiti. Their steadfastness must have become a model in times of persecution, and in a number of Coptic martyrs' legends where the saint is thrown into a furnace, a similar pattern in the narrative is repeated: an angel (usually identified as Michael) appears, and protects and saves the saint. In some cases the same formulation is repeated: the fire is turned into cool morning dew.[85] The child in the *apophthegma* fits in the model of the innocent victim, but as a completely passive character can hardly be identified as a model of self-sacrifice. The parallel with Isaac's sacrifice seems in the first place to focus on obedience, not on the sacrifice of the first-born.

Schroeder compares these *apophthegmata* not only to Isaac's sacrifice, but also to the sacrifice of Jephthah's daughter.[86] As mentioned above, the theme of Jephthah's sacrifice is rare in Christian art and occurs as a mural painting in the sanctuaries of only two monasteries. Despite the condemnation of many authors, there are others who appreciate Jephthah's act and respect his daughter's obedience.[87] It is beyond doubt that in both churches the story of Jephthah is depicted as a prefiguration of Christ's death and of the Eucharist. But also here there is more than one layer. It is probably no coincidence that the two representations are found in monastic churches and seem to be pictorial allusions to the relationship between child sacrifice and the monastic life, as Schroeder concludes. But with whom does the monk identify himself? With the daughter, a virgin who dies in obedience?[88] This is a logical possibility. On the other hand, there are reasons to presume that Jephthah was considered a role model for the monk or hermit. He was the warrior who overcame the enemy by sacrificing his 'own flesh and blood', which is a possible parallel for the monk who renounces his own flesh and battles the devil and his temptations. There is no proof for a direct connection between the stories of 'child sacrifice' mentioned above and the paintings of Jephthah's sacrifice, but given the popularity of the *Apophthegmata Patrum*, many of the viewers must have made the connection, whether or not this was the intention of the makers.

There is another form of 'human sacrifice' in a monastic context that deserves mentioning. This sacrifice is not a form of ritual killing, but a donation or dedication of a child to a monastery as a pious act, in certain cases as the redemption of a vow.[89] Although probably common in other monasteries in Egypt and elswhere, this practice is known in detail from the archive of the monastery of St Phoibammon of Preht, founded around 590 on the ruined mortuary temple of Queen Hatshepsut at Deir al-Bahari. The monastery was functioning until the end of the eighth century, and from that century twenty-six documents have

---

83 N. 295/14.28, Wortley, *The Anonymous Sayings*, 198-201.

84 Schroeder, 'Child Sacrifice in Egyptian Monastic Culture', 279-280. A third apophthegma, Apollo 2 (Ward, *The Desert Christian*, 36) describing how a shepherd killed a pregnant woman and her unborn child, and did penance for this murder as a monk, is also interpreted by Schroeder (p. 289) as an example of child sacrifice. Here this conclusion seems even more doubtful.

85 For instance in the martyrdoms of St Paese, (Till, *Koptische Heiligen- und Martyrerlegenden*, 89-90) and St Bafamus (Forget, *Synaxarium Alexandrinum*, 428).

86 Schroeder, 'Child Sacrifice', 272-279.

87 Van Loon, *The Gate of Heaven*, 156-157.

88 Schroeder, 'Child Sacrifice', 292.

89 Wipszycka, 'Child Donation'.

been preserved that concern donations of a child by its parents. The child (a boy in all cases) was not meant to become a monk and was not given to the monastery itself, but more precisely, to the shrine of St Phoibammon that was run by the monastery, in order to work there as a serf. This was done as a token of gratitude for the miraculous healing of the boy by the saint.[90] In a number of documents the term *prosphora* (offering) for the sake of the souls of the parents is mentioned, so that such donations can indeed be categorised as a kind of sacrifice. God has cured the child and in gratitude the parents give it back, as it were, to God. This practice is reminiscent of a number of biblical stories. First association is the sacrifice of Isaac, but the donations bear an even closer resemblance to the story of Hannah, who donated her child Samuel to the temple after her prayer was answered and she conceived (1 Sam. 1:2-2:21). The apocryphal Protoevangelium of James relates how in a similar way Joachim and Anna presented their daughter Mary to the temple.[91] There is yet another parallel with an Old Testament story that comes to mind in one of the legends connected to St Phoibammon. In the martyrdom of the saint in Pierpont Morgan Codex M 582 (produced between the years 822 and 913/914), he is shown as someone who can both punish and reward parents through harming or curing their children. A Roman *dux*, who had persecuted the Christian community of Assiut, is punished when his son, on his way to the *praetorium* where the saint is interrogated, dies under a collapsing wall. Likewise, those who do not keep their vow to the saint after a miracle has been granted are punished by inflicting harm to their child.[92] It reminds of the death of the first-born of Pharaoh in Exodus and the threat of harm to the Israelite first-borns in case the instructions of God were not exactly followed (Ex. 12:22-23).

6.3.5. The Melismos in texts and iconography

Accusations of cannibalism and child sacrifice against Christians in the pre-Constantinian era were apparently not uncommon. As mentioned above, this must have been quite understandable, given the metaphors that were used for the Eucharist: flesh and blood. The consubstantiality of bread and wine with the body and blood of Christ have been a subject of discussion from the very beginning of the history of Christianity and those who considered them mere symbols could be excommunicated as heretics if they remained insensitive to the arguments of the 'true' believers.[93] Such doubts were apparently of all centuries, and the arguments in favour of transubstantiation were not always subtle in character. In a number of texts and in an iconographical theme known as *melismos*, the bread and wine are replaced by or take the shape of a small child that is cut to pieces and consumed by the congregation or the individual who refused to accept transubstantiation.[94] The details in the various versions of the narratives and representations vary, but the main element -the child being dismembered- is the central point.

Possibly the earliest version of the theme can be found in the *Apophthegmata Patrum*. Here, Abba Daniel repeats a story that he heard from Abba Arsenius about a devout, but simple-minded old monk who refused to believe that the Eucharistic gifts were more than a symbol of Christ. Two fellow monks were aware of this but refused to criticise him, and instead prayed to God to reveal the truth to the old man. During the liturgy, at the moment of the communion, an angel appeared to the three monks, the Eucharistic bread turned into a small child that was cut to pieces by the angel, and the incredulous monk received a morsel of bloody flesh from the priest instead of bread. This shocking experience made the monk believe in transubstantiation, and at that moment the flesh turned again into the Eucharistic bread.[95] Caroline Schroeder treats this passage as a fourth example of child sacrifice in the *Apophthegmata*.[96] It is, however, of a different kind than the other narratives that she discusses. The other three stories deal with the actual killing of a child or an attempt to do so, while here the narrative concerns a vision, only seen by three people; the children in the former are human children, while in the latter it is obvious that the child represents Jesus Christ. Although the story of the old monk's experience is set in a monastic environment, the theme as such is repeated a number of times in other settings and with other actors, so that we could call it a genre in itself.[97] A comparable story is told in the *Vita Sancti Basilii*.[98] Here a Jew sneakily attends a liturgy celebrated by Basilius the Great; at the moment when the bishop breaks the Eucharistic bread, the Jew sees an infant being torn to pieces and the congretion consuming its flesh and blood. Two comparable stories, one from the *Logos Historikos* of Gregorios Dekapolites (before 797-842), and a second

---

90 Papaconstantinou, 'ΘΕΙΑ OIKONOMIA'; eadem, 'Notes sur les actes de donation'. One of the documents, P.KRU 104, concerns the self-donation of an adult. Where Papaconstantinou interprets these cases as donations to the monastery, Gesa Schenke ('The Healing Shrines of St. Phoibammon') has shown that the donations were in fact made to the shrine of the saint.

91 Hennecke and Schneemelcher, *Neutestamentliche Apokryphen* I, 280-283.

92 Schenke, 'The Healing Shrines of St. Phoibammon', 499-500.

93 For the history of the Eucharist, see note 47.

94 A number of references in this paragraph are based on the unpublished MA thesis of Nicole Kraan (Leiden University, 1989), entitled *Melismos. De Transsubstantiatie tot Verbeelding*.

95 Daniel 7, Ward, *The Desert Christian*, 53-54.

96 Schroeder, 'Child Sacrifice', 286-287.

97 For a number of medieval western versions of the legend, see Burns, 'Child sacrifice'.

98 Migne, PL 73, 301-302. The text is falsely attributed to Amphilochius of Iconium (d. ca. 400), but must date from around 800. Barringer, 'The Pseudo-Amphilochian Life of St. Basil'.

one, possibly based on the *Logos* and known from church-Slavonic texts as the *Vision of Amphilogos*, relate how a high Saracen official forcibly enters a church in Thebes with his camels, which drop dead as a punishment for his brutal intrusion. In spite of this he insists to attend the liturgy and sees how the priest cuts a small child to pieces and drinks his blood. Horrified by what he has seen, he calls the priest to account; the priest, in turn, explains to the Saracen the background of the miracle he has witnessed. The Saracen eventually converts and even becomes a monk.[99] The western tradition has preserved similar legends. In the *vita* of Gregory the Great, written by a monk from Whitby between 680 and 704, the story is told of how a Roman matron baked the bread that would be consecrated for the communion during the liturgy. When she smiles in disbelief at the moment when Gregory gives her 'the body of the Lord', he withholds the communion from her and hides the piece of bread on the altar. After she explains her doubts and Gregory prays with the congregation to strengthen her faith, the piece of bread turns out to be transformed into a bloody fragment of a little finger.[100] In the *Speculum Ecclesiae* by Honorius Augustodunensis, also known as Honorius of Autun (ca. 1080-1154), the motif of the Jewish unbeliever is brought up again: a Jewish boy secretly attends a liturgy and sees a child being cut to pieces and receives a piece of flesh, which he takes home. His father is so angered by this that he throws the boy into the furnace, in which he miraculously survives, protected by God.[101]

These legends, of which more variations must have been circulating in the oral tradition, have in common that disbelievers, whether they are Christian, Muslim, or Jewish, are being convinced of transubstantiation by the shock-effect of seeing a child being killed, or a piece of bloody flesh. The remarkable element is that the bread and wine are not transformed into the body of the crucified adult Christ, but that Christ is represented as an infant. This is also the case in an iconographical theme known as *melismos*, a term meaning 'fracturing' or 'dismembering'. It refers to the Byzantine liturgy where during the communion the priest speaks the following words over the *amnos* (lamb), the square piece of bread cut from the middle of the *prosphora* (liturgical bread):

Broken and distributed is the Lamb of God; broken yet not divided; forever eaten yet never consumed, but sanctifying those who partake thereof.

One would therefore expect that in methaphorical representations of the Eucharist a lamb would be represented instead of the *prosphora*, and indeed the sacrificial lamb occurs in Christian art frequently as a symbol of Christ and the Eucharist. In the East, however, this stopped almost completely after the Quinisext Council (692) forbade the representation of the lamb. The 82nd canon says:

In some pictures of the venerable icons, a lamb is painted to which the Precursor (John the Baptist) points his finger, which is received as a type of grace, indicating beforehand through the Law, our true Lamb, Christ our God. Embracing therefore the ancient types and shadows as symbols of the truth, and patterns given to the Church, we prefer grace and truth, receiving it as the fulfilment of the Law. In order therefore that that which is perfect may be delineated to the eyes of all, at least in colored expression, we decree that the figure in human form of the Lamb who takes away the sin of the world, Christ our God, be henceforth exhibited in images, instead of the ancient lamb, so that all may understand by means of it the depths of the humiliation of the Word of God, and that we may recall to our memory his conversation in the flesh, his passion and salutary death, and his redemption which was wrought for the whole world. [102]

As has been said above, the decoration of the sanctuary of churches usually has a symbolic character, with typological images referring to the Eucharist. Especially the lower zone of the apse is a suitable place for images with a Eucharistic symbolism, such as the communion of the apostles. The northern sideroom of the sanctuary, called *prothesis* after the ritual of preparation of the holy gifts, can also contain a representation of the *melismos*. The image of Christ as the Eucharistic sacrifice in human form occurs, as far as known, for the first time in the apse of the church of St George in Kurbinovo (North-Macedonia), painted in 1191 (fig. 6.2). Here he is depicted as an adult, lying on an altar and apparently with closed eyes. [103]

In the centuries to follow the *melismos* would be depicted in numerous churches in various compositions, especially in the Balkan region, but also on Crete and Cyprus. The composition usually contains an altar with a chalice and a paten on which a small figure of a child is lying, sometimes partly covered by a veil, sometimes with an *asterisk* on his body.[104] Flanking the altar there can be

---

99   Migne, PG 100, 1201-1212. The story of Amphilogos is known from Slavonic texts and is set in Jerusalem. A number of details are added, but the main line is similar. Kaluzniacki, 'Die Legende von der Vision Amphilogs'.
100 Colgrave, *The Earliest Life of Gregory the Great*, 105-109.
101 Migne, PL 172, 852.
102 Canon 82, *Nicene and Post-Nicene Fathers*, Second Series, Vol. 14, https://www.newadvent.org/fathers/3814.htm accessed 15-12-2020.
103 Haderman-Misguich, *Kurbinovo*, 74-78, figs. 21, 29.
104 An asterisk is a small, folding metal covering that keeps the veil and *aër* (larger veil) from disturbing the particles of bread on the paten.

Figure 6.2 Christ lying on an altar, *melismos* painting in the church of St George, Kurbinovo. Photo: author.

Figure 6.3 Melismos painting (fourteenth century) in the prothesis of the Church of St George, Staro Nagoričane. Photo: author.

two angels, dressed as deacons and holding liturgical fans known as *rhipidia*, which is an allusion to the procession of the Great Entrance (fig. 6.3).

During this procession bread and wine are brought to the altar, accompanied by deacons carrying the *rhipidia*. There can also be church fathers depicted in episcopal garments, performing the rite of the *prothesis*. During this preparation the priest cuts the square central part out of the round prosphora, and it is this part, called *amnos* (lit. 'lamb'), that is consecrated. He does this with a pointed knife called the lance, a reminder of the lance that pierced the side of Christ during the crucifixion. One would expect that a depiction of Christ as the sacrificial lamb would show him crucified, as in western iconography, but this is in fact rare. Apart from the painting in the apse of St George's church in Kurbinovo, there is only one other known example of a *melismos* scene in the *prothesis* that features the dead adult Christ on the altar. The scene in question is found in the fourteenth century church of St Demetrios in Markov Manastir (North-Macedonia) (fig. 6.4).[105]

---

105   Tomić Djurić, 'To picture and to perform', 123-141.

In all other depictions there is a live child on the paten.[106] In a number of paintings, the church fathers do not merely flank the table or altar on which the child lies, but they actually drive the lance into the child's body, an image that seems to be inspired by the legends of the visions of infanticide.[107] An extreme and literal depiction of the *melismos* comes from the church of St Photini at Kalini, Pediada (Crete). The fragment from the apse, now in the Historical Museum of Iraklion, shows a chalice in which a dismembered body, two arms and two legs are depicted.[108] This means that, instead of referring to the historical crucifixion as the sacrifice of Christ, prevalence is given to the ritual of *prothesis* as a reenactment of the death of Christ. The hierarchs who are depicted 'kill' the Eucharistic bread with the same lance that once pierced the side of Christ. However, while ritual as a reenactment is usually a stylised performance, here, as in the popular legends, the way of depicting the *melismos* is confronting and almost realistic. The 'bloodless sacrifice' of the Eucharist is now depicted in a bloody metaphor, which is all the more staggering since it shows the 'killing' of a child, not the adult Jesus Christ. It seems as if a circle has been closed: the first-born child is sacrificed, the beloved son, not the adult Christ who is priest and victim at once, but the infant, who, like Isaac, is led as a lamb to the slaughter. This aspect is also expressed in the words that are spoken by the priest when he cuts the *amnos* from the bread:

He was oppressed and he was afflicted, yet He opened not His mouth; He was led as a lamb to the slaughter, and as a sheep before its shearers is silent, so He opened not His mouth. (Isa. 53:7)

---

106   For instance in Donja Kamenica and Studenica; Walter, *Art and Ritual*, figs. 55, 56.

107   This can be seen in two Serbian churches, the one in Ljuboten (1344/1345), where St Peter of Alexandria and St Athanasius perform the *prothesis*, and the other in Matejič (1348/1352), where St John Chrystom and St Basil the Great are depicted. Tomić Djurić, 'To picture and to perform', 126.

108   *Byzantine and Post-Byzantine Art*, 53, fig. 49.

As mentioned, a theme that was popular as a representation in the lower area of the sanctuary before the *melismos* was introduced, is the communion of the apostles.[109] In this composition, which is a ritualised version of the Last Supper, we see Christ officiating as a bishop, giving bread and wine to the apostles. Instead of sitting at a dining table, they approach an altar. It is one of the themes where Christ is emphatically shown as patriarch/high priest. This stands in sharp contrast with the theme of the *melismos*, where Christ is the sacrificial victim while the doctors of the Church and other bishops are carrying out the symbolical killing. Both views on the Eucharist are in accordance with the official teachings of the Church, only the accents are differently placed. In the *melismos*, the priestly authority of the Church and its founding fathers is underscored, while the transubstantiation is displayed in its most outspoken form. Nicole Kraan believes that the sudden popularity of the theme may be explained by the challenge that the Bogomil movement presented to the Orthodox Church.[110] This movement, which had gnostic characteristics and rejected the authority of the Byzantine Church and the value of the Eucharist, was active from the late tenth to the fourteenth centuries, especially in the Balkans. The iconography of the *melismos* expresses two important points in the doctrine of the Orthodox Church: the role of the clergy, personified by church fathers, and the consubstantiality of the Eucharist and the body of Christ. Depicting the sacrificed Christ as an infant adds to the dramatic effect of this message.

6.4. Concluding remarks

Ritual killing, especially the sacrifice of children, was an element that played a role in the religion of ancient Israel and its neighbours. Children could be actually killed as sacrificial victims or replaced by an animal. Although archaeological evidence is absent so far, it cannot be excluded that first-born children were sacrificed to YHWH, not in the first place as an institutionalised part of the cultus, but rather as a traditional form of worship that took place also in the cults of neighbouring peoples. It is only in the post-exilic period that Judaism rejected child-sacrifice as pagan and abhorrent. The sacrifice of the 'beloved first-born son', however, was still an important part of Jewish cultural memory, and was adopted by early Christianity in a transformed model and applied to the death of Jesus Christ. It is the inversion of the sacrifice of the Paschal lamb, God sacrificing his son, that brings back human sacrifice in its literal form. Although from Christian perspective the sacrifice of the Son of God makes all other sacrifices superfluous, the *imitatio Christi* gave rise to the ideal of self-sacrifice that took shape initially in (voluntary) martyrdom and later in (monastic) asceticism.

The typological mirror through which the Old Testament was seen explains why not only Abraham's intended sacrifice of Isaac, but also Jephthah's sacrifice of his daughter was seen as a prefiguration of the death of Christ. The Eucharist, although called a 'bloodless sacrifice', is in fact a ritual with a complicated structure and history, in which not only the re-enactment of the Last Supper, but also the death of Christ and his physical presence in his sacrificed body and blood are central. In order to underscore the crude reality of a father sacrificing his only child, both Christian folk-legends and official iconography return to realistic images of the *melismos*, in which a small child is killed and dismembered. Here a circle seems to be closed: the sacrifice of the first-born, later redeemed by the sacrifice of a lamb, has returned in its purest form: not the crucifixion of Christ or the self-sacrifice of a consenting adult, but an infant killed on a Christian altar.

6.5. Acknowledgments

My thanks go to Joanna Wegner for her critical and encouraging comments on chapters 1 and 6.

---

109   Walter, *Art and Ritual*, 215-217.
110   Kraan, *Melismos*, 53-59.

6.6. References

Apollodorus, *The Library* II, translation by J.G. Frazer (London, 1921).

Barringer, R. 'The Pseudo-Amphilochian Life of St. Basil: Ecclesiastical Penance and Byzantine Hagiography', *Theologia Athinai* 51.1 (1980), 49-61.

Beck, Edmund (transl.), *Des heiligen Ephraem des Syrers Sermones IV*, Corpus Scriptorum Christianorum Orientalium 335 (Louvain, 1973).

Bradshaw, P., *Eucharistic Origins* (Oxford, 2004).

Brakke, David, *Athanasius and Asceticism* (Baltimore, London, 1995).

Burns, Paul C., 'Child sacrifice, a polyvalent story in early eucharistic piety', in V. Daphna Arbel et al., eds, *Not Sparing the Child, Human Sacrifice in the Ancient World and Beyond* (London, New York, 2016), 141-164.

Byzantine and Post-Byzantine Art (exhibition catalogue Byzantine Museum) (Athens 1986).

Clement of Alexandria, *The Writings of Clement of Alexandria*, II. Miscellanies (William Wilson transl.), Ante-Nicene Christian Library XII (Edinburgh, 1869).

Cohen, Arthur A. *The Myth of the Judeo-Christian Tradition* (New York, 1970).

Colgrave, Bertram (transl.), *The Earliest Life of Gregory the Great* (Cambridge, 1985).

Day, J., *Molech: a God of Human Sacrifice in the Old Testament* (Cambridge, 1989).

De Ste. Croix, G.E.M., 'Voluntary Martyrdom in the Early Church', in G.E.M. De Ste. Croix, Michael Whitby, and Joseph Street, eds, *Christian Persecution, Martyrdom, and Orthodoxy,* (Oxford, 2006), 153-200.

De Ste. Croix, G.E.M., 'Why Were the Early Christians Persecuted?', *Past and Present* 26 (1963), 6-38, reprinted in G.E.M. De Ste. Croix, Michael Whitby, and Joseph Street, eds, *Christian Persecution, Martyrdom, and Orthodoxy* (Oxford, 2006), 105-152.

Dearman, J.A., 'The Tophet in Jerusalem: Archaeology and Cultural Profile', *Journal of Northwest Semitic Languages* 22.1 (1996), 59-71.

Demus, Otto, *Byzantine Mosaic Decoration* (Londo, Henly, 1978).

Dewrell, H.W., *Child Sacrifice in Ancient Israel and its Opponents*, Ph.D. thesis, John Hopkins University, Baltimore, 2012.

Eckhardt, Benedikt, '"Bloodless Sacrifice": A Note on Greek Cultic Language in the Imperial Era', *Greek, Roman, and Byzantine Studies* 54 (2014) 255-273.

Eissfeldt, Otto, *Molk als Opferbegriff im Punischen und Hebraischen und das Ende des Gottes Moloch* (Halle, 1935).

Ephrem, *Carmina Nisibena*, ed. E. Bickell (Leipzig, 1866).

Ephrem the Syrian, *Des Heiligen Ephraem des Syrers Sermones IV*, translation by E. Beck, Corpus Scriptorum Christianorum Orientalum 335 (Louvain, 1973).

Eusebius, *Historia Ecclesiastica*, transl. G.A. Williamson (Harmondsworth, 1983).

Faust, Avraham 'Israelite Temples: Where Was Israelite Cult Not Practiced, and Why', *Religions* 10.2 (2019), 106, accessed 10-11-2020, https://www.mdpi.com/2077-1444/10/2/106.

Finsterbusch, K., A. Lange, and K.F. Diethard Römheld, eds, *Human Sacrifice in Jewish and Christian Tradition* (Leiden, Boston, 2007).

Forget, I., ed., *Synaxarium Alexandrinum* I (Rome, 1921).

Green, Alberto, *The Role of Human Sacrifice in the Ancient Near East*, American Schools of Oriental Research Series 1 (Missoula, Montana, 1975).

Haderman-Misguich, Lydie, *Kurbinovo, Les fresques de Saint-Georges et la peinture byzantine du XIIe siècle* (Brussels, 1975).

Hennecke, Edgar, and Wilhelm Schneemelcher, *Neutestamentliche Apokryphen* I (Tübingen, 1968).

Hennessey, J.B., 'Thirteenth Century B.C. Temple of Human Sacrifice at Amman', *Studia Phoenicia*, vol. 3, *Phoenicia and Its Neighbours* (Leuven, 1985), 85-104.

Henten, Jan Willem van, 'Noble Death and Martyrdom in Antiquity', in Sebastian Fuhrmann and Regina Grundmann, eds, *Martyriumsvorstellungen in Antike und Mittelalter*, Ancient Judaism and Early Christianity 80 (Leiden, Boston, 2012), 85-110.

Henten, Jan Willem van, 'Self-sacrifice and Substitution in Greek and Roman Literature', in Michael Hüttenhof, Wolfgang Kraus, and Karlo Meyer, eds, *"...mein Blut für Euch" Theologische Perspektiven zum Verständnis des Todes Jesu heute* (Göttingen, 2018), 61-89.

Hirsch, E.G., M. Seligsohn, S. Schechter, and G.A. Barton, 'Jephthah', in *Jewish Encyclopedia* VII (New York London, 1904), 94-95.

Ignatius of Antioch, *Epistle to the Romans*, Alexander Roberts, James Donaldson, and A. Cleveland Coxe, eds, *Ante-Nicene Fathers* 1 (Buffalo, NY, 1885). Revised and edited for New Advent by Kevin Knight, accessed 10-12-2020, http://www.newadvent.org/fathers/0107.htm.

Kaluzniacki, E., 'Die Legende von der Vision Amphilogs und der Logos Historikos des Gregorios Dekapolites', *Archiv für slavische Philologie* 25 (1903), 101-108.

Klauser, Th., 'Die konstantinischen Altäre in der Lateranbasilika', in *Gesammelte Arbeiten* (Münster, 1974), 155-160.

Lampe, P., 'Human Sacrifice and Pauline Christology', in Finsterbusch, K., A. Lange, and K.F. Diethard Römheld, eds, *Human Sacrifice in Jewish and Christian Tradition* (Leiden, Boston, 2007), 193-209.

Lange, A, '"They Burn Their Sons and Daughters – That Was No Command o Mine" (Jer. 7:31)', in Finsterbusch, K., A. Lange, and K.F. Diethard Römheld, eds, *Human Sacrifice in Jewish and Christian Tradition* (Leiden, Boston, 2007), 109-132.

Levenson, J.D., *The Death and Resurrection of the Beloved Son, The transformation of Child Sacrifice in Judaism and Christianity* (New Haven, London, 1993).

Loon, Gertrud van, *The Gate of Heaven, Wall Paintings with Old Testament Scenes in the Altar Room and the Ḥūrus of Coptic Churches* (Istanbul, 1999).

Lucchesi Palli, E., 'Abraham', in E. Kirschbaum, ed., *Lexikon der christlichen Ikonographie* (Rome, Freiburg, Basel, Vienna, 1999), col. 20-35.

Malkiel, David J., 'Infanticide in Passover Iconography', *Journal of the Warburg and Courtauld Institutes* 56 (1993), 85-99.

Marinis, Vasileios, *Death and the Afterlife in Byzantium, the Fate of the Soul in Theology, Liturgy, and Art* (Cambridge, 2017).

McEntire, Mark, *Struggling with God: An Introduction to the Pentateuch* (Macon, GA., 2008).

McGowan, Andrew, 'Rethinking Eucharistic Origins', *Pacifica* 23 (2010), 173-191.

Menzies, Allan, ed., *Ante-Nicene Fathers*, Vol. 9 (Buffalo, NY, 1896.), accessed 20-11-2020, http://www.newadvent.org/fathers/101506.htm.

Moorsel, P.P.V. van, 'Jephthah? Or, an Iconographical Discussion Continued', in F. Geus and F. Thill, eds, *Mélanges offerts à Jean Vercoutter* (Paris, 1985), 273-278.

Moorsel, P.P.V. van, *Les peintures du monastère de Saint-Antoine près de la Mer Rouge* (Cairo, 1995).

Mosca, P.G., *Child Sacrifice in Canaanite and Israelite Religion, a study in* molk *and* למך, Ph.D. thesis, Harvard University, Cambridge, MA., 1975.

Moss, Candida R., 'The Discourse of Voluntary Martyrdom: Ancient and Modern', *Church History* 81,3 (2012), 531-552.

Moss, Candida R., *The Other Christs, Imitating Jesus in Ancient Christian Ideologies of Martyrdom* (Oxford, New York, 2010).

Musurillo, Herbert (transl.), *The Acts of the Christian Martyrs* (Oxford, 1972).

Nathan, Emmanuel and Anya Topolski, eds, *Is there a Judeo-Christian Tradition?: A European Perspective* (Berlin, Boston, 2016).

Noort, E., 'Child Sacrifice in Ancient Israel: The status quaestionis', in J. N. Bremmer, ed., *The Strange World of Human Sacrifice* (Leuven, 2007), 103-125.

O'Connell, Elisabeth, 'Transforming Monumental Land-scapes in Late Antique Egypt: Monastic Dwellings in Legal Documents from Western Thebes', *Journal of Early Christian Studies* 15 (2007), 239-273.

Papaconstantinou, Arietta, 'ΘΕΙΑ ΟΙΚΟΝΟΜΙΑ, les actes thébains de donation d'enfants ou la gestion monastique de la penurie', in Vincent Déroche et al., eds, *Mélanges Gilbert Dagron* (Paris, 2002), 511-526.

Papaconstantinou, Arietta, 'Notes sur les actes de donation d'enfant au monastère thébain de Saint-Phoibammon', *The Journal of Juristic Papyrology* 32 (2002), 83-106.

Pesthy-Simon, Monika, *Isaac, Iphigenea, Ignatius, Martyrdom and Human Sacrifice* (Budapest, New York, 2017).

Pongratz-Leisten, B., 'Ritual Killing and sacrifice in the Ancient Near East', in Finsterbusch, K., A. Lange, and K.F. Diethard Römheld, eds, *Human Sacrifice in Jewish and Christian Tradition* (Leiden, Boston, 2007), 3-33.

Reynolds, B., 'Molek: Dead or Alive? The Meaning and Derivation of *mlk* and למך', in Finsterbusch, K., A. Lange, and K.F. Diethard Römheld, eds, *Human Sacrifice in Jewish and Christian Tradition* (Leiden, Boston, 2007), 133-150.

Roig Lanzilotta, R., 'The Early Christians and Human Sacrifice', in Jan Bremmer, ed., *The Strange World of Human Sacrifice* (Leuven, Paris, Dudley, MA, 2007), 81-102.

Robinson, Jed, 'The God of the Patriarchs and the Ugaritic Texts: A Shared Religious and Cultural Identity', *Studia Antiqua* 8.1 (2010), 25-33, accessed 15-11-2020, https://scholarsarchive.byu.edu/studiaantiqua/vol8/iss1/4.

Rordorf, W. and A. Tuiller, *La doctrine des douze apôtres* (Paris, 1978).

Sales, R.H., 'Human Sacrifice in Biblical Thought', *Journal of Bible and Religion* 25 (1957), 112-117.

Schaff, Philip and Henry Wace, eds, *Nicene and Post-Nicene Fathers*, Second Series, Vol. 13 (Buffalo, NY, 1890). Revised and edited for New Advent by Kevin Knight, accessed 20-1-2020, http://www.newadvent.org/fathers/370121.htm.

Schaff, Philip and Henry Wace, eds, *Nicene and Post-Nicene Fathers*, Second Series, Vol. 14 (Buffalo, NY, 1900). Revised and edited for New Advent by Kevin Knight, accessed 20-1-2020, http://www.newadvent.org/fathers/3814.htm.

Schenke, Gesa, 'The Healing Shrines of St. Phoibammon: Evidence of Cult Activity in Coptic Legal Documents', *Zeitschrift für antikes Christentum* 20.3 (2026), 496-523.

Roberts, Alexander, James Donaldson, and A. Cleveland Coxe, eds, *Ante-Nicene Fathers*, Vol. 1 (Buffalo, NY, 1885). Revised and edited for New Advent by Kevin Knight, accessed 14-11-2020, http://www.newadvent.org/fathers/0107.htm.

Schoedel, W. R., *Ignatius of Antioch. A Commentary on the Letters of Ignatius of Antioch* (Philadelphia, 1985).

Shanks, Hershel, 'First Person: Human Sacrifice to an Ammonite God?', *Biblical Archaeology Review* 40.5 (September /October 2014), accessed 10-11-2020, https://www.biblicalarchaeology.org/daily/ancient-cultures/daily-life-and-practice/first-person-human-sacrifice-to-an-ammonite-god/.

Sheridan, M., ed., *Acient Christian Commentary on Scripture, Old Testament* II (Genesis 11-50) (Downers Grove Ill., 2002).

Schroeder, C. T., 'Child Sacrifice in Egyptian Monastic Culture: from Familial Renunciation to Jephthah's Lost Daughter', *Journal of Early Christian Studies* 20.2 (2012), 269-302.

Schwartz, Joshua, 'Jubilees, Bethel and the Temple of Jacob', *Hebrew Union College Annual*, 56 (1985), 63-85.

Stavrakopoulou, F., *King Manasseh and Child Sacrifice, Biblical Distortions of Historical Realities* (Berlin, New York, 2004).

Thompson, J.L., *Writing the Wrongs, Women of the Old Testament Among Biblical Commentators from Philo through the Reformation* (Oxford, New York, 2001).

Thompson, Thomas L., *Early History of the Israelite People: From the Written & Archaeological Sources* (Leiden, Boston, Köln, 1994).

Till, W., *Koptische Heiligen- und Martyrerlegenden* I (Rome, 1935).

Tomić Djurić, Marka, 'To picture and to perform: the image of the Eucharistic Liturgy at Markov Manastir (I)', *Zograph* 38 (2014), 123-142.

Walter, Ch., *Art and Ritual of the Byzantine Church* (London, 1982).

Ward, Benedicta S.L.G., *The Desert Christian. Sayings of the Desert Fathers, The Alphabetical Collection* (New York, 1975).

Waszkowiak, Jakub, 'Pre-Israelite and Israelite Burnt Offering Altars in Canaan – Archaeological Evidence', *The Polish Journal of Biblical Research* 13.1-2 (2014), 43-69.

Weitmann, Kurt, 'The Jephthah Panel in the Bema of the Church of St. Catherine's Monastery on Mount Sinai', *Dumbarton Oaks Papers* 18 (1964), 341-352.

Wipczycka, Ewa, 'Child Donation', in Aziz Atiya, ed., *Coptic Encyclopedia* (New York, Toronto, 1991), 918a-919b.

Wortley, John, (ed. and transl.), *The Anonymous Sayings of the Desert Fathers* (Cambridge, 2013).

Chapter 7

Deconstructing the Aztec human sacrifice[1]

Maarten E.R.G.N. Jansen*

and Gabina Aurora Pérez Jiménez*

7.1. Introduction: colonial sources

Human sacrifice has become emblematically associated with the ancient civilisation of Mexico and Central America, a region also known as Mesoamerica.[2] Particularly the Aztecs, protagonists of the last imperial expansion in that region before the Spanish conquest of 1521, have been portrayed as carrying out sanguinary sacrifices on a daily basis. The custom was reported in abhorrent detail by Spanish authors and explicitly identified as "sacrifice" already in their earliest references. Recalling his first entry in the Aztec capital, one of the conquistadors, Bernal Díaz del Castillo (1492-1581), writes:

> Respecting the abominable human sacrifices of these people, the following was communicated to us: The breast of the unhappy victim destined to be sacrificed was ripped open with a knife made of sharp flint; the throbbing heart was then torn out, and immediately offered to the idol-god in whose honour the sacrifice had been

---

1   The present article is a result of the project 'Time in Intercultural Context: the indigenous calendars of Mexico and Guatemala', which we have carried out at the Faculty of Archaeology, Leiden University (The Netherlands), together with a team of PhD candidates and postdocs, funded by the European Research Council (ERC) in the context of the European Union's Seventh Framework Programme (FP7/2007-2013) under grant agreement n° 295434. This project builds on the long-term research concerning the interpretation of Mesoamerican visual art and oral tradition, paying special attention to time symbolism, sacred landscape and cultural memory in Central and Southern Mexico (cf. Jansen and Pérez Jiménez, *Time and the Ancestors*).

2   For an overview of the archaeology and history of this region see for example Evans, *Ancient Mexico*. For synthetic studies of Aztec human sacrifice, see Duverger, *Fleur létale*, *Nájera, Don de Sangre*, and Graulich, *Sacrifice humain*. Anders, Jansen and Reyes García discuss the main points in their book *El Libro del Ciuacoatl* (ch. 8). The volume *El sacrificio humano en la tradición religiosa meso-americana*, edited by Leonardo López Luján and Guilhem Olivier, reviews earlier literature and provides a timely analytic and comparative overview. Compare the contributions by Laura Rival and David Brown to the volume *Sacrifice and Modern Thought*, edited by Meszaros and Zachhuber, and see also Olivier, *Cacería, sacrificio y poder*. Dehouve, *Offrandes et Sacrifices*, analyses sacrifice in the context of ritual deposits, paying attention to cultural continuity.

*Leiden University

Figure 7.1 Colonial representation of Aztec human sacrifice (Codex Magliabechi, 70). After: Anders and Jansen, *Libro de la Vida*.

Figure 7.2 Colonial representation of Aztec cannibalism (Codex Magliabechi, 73). After: Anders and Jansen, *Libro de la Vida*.

instituted. After this, the head, arms, and legs were cut off and eaten at their banquets, with the exception of the head, which was saved, and hung to a beam appropriated for that purpose.[3]

Similarly another chronicle, written by an unidentified conquistador, describes the ritual in even more detail:

They take him who has to be sacrificed, and first they carry him through the streets and squares, very finely adorned, with great festivities and rejoicing. Many a one recounts to him his needs, saying that since he is going where his God is, he can tell him so that he may remedy them. Then he gives him refreshments and other things. ... They lead him to the temple, where they dance and carry on joyously, and the man about to be sacrificed dances and carries on like the rest. At length the man who offers the sacrifice strips him naked, and leads him at once to the stairway of the tower [pyramid] where is the stone idol. Here they stretch him on his back, tying the hands to the sides and fastening the legs. Then all commence to sing and dance around him, chanting the principal message which he is to bear to the God. Soon comes the sacrificing priest – and this is no small office among them – armed with a stone knife, which cuts like steel, and is as big as one of our large knives. He plunges the knife into the breast, opens it, and tears out the heart hot and palpitating. And this as quickly as one might cross himself. At this point the chief priest of the temple takes it, and anoints the mouth of the principal

idol with the blood; then filling his hand with it he flings it towards the sun, or towards some star, if it be night. Then he anoints the mouths of all the other idols of wood and stone, and sprinkles blood on the cornice of the chapel of the principal idol. Afterwards they burn the heart, preserving the ashes as a great relic, and likewise they burn the body of the sacrifice, but these ashes are kept apart from those of the heart in a different vase.[4]

Bernal Díaz and several other sources insist on the connection between human sacrifice and cannibalism: "arms and legs were cut off and eaten at their banquets". This is also the prominent thread in the early colonial accounts by Spanish missionaries, such as the Franciscan friar Bernardino de Sahagún (1499-1590) or the Dominican friar Diego Durán (ca. 1537-1588), who presented detailed descriptions of Aztec rituals in their "crusade" against the Mesoamerican religion, which they basically saw as the work of the devil.

The practice of human sacrifice was further illustrated in early-colonial (sixteenth century) pictorial manuscripts that continued the pre-colonial pictographic tradition but were produced for the purposes of Christianisation (the "spiritual conquest") and under the supervision of the missionaries. A famous example is the so-called Book of Life (*Libro de la Vida*) or Codex Magliabechi, which shows the stereotypical representation of the human sacrifice: cutting out the heart and throwing the body down the stairs of the temple-pyramid (page 70) while elsewhere (page 73)

---

3   Díaz del Castillo, *Memoirs*, ch. 91, 1844, 232-233; English translation by John Ingram Lockhart, published in 1844 and now a Project Gutenberg EBook.

4   Anonymous conqueror, ch. 15, 1917, 51; We cite the 1917 translation by Marshall H. Saville, reproduced by Alec Christensen [http://www.famsi.org/research/christensen/anon_con/section16.htm].

Figure 7.3 De Bry's fanciful rendering of the Aztec main temple. After: De Bry, *Conquistadores, Aztecs and Incas.*

Figure 7.4 De Bry's fanciful rendering of Aztec bloody and cannibalistic rituals. After: De Bry, *Conquistadores, Aztecs and Incas.*

people are sitting in front of the temple eating human flesh (figs. 7.1 and 7.2).[5]

During the same period in Europe the draughtsman Theodore de Bry (Liège 1528 – Frankfurt 1598) produced engravings for editions of chronicles of the Spanish conquest. De Bry himself had never been in the Americas, so his drawings were largely the product of his imagination based on texts, but, as he had a good feeling for the expectations and taste of his audience, his work caused sensation and impact, and profoundly influenced the image of the Aztecs in European perception. Here we see, for example, an image of priests ripping open the belly of a victim on top of a temple platform decorated with human skulls and throwing the corpse down the stairs, and a scene in which the body is flayed and pieces are cut from it to be served at a banquet (figs. 7.3 and 7.4).[6]

Today these descriptions and illustrations are still the basis for popular publications and films such as Mel Gibson's widely debated *Apocalypto* (2006), but they also remain influential in scholarly literature. U.S. anthropologist Marvin Harris, for example, in his widely read book *Cannibals and Kings* (1978) sketched a synthetic image:

> Nowhere else in the world had there developed a state-sponsored religion whose art, architecture and ritual were so thoroughly dominated by violence, decay, death and disease. Nowhere else were walls and plazas of great temples and palaces reserved for such a concentrated display of jaws, fangs, claws, talons, bones and gaping death heads. The eyewitness accounts of Cortes and his fellow conquistador, Bernal Diaz, leave no doubt concerning the ecclesiastical meaning of the dreadful visages portrayed in stone. The Aztec gods ate people. They ate human hearts and they drank human blood. And the declared function of the Aztec priesthood was to provide fresh human hearts and human blood in order to prevent the remorseless deities from becoming angry and crippling, sickening, withering, and burning the whole world.[7]

There are quite a few problems in the records about the Aztec human sacrifice, however. The few Spanish chroniclers who took part in the conquest themselves and were in a position to watch those sacrifices, were still limited in their understanding of Mesoamerican culture: they did not speak the local languages and the translation process was cumbersome. Furthermore, they wrote their texts not as "objective" descriptions but with the clear motive of justifying their (very violent and unjust) enterprise of conquest. The vast majority of the more detailed information does not actually come from eye-witness accounts, but was collected several decades after such practices had become totally prohibited by the Spanish colonial regime.[8] The missionaries who reported these rituals also had ulterior motives, essentially to convince the Spanish authorities in their homeland about the horrible aspects of native "idolatry" and the urgent necessity of sending enough human and material resources for the "spiritual conquest".[9] Enough of a reason to analyse these sources with care and historical critique!

7.2. Cannibals and Witches

The early-colonial sources connected the Aztec human sacrifice intimately to the practice of anthropophagy, which had first and foremost been attributed to the native peoples of the Caribbean and the wider Amazonian region. De Bry visualised cannibalistic banquets in his illustrations of the account of Hans Staden about his stay among the Tupinambá people (Brazil). Following in his footsteps, the Dutch painter Albert Eeckhout (1610-1666) made a famous painting of a native Brazilian woman walking around holding a severed human arm and carrying a basket with human limbs for consumption. The style is so precise and naturalistic that it seems to be a photograph, but one moment of reflection is enough to understand that this is not a realistic image at all: it is highly unlikely that cannibalistic women were wandering around under Dutch colonial rule with its protestant ethics.[10]

In the minds of the colonizers, cannibalism on the Mesoamerican mainland was an expected continuation of macabre practices known from the Caribbean, but even more dramatic as it was combined with the sanguinary act of human sacrifice.

In the framework of proposing a scientific theory about cultural differences, Harris saw the occurrence of human sacrifice among the Aztecs as a function of

---

5   For a facsimile edition and commentary see Anders and Jansen, *Libro de la Vida*.

6   De Bry, illustrations VIII and IX of the *Idea Vera et Genuina praecipuarum historiarum omnium, ut et variorum rituum, ceremoniarum, consuetudinumque gentis Indicae* (published in Frankfurt 1602), reproduced in De Bry, *Conquistadores, Aztecs and Incas*. On the work of De Bry and its influence on the image of the indigenous peoples and cultures of the Americas, see Bucher, *Icon and Conquest*, and Van Groesen, *Representations*. For an overview of how Aztec culture has been perceived through time, see the classic monograph by Keen, *Aztec Image in Western Thought*. A recent article by Klein, 'Death at the Hand of Strangers', focuses on the Western representation of Aztec human sacrifice.

7   Harris, *Cannibals*, ch. 9, 147-148.

8   For example: Sahagún arrived several years after the conquest (1529) and started the research for his book some thirty years later, while Durán was born in Mexico in ± 1537 and wrote his work in the 1570s.

9   Cf. Jansen and Pérez Jiménez, *Tiempo, Religión, Interculturalidad*.

10 Buvelot, *Eckhout*; cf. Mason, *Infelicities*.

cannibalism and, following suggestions of another anthropologist, Michael Harner, explained the habit of cannibalism by linking it to a supposed absence of protein sources (Harris, *Cannibals*, ch. 10). The subjective reason for procuring these proteins through sacrifice, in Harris' interpretation, would have been the primitive people's fear of "remorseless deities".[11]

Ironically, at the same time, other authors focused on analysing how and why cultural differences were observed, constructed and valued in the first place. In an intellectual context of questioning the motivations behind stereotyping "the Other", epitomized by the critical works of Edward Said and Michel Foucault, the long accepted presence of cannibalism came under scrutiny.

Puerto Rican author Jalil Sued Badillo wrote a ground-breaking cultural-historical analysis *Los Caribes: realidad o fábula* (1978), which questioned the existence of anthropophagy among the Caribs, as the vast majority, if not all, of testimonies seemed to be based on hearsay and misinterpretations of native customs. Human remains found preserved in baskets or vessels, for example, do not indicate that the bodies had been consumed at a banquet, but rather a form of keeping bones of deceased family members in a context of ancestor worship. Similarly the Spaniards interpreted the location of human bodies on a *barbacoa* installation above a fire as "cooking" the body for consumption, while in fact it was a form of drying the body as part of a mummification process.[12] William Arens goes even further in his book with the eloquent title *The Man-Eating Myth: anthropology and anthropophagy* (1979), and questions the existence of cannibalism in human cultures in general. He argues that many reports were inspired by a desire to justify conquest and colonisation (with its cruel, destructive and genocidal character) by representing the "newly discovered" peoples as wild cannibals and consequently as inhuman, even anti-human. In order to "save" them from the devil, they should be brought under European rule, so they could be "civilized" and educated in the "true religion".

The works of Sued Badillo and Arens caused visceral criticism and emotional polemics. Opponents argued

that the critique of cannibalism was too superficial and that cannibalism existed, though they admitted that it was probably less frequent than commonly thought, and that where it occurred it was probably part of a much more complicated cultural set of ideas and practices and certainly could not be described adequately as a primitive culinary custom. The whole discussion shows that these books were successful in unmasking a stereotype that until then had remained largely unquestioned.[13]

A number of follow-up studies have indeed made it clear that reports and representations of "other people" are often deeply influenced by all kinds of stereotypes, engrained as pre-understandings in the mind of the colonizers and missionaries as well as in that of their "successors", the modern anthropologists. The basic element in this lack of good intercultural understanding is the tendency of seeing "the Other" as less rational (and therefore less human) than "Self". Thus the religion of "Self" is felt as a profound and comforting spiritual guidance in life, but the religion of "the Other" is typically considered irrational, weird, caused by fear and horror-inspiring.[14]

The first European impressions of the indigenous peoples of the Americas followed cognitive templates already put in place by fanciful (even hoax-like) medieval travel accounts such as the 14th-century book of John Mandeville, who, following Pliny the Elder, described the inhabitants of far-away islands as strange and monstrous creatures.[15] This work, very popular in its time, mentioned instances of human sacrifice and anthropophagy:

In that country they make idols, half man half ox. And in those idols evil spirits speak and give answer to men of what is asked them. Before these idols men slay their children many times, and spring the blood upon the idols; and so they make their sacrifice.[16]

And then for the love and in worship of that idol, and for the reverence of the feast, they slay themselves, a two hundred or three hundred persons, with sharp knives, of which they bring the bodies before the idol. And then they say that those be saints, because that they slew themselves of their own good will for love of their idol... they go before the idol leading him that will slay himself for such devotion between them, with great reverence. And he, all naked, hath a full sharp knife in his hand, and he cutteth a great piece

---

11   See Harner, 'Ecological Basis'. This theory has been elaborated upon by Winkelman ('Aztec Human Sacrifice'), who, applying a cross-cultural analysis, brought to the fore an interplay with factors such as population pressure, societal stratification, and psychocultural dynamics. Following a similar comparative approach, an article in Nature by Watts et al. ('Ritual Human Sacrifice') also examines the possible connection of human sacrifice, the legitimation of authority and the evolution of stratified societies. The problem of developing such general theoretical models, however, is that at this stage the argument is often based on uncertain, debatable and pluri-interpretable data.

12   See Sued Badillo's intelligent and convincing analysis of the source texts (*Los Caribes*, 41-46).

13   See the contributions by Peter Hulme and William Arens in Barker, Hulme and Iversen, *Cannibalism and the Colonial World*.

14   See for example Jarich Oosten, 'Prime mover', in Jansen et al., *Continuity and Identity*, as well as Churchill, *Fantasies of the Master Race*.

15   See on this topic Mason, *Deconstructing America*.

16   Mandeville, *Travels*, ch. 18.

of his flesh, and casteth it in the face of his idol, saying his orisons, recommending him to his god. And then he smiteth himself and maketh great wounds and deep, here and there, till he fall down dead. And then his friends present his body to the idol.[17]

But in that country there is a cursed custom, for they eat more gladly man's flesh than any other flesh; and yet is that country abundant of flesh, of fish, of corns, of gold and silver, and of all other goods. Thither go merchants and bring with them children to sell to them of the country, and they buy them. And if they be fat they eat them anon. And if they be lean they feed them till they be fat, and then they eat them. And they say, that it is the best flesh and the sweetest of all the world.[18]

The act of killing and eating children was also attributed by the Catholic inquisitors to "witches", as registered in the infamous persecution manual *Malleus Maleficarum* written by the Dominican monks Heinrich Kramer and Jacobus Sprenger, published only a few years before Columbus' first voyage:

... the fact that certain witches, against the instinct of human nature, and indeed against the nature of all beasts, with the possible exception of wolves, are in the habit of devouring and eating infant children. And concerning this, the Inquisitor of Como, who has been mentioned before, has told us the following: that he was summoned by the inhabitants of the County of Barby to hold an inquisition, because a certain man had missed his child from its cradle, and finding a congress of women in the night-time, swore that he saw them kill his child and drink its blood and devour it.[19]

We should keep in mind that the European conquest and colonisation of the Americas took place at the same time as the witch-craze in Europe. Treatises against witchcraft such as the *Malleus Maleficarum*, or the *Reprovación de las supersticiones y hechizerías* of Pedro Ciruelo (1538) were certainly known to the missionaries and must have had a determining influence on the way in which they saw native religion as "idolatry" and a "pact with the devil". Witches were also a popular stereotypical theme in literature, paintings and engravings.[20]

Nowadays, after much critical research, the scholarly consensus is that "witches" as such – *i.e.* as the created stereotype – did not exist but were a product of the fantasies and fears of their persecutors. This witch-craze caused the torture and death of tens of thousands of innocent victims – in itself it is illustrative that nobody really knows how many, because records have been lost and were not always kept consistently (certainly not in cases where the perpetrators themselves felt that they were actually acting anti-ethically or in a criminal way). On the basis of a collection of inquisition documents Carlo Ginzburg (*Benandanti, Storia Notturna*) has analysed the phenomenon in depth, demonstrating how the inquisitors interpreted information about agricultural rites and beliefs (focusing on protection of community and harvest) in accordance with their preconceived image of the witches' Sabbath (cult of the devil) and made local people confess to that.

We should remember that the persecution of indigenous religion (the "spiritual conquest") in the Americas and the persecution of witches in Europe were not only contemporaneous, but were two aspects of the same historical phenomenon, with the same ideology and demonology. In fact, sometimes the protagonists were the same. For example, the first bishop of Mexico, friar Juan de Zumárraga (OFM), had been the leading inquisitor in the persecution campaign against the "witches" of Vizcaya, Spain, in 1527. He was accompanied in this enterprise by friar Andrés de Olmos (OFM), who would later follow him to Mexico and become an important author of a grammar and a vocabulary of the Aztec language. Olmos would even write in the Aztec language a treatise on witchcraft, *Tratado de hechicerías y sortilegios* (1553), which was a translation and adaptation of the *Tratado de las Supersticiones y Hechizerías* (1529) that his confrere Martin de Castañega had written after the experiences of the campaign against the Vizcaya witches.[21] Spanish authors of the 16th Century refer consistently to Mesoamerican Gods as "demons" and to religious practice in terms of witchcraft (*brujería*), and so do many people today: common citizens but also anthropologists.[22]

Taking it for granted that such practices were common in the "New World", and having only a very limited understanding of the people there, the conquistadors and

---

17   Mandeville, *Travels*, ch. 19, 118.
18   Mandeville, *Travels*, ch. 20, 120.
19   *Malleus Maleficarum*, Part I, Question XI
20   See Vervoort and Vanysacker, *Bruegel witches*. An example of a literary and philosophical treatment is the work *Dialogus Strix sive de ludificatione Daemonum* (1523) by Giovanni Francesco Pico della Mirandola (1470-1533). Cohn, *Europe's Inner Demons*, offers a classic evaluation of the phenomenon.

21   See the edition and Spanish translation of Olmos' work by Georges Baudot (1990). Bishop Zumárraga is famous for his role in the appearance of the Virgin of Guadelupe, but he also wrote a *Doctrina Cristiana* (1543); for his relations with the inquisition, see Greenleaf, *Zumárraga*. Cervantes' *Devil in the New World* offers an overview of the cultural-historical context.
22   Cf. Christensen and Martí, *Witchcraft and pre-Columbian Paper*, Madsen and Madsen, *Guide to Mexican Witchcraft*, Nutini and Roberts, *Bloodsucking Witchcraft*. The Mesoamerican landscape is full of places called *"cueva del diablo"* etc.

the missionaries interpreted and represented what they saw of the local customs through this lens. Particularly since the hostile image of the cannibal and idolater was a welcome device to discredit other peoples and consequently deny them human status and rights.[23] The Royal *Cédula* of King Ferdinand of Spain (1511) accused the Caribs of being unwilling to receive the Europeans and of being aggressors who made war on the indigenous population "in our Service", taking them prisoner, killing them, dismembering and eating them and inciting them to commit many evils. Therefore the Royal *Cédula* gave the Spaniards permission to make war on those Caribs, take them prisoner and sell them (as slaves).[24] Undeniably, this was a very strong motive for the conquistadors – determined to usurp indigenous lands and resources – to dismiss the indigenous inhabitants as murderers and man-eaters. It is precisely for this reason that we cannot trust such allegations without further proof. And, as Sued Badillo, Arens and others have pointed out, that proof is conspicuously lacking.

7.3. The European invention of Aztec human sacrifice

Now, as we know that the diverse accusations related to witchcraft and the cult of demons in Europe – concretely the alleged acts of sacrificial killing and cannibalism – were generally false, and that the conquistadors were not only prejudiced and biased, but also had a persuasive self-interest to create such a gory image, how should we consider the descriptions of such matters in Mesoamerica?

As in the case of the anthropophagy attributed to the Caribbean, in the case of Mesoamerica the reports on human sacrifices and related cannibalism are generally written long after the facts and are not trustworthy eyewitness accounts.[25] In order to uncover original observations we must turn to pre-colonial sources, which indeed contain several depictions of the act described by the Spanish authors as "human sacrifice", both in the pre-colonial painted manuscripts and in sculptures: a priest killing a person in front of a deity by cutting out the heart with a flint or obsidian knife. The frequency, scale, time-depth, context, purpose and meaning of these acts, however, are not self-evident.

In Codex Mictlan (Laud), p. 17, for example, we see a priest killing a man on an altar by stabbing a flint knife

Figure 7.5 The sacrificing priest in Codex Mictlan (Laud), p. 17. After: Anders and Jansen, *Pintura de la Muerte*.

into his breast (fig. 7.5). This is not a historical action, however, but a way of referring to the title of a priest, who happens to be a participant in a procession leading to a cave, where he will present an offering of firewood.[26]

Some conquistadors claimed to have witnessed such events – or their remains – but the circumstances are generally not clear. They were all children of their time and thus their observations were predetermined and biased by all kinds of imaginations and prejudices about unknown non-Christian "other peoples". Besides, it is obvious that the conquistadors, the missionaries and the colonial officials, all had reasons to promote the image of the cruel barbarian sacrificers and cannibals as a justification for their own military and spiritual conquest.[27]

In 1992 an in-depth critical review of the problematic character of these testimonies appeared: the PhD thesis of Peter Hassler, *Menschenopfer bei den Azteken? Eine quellen- und ideologiekritischer Studie*. Since then, several specialists (such as Elizabeth Graham and Antje Gunsenheimer) have equally presented critical analyses and have noted the need to re-examine the stories about human sacrifices in Mesoamerica, but their observations have not received adequate attention in the mainstream literature.

Here we will try to reconstruct the origin and early development of the now widely accepted image of such practices. An important testimony in this respect comes from Bernal Díaz del Castillo, who participated in the conquest campaign (1518-1521). He started writing

---

23   For a historical critical review of ideas surrounding the Spanish conquest of Mexico, see Restall, *Seven Myths*. Already the ancient Romans accused the early Christians of killing and eating children during their religious ceremonies (Minucius Felix, Octavius IX, 5, quoted by Widengren *Religionsphänomenologie*, 310).

24   See Jesse, *Spanish Cédula*, for the full text of the document in question.

25   See for example Jacobs, *Cannibalism paradigm*.

26   See the edition and commentary by Anders and Jansen, *Pintura de la Muerte*. We follow the new nomenclature we have proposed for the pre-colonial Mexican codices (Jansen and Pérez Jiménez, *Mixtec Pictorial Manuscripts*).

27   Cf. Bataillon et al., *Teorías de la guerra justa*.

his *Memoirs* in 1568 in order to correct the work of Francisco de Gómara (chaplain of Hernán Cortés), which in his opinion contained many errors and mistakes – an indication of how the Spaniards themselves recognised that the existing reports were far from precise and objective. Although several decades after the facts, Bernal Díaz del Castillo wrote a vivid report directly from memory that transports the reader to the places, times and events described. Until now his chronicle has had a determining influence on the way the conquest of Mexico is perceived.[28]

The first references to religious monuments and blood sacrifice appear in the description of the first Spanish incursion into Mexico, the expedition led by Francisco Hernández de Córdoba (1517), visiting the coast of Campeche. Bernal Díaz del Castillo writes:

> They [the local people] took us to some large edifices, which were strongly put together, of stone and lime, and had otherwise a good appearance. These were temples, the walls of which were covered with figures representing snakes and all manner of gods. Round about a species of altar we perceived several fresh spots of blood. On some of the idols there were figures like crosses, with other paintings representing groups of Indians. All this astonished us greatly as we had neither seen nor heard, of such things before. It appeared to us that the inhabitants had just been sacrificing some Indians to their gods, to obtain from them the power to overcome us.[29]

Expressions such as "All this astonished us greatly" and "It appeared to us that … " indicate that the Spaniards were not sure what to make of these "fresh spots of blood" and just speculated that they represented some form of sacrifice, probably because of their general expectation pattern (nurtured by Mandeville and similar literature). From the blood itself it is not clear, however, whether humans really had been killed on that occasion or if the blood came from bloodletting or from killed animals. Much more explicit is the next reference:

> We found two houses, which were strongly built of stone and lime; both were ascended by a flight of steps, and surmounted by a species of altar, on which stood several abominable idols, to whom, the previous evening, five Indians had been sacrificed. Their dead bodies still lay there, ripped open, with the arms and legs chopped off, while everything near was

besmeared with blood. We contemplated this sight in utter astonishment, and gave this island the name of Isla de Sacrificios.[30]

Thus Bernal Díaz presents himself as personally having witnessed the dead bodies of five persons. The reason for the killing (and for the dismembering) is actually unknown, but the Spaniards immediately supposed that it had been a sacrifice. They even established and commemorated this in naming the place the "Island of Sacrifices".

The Spanish arrival at Isla de Sacrificios has also been described by Juan Díaz, who participated in Grijalva's expedition as chaplain. An Italian translation of his account, entitled 'Itinerario de l'armata del Re Catholico in India verso la isola de Iuchathan del anno MDXVIII', was included as an appendix in the *Itinerario de Ludovico de Varthema Bolognese*, published in Venice with the date 3 March 1520.[31]

> We all went ashore on this small island, which we called the Island of the Sacrifices: … we found some buildings of lime and sand, very large, and a piece of a building also of that material, made in the same way as an ancient arch that stands in Mérida, and another buildings with foundations of the height of two men, ten feet wide and very long; and another tower-shaped building, round, of fifteen paces wide, and on top it had marble like that of Castile, on which was an animal like a lion, also made of marble, which had a hole in the head in which they put the perfumes; and that lion had its tongue out of its mouth, and near it was a vessel of stone with blood, which might have been eight days old, and here were two poles of the height of a man, and among them there were some clothes made of silk similar to the Moorish almaizares; and on the other side there stood an idol with a feather on its head, with its face turned toward the above-mentioned stone, and behind this idol there was a large pile of stones; and between these poles, near the idol, were two dead Indians of young age wrapped in a painted blanket; and behind the cloth were two other dead Indians, who seemed to have been killed three days before, while the before-mentioned other two apparently were already dead for twenty days.

> Near these Indians and the idol there were many skulls and bones, and there were also many bundles of pine wood, and some large stones on which they killed the said Indians…

---

28   For a thorough, critical analysis of these early sources and their influence, see Solis Salcedo, *Sacrifices Humains*.

29   Díaz del Castillo *Memoirs*, ch. 3, 1844, 7.

30   Díaz del Castillo, *Memoirs*, ch. 13, 1844, 31.

31   Jiménez del Campo, 'Sobre el Itinerario'. The Italian text has been translated back into Spanish and both texts have been published by García Icazbalceta in his *Colección*.

When the captain and the people had seen this, he wanted to be informed if this had been done as sacrifice, and sent to the ships for an Indian who was from this province, the one who came to where the captain was, he suddenly passed out and fell on the road, thinking that they were taking him [there] to kill him.

Arrived at the mentioned tower the captain asked him, why was such a thing done in that tower, and the Indian replied that it was done as a form of sacrifice; and according to what was understood, they [the local inhabitants] cut the throats of people on that large stone, poured the blood into the vessel, and pulled out the heart from the chest, and burned it and offered it to that idol; they cut off the fleshy parts of the arms and legs and ate them; and that they did with their enemies with whom they were at war.[32]

We notice some interesting differences in these accounts, Bernal Díaz refers to the dismembered bodies of five persons, which (apparently) had been killed the evening before. Juan Díaz describes the place in more detail and mentions a vessel of stone with blood (not specifying whether it was human or animal blood), two youngsters who had already been dead for some twenty days and two others (adults?), who had been dead for three days (so in total four persons). Their bodies were wrapped in cloth and apparently not ripped open. There were also skulls and bones. In referring to the human remains Juan Díaz himself does not clarify the cause or circumstances of their death. But he does tell how the captain had the idea that this represented an act of sacrifice and interrogated a local person about that. The phrase 'according to what was understood' indicates that communication was problematic. Anyway, the Spaniards got the confirmation of what they suspected: a first description of human sacrifice (offering of the heart to the idol) and cannibalism. One starts wondering how much of their accounts was influenced by this pre-conceived notion.

A little later in his chronicle Bernál Díaz del Castillo gives a somewhat more detailed description of such sacrificial acts, now situated in the harbour town now known as San Juan de Ulua:

Here we found a temple on which stood the great and abominable-looking god Tetzcatlipuca, surrounded by four Indians, dressed in wide black cloaks, and with flying hair, in the same way as our canons or Dominicans wear it. These were priests, who had that very day sacrificed two boys, whose bodies they had ripped up, and then offered their bleeding hearts to the horrible idol. They were going to perfume us in the same way they had done their gods; and though it smelt like our incense, we would not suffer them, so shocked were we at the sight of the two boys whom they had recently murdered, and disgusted with their abominations. Our captain questioned the Indian Francisco whom we had brought with us from the Bandera stream as to what was meant by all this, for he seemed rather an intelligent person; having, at that time, as I have already stated, no interpreter, our captain put these questions to him by means of signs. Francisco returned for answer that this sacrifice had been ordered by the people of Culua; but, as it was difficult for him to pronounce this latter word, he kept continually saying Olua.[33]

Here Bernal Díaz mentions the name of the deity in question (Tezcatlipoca, the Burning and Smoking Mirror), which he probably introduces in retrospect. The communication was severely limited because of the lack of an interpreter, but he learned the names of indigenous Gods later during his stay in the Aztec capital. Again Bernal Díaz states that he himself saw the ripped up bodies – in this case of two boys. He attributes the killing to the four priests but has not seen the act himself. Interrogation through signs and words made the Spaniards think that the killing was a sacrifice that had happened on the orders of the people of Culua, *i.e.* the Aztecs who would become the main adversary once the expedition of Cortés was under way. All of this happened during an earlier reconnaissance trip that preceded the conquest campaign itself. We may suppose that such accounts coloured the expectations that the Spaniards still in Cuba had about the lands they were soon going to invade in search for gold.

Thus, we find here the beginning of an argument that the human sacrifices were an imposition of the Aztec empire (and therefore not something the local population really wanted to do). Later on, Bernal Díaz will confirm that human sacrifices took place first and foremost and continuously in the Aztec capital (Tenochtitlan) and that the ruler Motecuhzoma, generally known as Moctezuma or also Montezuma, was himself actively involved. We also find here the reference to the sacrifice of children (boys), which was particularly barbarian and in line with the alleged crimes of witches.

Even before describing the Spanish arrival in Tenochtitlan Bernal Díaz (with hindsight) observes the customs and plans of the Aztec monarch:

---

32 Juan Díaz, in García Icazbalceta, *Colección*.

33 Díaz del Castillo, *Memoirs*, ch. 14, 1844, 32.

These [deities] were named Tetzcatlipuca and Huitzilopochtli, the former being the god of hell and the latter the god of war, to whom Motecusuma daily sacrificed some young children, that they might disclose to him what he should do with us. His intention was to take us prisoners if we would not re-embark, and employ some to educate children, while others were to be sacrificed.[34]

The explicit accusation that Motecuhzoma was a murderer of children is connected to a speculation about his intentions, which, however, the Spanish author had no way of knowing. The theme of child sacrifice, which we know from the accusations of Romans against the early Christians and from the inquisitors' accusations against the alleged witches, is elaborated upon in the following statement about an expedition by one of the Spanish captains, Pedro de Alvarado:

Alvarado, during this expedition, visited some small townships which were subject to a greater one, called, in the Aculhua language, Costatlan. This language is that of Mexico and Motecusuma; and when we speak of persons of Aculhua, we must always understand subjects of his empire. Alvarado nowhere met with any inhabitants, but found sufficient proofs in the temples that boys and full-grown people had very recently been sacrificed; for the altars and walls were covered with drops of fresh blood. The flint knives with which the unfortunate victim's breast is cut open to tear the heart away, and the large stones on which they are sacrificed, still lay in their proper places. Most of the bodies thus seen by our men were without arms or legs, which, according to the accounts of the Indians, had been devoured. Our men were perfectly horror-struck at such barbarities: however, I will not waste another word on the subject, for we found the same thing over again in every district we visited in this country.[35]

Bernal Díaz himself did not participate in Alvarado's expedition but refers to what was "seen by our men" and what had occurred "according to the accounts of the Indians". Actually, Alvarado did not meet the locals but "found sufficient proofs". The sacrificial act is then described in more detail and qualified as "barbarity" which struck the Spaniards with "horror". The latter term sounds somewhat hypocritical if we think of the violent social reality of late medieval Spain.

Then Bernal Díaz stresses that the Spaniards found the same indications of manslaughter throughout the country: *"in every district we visited"*. Later he repeats:

... we marched on until we came to a small township, where a short time previous several human beings had been sacrificed. As the kind reader would be disgusted with hearing of the numbers of male and female Indians we found butchered along every road and in every village we passed through, I will be silent on that head... [36]

Clearly this theme had now become a generalisation, which makes it difficult to tell what and how much the author actually witnessed. At the same time Cortés made it a point to insist that the local rulers had to abandon these sacrifices immediately.

Cortes desired Doña Marina and Aguilar to acquaint him [the "fat cacique" of Cempoala] how grateful he was for so much kindness, and he had merely to inform him in what way he in return could be of service to him and his people. We were the vassals of the great emperor Charles, who had dominion over many kingdoms and countries, and who had sent us out to redress wrongs wherever we came, punish the bad, and make known his commands that human sacrifices should no longer be continued. To all this was added a good deal about our holy religion. After the fat cazique [local ruler] heard this he sighed deeply, and complained most bitterly about Motecusuma and his governors. It was not long ago that he had been subdued by the former, and robbed of all his golden trinkets. His sway was so excessively oppressive, that he durst not move without his orders; yet no one had sufficient courage to oppose him, as he possessed such vast towns and countries, such numbers of subjects and extensive armies. [37]

Again we see that the local rulers agreed quickly and blamed those bad customs on the oppression of the Aztec empire. The same picture is repeated in the next chapter:

While the first welcomings were going on it was announced to Cortes that the fat cazique of Sempoalla was approaching in a sedan, supported by numbers of distinguished Indians. Immediately upon his arrival he renewed his complaints against Motecusuma, in which he was joined by the cazique of this township and the other chief personages. He related so much of the cruelties and oppression they had to suffer,

34   Díaz del Castillo, *Memoirs*, ch. 41, 1844, 95.
35   Díaz del Castillo, *Memoirs*, ch. 44, 1844, 102.

36   Díaz del Castillo, *Memoirs*, ch. 44, 1844, 103.
37   Díaz del Castillo, *Memoirs*, ch. 45, 1844, 105.

and thereby sobbed and sighed so bitterly that we could not help being affected. At the time when they were subdued, they had already been greatly ill used; Motecusuma then demanded annually a great number of their sons and daughters, a portion of whom were sacrificed to the idols, and the rest were employed in his household and for tilling his grounds. His tax-gatherers took their wives and daughters without any ceremony if they were handsome, merely to satisfy their lusts.[38]

There is no way to prove or disprove this allegation. The Aztec tribute records in Codex Mendoza do not register that persons were rounded up to be sacrificed nor that women were kidnapped.[39] In such tribute records we rather find indications of services, such as weaving or other production activities.[40] It is also plausible that the tribute included local participation in bloodletting rituals and offerings to the Aztec deities. It is only logical that the local rulers would resent the Aztec tribute demands, as well as related religious impositions. But in the Spanish version everything may have become convoluted with a supposed obligation to deliver victims for human sacrifice. Anyway, it must have been clear to the local rulers that Cortés opposed the Aztec regime: this was an aspect they liked about him. Cortés, in turn, interpreted their welcoming reaction as a formal acceptance of Spanish rule.

The caziques and papas [priests] of Tzinpantzinco, with other inhabitants of the surrounding neighbourhood, having witnessed this act of justice, and seeing altogether how friendly Cortes was disposed, and the good deeds which he manifested, were the more susceptible of the things he told them about our holy religion, – respecting the abolishment of their human sacrifices and kidnapping, the discontinuation of other abominations and obscenities, with other matters salutary to their well being. They appeared so well inclined that they assembled the inhabitants of the surrounding districts, and formally declared themselves vassals of the emperor, our master. On this occasion, likewise, numerous complaints were made against Motecusuma, which all terminated with instances of his oppression similar to what we had heard from the Sempoallans and Quiahuitzlans.[41]

Bernal Díaz again stresses the continuous practice of human sacrifice directly related to anthropophagy, always in the same stereotypical manner:

Indeed, hardly a day passed by that these people did not sacrifice from three to four, and even five Indians, tearing the hearts out of their bodies, to present them to the idols and smear the blood on the walls of the temple. The arms and legs of these unfortunate beings were then cut off and devoured, just in the same way we should fetch meat from a butcher's shop and eat it: indeed I even believe that human flesh is exposed for sale cut up, in their tiangues, or markets.[42]

The addition "I even believe" indicates again that this rather drastic image is to a large extent based on the conquistador's speculation.

This is a crucial moment: it coincides with the redaction of Cortés' first letter (carta de relación), which obviously posed the challenge to justify the unjustifiable. As is well known, Cortés and his men had left for Mexico on their own initiative, without proper authorisation. They were now getting involved in nothing less than a full military attack on another country. As the realm they were invading was clearly a well-developed urban state, much richer in gold, art and resources than the Antilles, such an unprovoked aggression was bound to produce even more public and intellectual criticism (and problems for the Majesties' conscience) than the Spanish annexation and ruthless exploitation of the Antillean islands. In 1511, in a famous political sermon on Hispaniola, the Dominican friar Antonio de Montesinos had openly criticized the right of the Spaniards to conquer these lands and enslave and oppress its population. This led to soul-searching of the king and to the promulgation of the Laws of Burgos (1512), which in theory would recognise some minimal rights of the native inhabitants.

This critical milieu must have caused some serious headaches to Cortés in drafting his letters to the Royal Majesties. How to justify his position – and that of the Spanish authorities themselves? In the case of the Antilles the allegation of cannibalism had proved to be an excellent argument for making Spanish interference acceptable, so it could be used again in the case of the Aztec empire, but it might seem somewhat overused and certainly needed some expansion and reinforcement. Cortés found the following solution: connecting cannibalism to an even more dramatic and horrifying sign of diabolic presence: the human sacrifice. In his first letter he made the following argument:

---

38   Díaz del Castillo, *Memoirs*, ch. 46, 1844, 107.
39   Clark, *Codex Mendoza*.
40   See for example the manuscript of Tecomaxtlahuaca (Jansen, *Gran Familia*, ch. 2) or the Codex of Yanhuitlan (Jansen and Pérez Jiménez, *Mixtec Pictorial Manuscripts*, ch. 10).
41   Díaz del Castillo, *Memoirs*, ch. 51, 1844, 118.

42   Díaz del Castillo, *Memoirs*, ch. 51, 1844, 119-112.

They have another custom, horrible, and abominable, and deserving punishment, and which we have never before seen in any other place, and it is this, that, as often as they have anything to ask of their idols, in order that their petition may be more acceptable, they take many boys or girls, and even grown men and women, and in the presence of those idols they open their breasts, while they are alive, and take out the hearts and entrails, and bum the said entrails and hearts before the idols, offer that smoke in sacrifice to them.

Some of us who have seen this say that it is the most terrible and frightful thing to behold that has ever been seen. So frequently, and so often do these Indians do this, according to our information, and partly by what we have seen in the short time we are in this country, that no year passes in which they do not kill and sacrifice fifty souls in each mosque [temple]; and this is practised, and held as customary, from the Isle of Cozumel to the country in which we are now settled. Your Majesties may rest assured that, according to the size of the land, which to us seems very considerable, and the many mosques which they have, there is no year, as far as we have until now discovered and seen, when they do not kill and sacrifice in this manner some three or four thousand souls.

Now let Your Royal Highnesses consider if they ought not to prevent so great an evil and crime, and certainly God, Our Lord, will be well pleased, if, through the command of Your Royal Highnesses, these peoples should be initiated and instructed in our Very Holy Catholic Faith, and the devotion, faith, and hope, which they have in their idols, be transferred to the Divine Omnipotence of God; because it is certain, that, if they served God with the same faith, and fervour, and diligence, they would surely work miracles.[43]

In other words, it was Divine Providence that justified and dictated the conquest: the Catholic majesties were called upon by God himself to combat the influence of the devil and therefore just had to take over (invade and conquer) the "newly discovered" lands. At the same time, by attributing this custom to the Aztec domination Cortés further constructed the idea of an "evil empire" against which all (in principle "good") subject communities wanted to rebel: they were just waiting for the Spaniards to "liberate" them. Cortés involved his whole army of conquistadors in this complot:

Cortes spoke a long time to us upon the subject; he brought many holy and useful lessons to our mind, and observed that we could do nothing which would be more beneficial to this people, and more to the glory of God, than to abolish this idolatry with its human sacrifices.[44]

The fact that he needed such a long speech, suggests that Cortés indeed had to inculcate in his men a specific vision of the surrounding world and their "mission". It is here, we suspect, that the notion of the human sacrifice was fully developed as the essential justification and motivation for the conquest of the Aztec empire. Logically from now on the prohibition of these sacrifices becomes a recurrent topic in Cortés' rhetoric:

Doña Marina and Aguilar [the interpreters] told the inhabitants a good deal about our holy religion, and how we were subjects of the emperor Don Carlos the Fifth, who sent us out to bring them back from kidnapping and sacrificing human beings.[45]

The conquistadors understood that the political dimension of their success depended completely on the vision / representation of the "Other", *i.e.* the Aztecs, as inhuman barbarians who indulged in sacrificing people to the demons and in eating them. Simultaneously Cortés used the human sacrifice as a threat to manipulate and convince his men to participate in the act of war, which now had become inevitable. The argument was extra attractive as it also motivated the Spaniards to be alert and fight well in order not to fall victim to that horrible sacrifice themselves.

They had calculated, he [Cortés] said [to his troops], that we had already lost fifty-five of our men since our departure from Cuba. Neither did we know how matters stood with our garrison at Vera Cruz. Though the Almighty had everywhere granted us victory, it was merely out of the abundance of his mercy towards us. It was not right to calculate too long upon his mercy and forbearance, for that would be tempting him. The pitcher goes to the well until it is broken, and one morning or other we should undoubtedly be sacrificed to the idols.[46]

The rulers of Tlaxcala, a state that had been able to defend itself successfully against Aztec expansion, were probably informed beforehand of the Spanish antagonism towards the Aztecs. Having a common enemy, they welcomed the

---

43   Cortés, *First letter*, 1908: 163-164; We quote the English translation by Francis Augustus MacNutt (1908).

44   Díaz del Castillo, *Memoirs*, ch. 51, 1844, 120.
45   Díaz del Castillo, *Memoirs*, ch. 61, 1844, 139.
46   Díaz del Castillo, *Memoirs*, ch. 69.

Spaniards with open arms. Cortés repeated his position in order to win this people as an ally:

> Cortes answered, by means of our interpreters, that he was desirous of making peace, not war, which he had already made known to them. He was come into their country to beg of them, in the name of our Lord Jesus Christ, and of our great emperor Don Carlos, to abstain from human sacrifices. We were all human beings made of flesh and bone like themselves, and not teules [deities], but Christians. We killed no one, excepting when we were attacked, then, indeed, we destroyed our enemies, whether it happened to be day or night.[47]

Bernal Díaz repeatedly quotes Cortés speaking in similar terms to the local rulers (caciques) – and of course also to his own emperor and home front:

> I have no other reason than that I am bound first to fulfil my duty to the God whom we adore, and to the emperor our master, which is to require of you to abolish your idols, the human sacrifices, and other abominations practised among you, and exhort you to believe in him in whom we believe, who alone is the true God.[48]

The Spanish position is then connected with a promise of benefits. Choosing for or against the Spaniards becomes an existential and ethical choice between good and evil, heaven and hell:

> They [the local lords] must abandon their horrible idols, and believe in the Lord God whom we adore. They would soon discover the beneficial effect of this; blessings would be showered down upon them, the seasons would be fruitful, and all their undertakings would prosper; after death their souls would be transplanted to heaven, and partake of eternal glory; for, by the human sacrifices which they made to their idols, who were nothing but devils, they would be led to hell, where eternal fire would torment their souls.[49]

Arriving in the Aztec capital Tenochtitlan, Cortés made the same point to Motecuhzoma. Bernal Díaz suspected that human flesh – that of young children – must have been served at the banquets of that monarch:

> Above 300 kinds of dishes were served up for Motecusuma's dinner from his kitchen, underneath which were placed pans of porcelain filled with fire, to keep them warm. Three hundred dishes of various kinds were served up for him alone, and above 1000 for the persons in waiting. He sometimes, but very seldom, accompanied by the chief officers of his household, ordered the dinner himself, and desired that the best dishes and various kinds of birds should be called over to him. We were told that the flesh of young children, as a very dainty bit, was also set before him sometimes by way of a relish. Whether there was any truth in this we could not possibly discover; on account of the great variety of dishes, consisting in fowls, turkeys, pheasants, partridges, quails, tame and wild geese, venison, musk swine, pigeons, hares, rabbits, and of numerous other birds and beasts; besides which there were various other kinds of provisions, indeed it would have been no easy task to call them all over by name. This I know, however, for certain, that after Cortes had reproached him for the human sacrifices and the eating of human flesh, he issued orders that no dishes of that nature should again be brought to his table.[50]

There is no way of telling if what was told to the Spaniards about human flesh being served was a reality or rather a misunderstanding or even a joke. The conquistador recognises this explicitly. Anyway, a text like this illustrates that in principle there was no lack of protein in Mesoamerica.

In the ceremonial centre of Tenochtitlan the issue of human sacrifice came up again, of course. Bernal Díaz reports several details. Speaking about the Templo Mayor:

> Around Huitzilopochtli's neck were figures representing human faces and hearts made of gold and silver, and decorated with blue stones. In front of him stood several perfuming pans with copal, the incense of the country; also the hearts of three Indians, who had that day been slaughtered, were now consuming before him as a burnt-offering. Every wall of this chapel and the whole floor had become almost black with human blood, and the stench was abominable...

> This platform was altogether covered with a variety of hellish objects, – large and small trumpets, huge slaughtering knives, and burnt hearts of Indians who had been sacrificed: everything clotted with coagulated blood, cursed to the sight, and creating

---

47   Díaz del Castillo, *Memoirs*, ch. 70, 1844, 166

48   Díaz del Castillo, *Memoirs*, ch. 77, 1844, 180.

49   Díaz del Castillo, *Memoirs*, ch. 77, 1844, 181.

50   Díaz del Castillo, *Memoirs*, ch. 91, 1844, 229.

horror in the mind. Besides all this, the stench was everywhere so abominable that we scarcely knew how soon to get away from this spot of horrors.[51]

I cannot, however, pass by in silence a kind of small tower standing in its immediate vicinity, likewise containing idols. I should term it a temple of hell; for at one of its doors stood an open-mouthed dragon armed with huge teeth, resembling a dragon of the infernal regions, the devourer of souls. There also stood near this same door other figures resembling devils and serpents, and not far from this an altar encrusted with blood grown black, and some that had recently been spilt. In a building adjoining this we perceived a quantity of dishes and basins, of various shapes. These were filled with water and served to cook the flesh in of the unfortunate beings who had been sacrificed; which flesh was eaten by the papas. Near to the altar were lying several daggers, and wooden blocks similar to those used by our butchers for hacking meat on.[52]

The serpent in Mesoamerican art is a symbol of the liminal sphere in which the deities dwell. For the Spaniards, however, the use of this image was proof that the devil was present in all of this. Again we note: the conquistador just sees vessels in a temple, but thinks they serve for cooking flesh. Similarly he sees knives and wooden blocks and understands them as butchers' knives, in this context as knives for making human sacrifices.

According to Bernal Díaz, the religious difference was the central cause of distancing between Motecuhzoma and Cortés. When both visited the Templo Mayor, Cortés again brought up the subject, but:

Motecusuma knew what the image of the Virgin Mary was, yet he was very much displeased with Cortes' offer, and replied, in presence of two papas, whose anger was not less conspicuous, 'Malinche, could I have conjectured that you would have used such reviling language as you have just done, I would certainly not have shown you my gods. In our eyes these are good divinities: they preserve our lives, give us nourishment, water, and good harvests, healthy and growing weather, and victory whenever we pray to them for it. Therefore we offer up our prayers to them, and make them sacrifices. I earnestly beg of you not to say another word to insult the profound veneration in which we hold these gods'.[53]

The issue became the ground for Cortés' daring action to overtake the temple and later to take Motecuhzoma prisoner:

Thus determined, Cortes, accompanied by seven officers and soldiers, repaired to Motecusuma, and spoke to him as follows: 'Great monarch, I have already so many times begged of you to abolish those false idols by whom you are so terribly deluded, and no longer to sacrifice human beings to them; and yet these abominations are continued daily: I have, therefore, come to you now, with these officers, to beg permission of you to take away these idols from the temple, and place in their stead the holy Virgin and the cross. The whole of my men feel determined to pull down your idols, even should you be averse to it; and you may well suppose that one or other of your papas will become the victim'.[54]

Cortés effectively took Motecuhzoma prisoner and argued several times with him to give up his sacrifices, but without success:

Motecusuma readily agreed to this, as he did in everything else we desired, save the sacrificing of human beings, which nothing could induce him to abolish; day after day were those abominations committed: Cortes remonstrated with him in every possible way, but with so little effect, that at last he deemed it proper to take some decided step in the matter. But the great difficulty was to adopt a measure by which neither the inhabitants nor the priesthood would be induced to rise up in arms. We, however, came to the determination, in a meeting called for the purpose, to throw down the idols from the top of Huitzilopochtli's temple; and should the Mexicans rise up in arms for their defence, then to content ourselves by demanding permission to build an altar on one side of the platform, and erect thereon the image of the holy Virgin with the cross.[55]

In his second letter, directed to the King of Spain (Charles V), Cortés also reports how he immediately banned the sacrifices in the Aztec capital and realm:

Montezuma and many chiefs of the city remained with me until the idols were taken away and the chapels cleansed, and the images put up, and they all wore happy faces. I forbade them to sacrifice human beings to the idols, as they were accustomed to do, for besides its being very hateful to God, Your Majesty had

---

51   Díaz del Castillo, *Memoirs*, ch. 92, 1844, 239-240.
52   Díaz del Castillo, *Memoirs*, ch. 92, 1844, 242.
53   Díaz del Castillo, *Memoirs*, ch. 92, 1844, 240.

54   Díaz del Castillo, *Memoirs*, ch. 107, 1844, 285.
55   Díaz del Castillo, *Memoirs*, ch. 107, 1844, 284-285.

also prohibited it by your laws, and commanded that those who killed should be put to death. Henceforth they abolished it, and, in all the time I remained in the city, never again were they seen to sacrifice any human creature.[56]

This last phrase ("y en todo el tiempo que yo estuve en la dicha ciudad, nunca se vio matar ni sacrificar criatura alguna") is illuminating. Cortés not only used the human sacrifice as justification, but also anticipated the absence of evidence that was going to be observed later, by explaining that all traces had been removed precisely because of his – Cortés' – pious dedication to the good cause and his drastic and effective prohibition of this practice!

When we combine all these testimonies stemming from memories of the first hour, we come to the following reconstruction. Texts such as the book about the travels of John of Mandeville and the *Malleus Maleficarum* had prepared the Spaniards to expect that the peoples in that exotic land were likely to indulge in cannibalism and bloody sacrifice. When they found remains of persons that had been killed in a temple they interpreted that as evidence for anthropophagy, and, as those bodies were lying in front of "idols", they interpreted the killing itself as a human sacrifice, *i.e.* an act that purely served to venerate and feed the "demons". The Spaniards needed very little to confirm their pre-understandings, stemming from previous fanciful literature: they simply saw their suspicions fulfilled and were furthermore motivated to see things this way because of the colonial propaganda of their leaders. They did not try to obtain additional information from the locals in order to understand the sacrifice as such but only to find out who had ordered such a horrible act. From the difficult communications (by signs and through two interpreters) the Spaniards gathered that the culprits were the Culhua, *i.e.* the Aztecs. Cortés declared the human sacrifice in combination with cannibalism as the main reason and fundament for the enterprise of conquest. This resulted in a general tacit understanding of all conquistadors – and of the Spaniards who arrived after them – that they had to emphasize those practices as an integral part of the ancient Mexican culture, in order to legitimise the oppression and elimination of that culture.

This analysis concurs with the statement of friar Bartolomé de Las Casas, who already observed that the Spanish stories about human sacrifices were fabrications in order to excuse, *i.e.* justify, the crimes of the conquistadors themselves:

As for this allegation that they sacrificed humans and ate them, as Gómara says, I believe that there is no truth in it, because in that realm of Yucatán I always heard that there were no human sacrifices, nor was it known what it was to eat human flesh, and the statement of Gómara, who did not see nor hear it, but got it from the mouth of Cortés, his master, who maintained him, has little authority, as it is in his favour and an excuse for his crimes; this is from the talk of the Spaniards and from those who wrote down their horrible deeds, to defame all these nations to excuse the violence, cruelties, robberies and massacres that they have perpetrated, and that every day and even today they continue to do.[57]

7.4. Missionary elaborations

Our main written source on the Aztec world is the work of the Franciscan friar Bernardino de Sahagún, who arrived in "New Spain" in 1529, some eight years after the consummation of the conquest. He started his formal research for this work some thirty years after his arrival and the completion of two successive versions (known as the *Primeros Memoriales* and the *Florentine Codex* or *Historia General de las Cosas de la Nueva España* respectively) took him some twenty-five years. This encyclopaedic work is written in the Aztec language (Nahuatl), which gives it a unique importance and flavour of authenticity, the reason that he is often hailed as the father of Mexican ethnography. Indeed it records many traditional data, customs and ideas. But in composing this book, Sahagún was mainly assisted by young members of the native nobility that were already converted to Catholicism and were strongly committed to the new religion (connected to the ideology of the colonizers).[58] By the time the Franciscan friar started this project, the conviction that the pre-colonial culture included a lot of human sacrifice and cannibalism had become engrained

---

56   Cortés, *Second letter*, 1908, 261-262.

57   Las Casas, *Historia de las Indias*, vol. III, cap. 117, 427, cited by Hassler, 108. This testimony is relevant because Las Casas based this statement on his personal acquaintance with the Maya people. In his work *Apologética Historia* he recognised the existence of human sacrifice among the Aztecs, probably because he followed and transcribed the descriptions by the Franciscan friar Toribio de Benavente Motolinia (Silva Tena, 'Sacrificio Humano'). Las Casas tried to rationalise and justify that form of sacrifice by pointing towards the wide distribution of this practice among many of the world's cultures and to the freedom of conscience (Zuluaga Hoyos, 'Discusión sobre el Canibalismo'; Lantigua, 'Religion within the Limits').

58   We agree with Restall, who in his erudite and innovative book *When Montezuma met Cortés* offers a critical view of Sahagún's work as a "quasi indigenous source", which "was misleadingly read for most of the twentieth century as an authentic Aztec or even "Indian" view of the Conquest".

in everyone's mind and kept everybody under its dramatic spell. Later Spanish interviews with indigenous Mesoamerican religious specialists continued to suffer from the complexities and difficulties of intercultural communication. If some indigenous elder dared to contradict this mainstream image in conversation, he would run the risk of being considered a sympathizer with pre-colonial (evil) paganism, a dissident in denial, so he would probably prefer to keep silent.

Moreover we find some indications that the Franciscan friar consciously misrepresented the facts. For example the first version of Sahagún's work, the *Primeros Memoriales*, summarises how during the month of *Cuauitleua* offerings were made to the Rain Gods: "the children died – they were called *tlacateteuhmê* – there on the mountain tops".[59] The term *tlacateteuhmê* (singular: *tlaca-teteuitl*) refers to anthropomorphic figures cut out of native paper (*amate*). We understand this by studying the ongoing traditional practice in the Sierra de Puebla, e.g. in the Hñahñu (Otomí) village of San Pablito near Pahuatlan: images of plant spirits or other deities are cut out of *amate* paper for agricultural rituals or curing ceremonies (fig. 7.6).[60]

In other words the so-called "children" were paper figures, which "died", *i.e.* were offered and ceremonially disposed of. But the final version of Sahagún's work, the *Florentine Codex*, gives a much more explicitly bloody and sensational image of the *Cuauitleua* feast:

> In this month they slew many children; they sacrificed them in many places upon the mountain tops, tearing from them their hearts, in honor of the gods of water, so that these might give them water or rain. The children whom they slew they decked in rich finery to take them to be killed; and they carried them in litters upon their shoulders... When they took the children to be slain, if they wept and shed many tears, those who carried them rejoiced, for they took it as an omen that they would have much rain that year.[61]

It is clear what happened: the first version describes a local tradition in which paper figures were used as offerings. Sahagún's aim was to convince the Spanish king of the awful and inhuman character of the Mesoamerican religion, so that he would send more (preferably Franciscan) missionaries to combat the persistence of the "idolatry". In the final version, therefore, he and his co-workers made the text

Figure 7.6 Contemporary paper figure of the Lord of the Mountain.

into a dramatically "embellished" testimony of the murder of innocent children to honour the pagan gods. In this way, Mesoamerican religion would be perceived as just another variant of the demonic practices of witches (to whom the *Malleus Maleficarum* also attributed the killing of children).

In a similar vein the Franciscan friar Juan de Torquemada (ca. 1562-1624) describes in his *Monarquía Indiana* (Book 2) that the plaster of the temple of Quetzalcoatl in Cholula consisted of chalk mixed with the blood of young children (of two or three years old), which had been sacrificed for this purpose.[62] Torquemada wrote his monumental work at the beginning of the 17th Century – needless to say: completely out of touch with the pre-colonial building techniques. Most likely this is a sensationalist misinterpretation of the red painted plaster that was widely used in Mesoamerica – abundantly present, for example, in Teotihuacan.

---

59 Jiménez Moreno, *Primeros Memoriales*, 19.

60 Jansen and Leyenaar, *Amate-geesten*. Cf. Christensen and Martí, *Witchcraft*; Sandstrom, *Corn is our Blood*. Sahagún himself mentions the ritual use of paper-cut figures in the *Florentine Codex* (Book IX, ch. 3).

61 Sahagún, *Florentine Codex*, Book II, ch.1; Cf. Jansen and Pérez Jiménez, *Mixtec Pictorial Manuscripts*, 269-270.

---

62 Torquemada mentions this idea in the context of the attack on the Spanish conquistadors when they passed through Cholula – see also McCafferty, *Cholula Massacre*.

Figure 7.7 The sacrifice of a Tree Spirit in front of the Temple of Heaven (inside which priests perform a bloodletting ritual), in Codex Yoalli Ehecatl (Borgia), p. 33. After: Anders, Jansen and Reyes García, *Templos del Cielo*.

Figure 7.8 The colonial representation of the inauguration of the Aztec main temple (Codex Telleriano-Remensis, p. 39). After: Quiñones Keber, *Codex Telleriano-Remensis*.

Sahagún does inform us that the Aztecs also sacrificed (indeed: "beheaded" and "killed") images of paste or dough. This may have led to a metaphoric use of sacrificial terminology also in other cases, which, however, in little-informed and biased descriptions from an outsider perspective, all became qualified as real bloody sacrifice.[63]

The same interpretive challenge can still be experienced today when studying enigmatic scenes in pre-colonial religious manuscripts. A fascinating example is the central chapter (the "Temple Scenes") of Codex Yoalli Ehecatl (Borgia), 29-47.[64] Here we find many ritual elements, which would be categorized as "objects" in western thought, represented as animated beings. For example, on page 30 we see Trees represented as Spirits (in a way that is comparable to the paper figures of San Pablito that represent Plant Spirits). On pages 33-34 priests sacrifice a Tree Spirit in front of the Temple of Heaven (fig. 7.7). Probably what is meant is the cutting and chopping of wood for the kindling of the (new) fire in the temple and for the meals that have to be prepared for the participants in the rituals. Still today, people in the Mixtec region after cutting a tree will put a stone on the trunk to keep the heart (life) inside.

In filling in the image of ancient human sacrifice, the various colonial authors outrivaled each other in giving high numbers of persons killed and eaten. Modern authors generally place less emphasis on the cannibalistic aspect and consider the amount of victims "exaggerated" (as these are indeed unrealistic). The term "exaggeration" is actually not an apt one because it would imply that the colonial authors had some notion of the real number, while in fact, the large majority of them had never been present at those acts, had never seen the victims and thus could not have been able to count them! So we should not treat these numbers as historical facts, not even as exaggerated ones, but as *imaginations* that were part of colonial propaganda.

We can reconstruct the procedure taking as an example the inauguration of the extension and renewal of the Main Temple (Templo Mayor) in the Year 8 Reed (1487 CE). The early-colonial sources give different numbers of individuals sacrificed on that occasion. Friar Diego Durán, for example, speaks of 80,400 victims, which sounds quite impossible when we think of the practical conditions and the time needed. Obviously, no Spaniards had been present on that occasion and only a few indigenous eyewitnesses would have still been alive in the mid 16th century.

Figure 7.9 The Dedication Stone of the Aztec main temple. After: Seler, *Gesammelte Abhandlungen.*

The Codex Telleriano-Remensis and its later copy Codex Vaticanus A depict the event.[65] The Spanish commentary of Codex Telleriano-Remensis, p. 39, says that in the year 1487 the construction or rather enlargement of the Templo Mayor of Mexico was finished and that the old men say that 4000 men were sacrificed in that year, assembled from the provinces that had been subjugated through war. The corresponding pictorial text (fig. 7.8) shows the new fire that was kindled in the Templo Mayor and the presence of the Aztec ruler Ahuizotl and three men approaching. The ethnic identity of these three men is registered in the painting by specific signs accompanying them: Mazatecs (identified by the head of a deer, standing for *mazatl*, "deer") combined with the people of Xiuhcoac ("Place of the Turquoise Serpent"), as well as Tlapanecs (from Tlapa, "Red Place") and Zapotecs (identified by a *zapote* tree). All three are attired with white down-balls

---

63   Jiménez Moreno, *Primeros Memoriales*, 58.

64   See Anders, Jansen and Reyes García, *Templos del Cielo* and our new interpretation of the chapter in question (Jansen and Pérez Jiménez, *Time and the Ancestors*, 431-530).

65   For an edition of the Codex Telleriano-Remensis with commentary see the publication by Quiñones Keber (1995). For the Codex Vaticanus A see the edition and commentary by Anders and Jansen (1996).

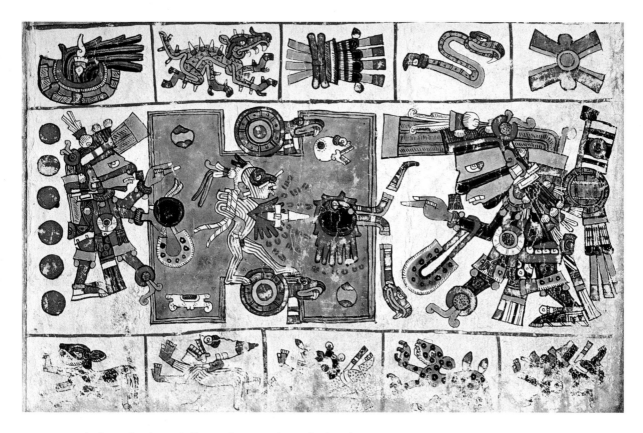

Figure 7.10 A bad time for playing ball, according to Codex Yoalli Ehecatl (Borgia), p. 21.

on the head and a vertical black band through the eye, while holding a white banner. These signs are indeed associated with ritualised killing.[66] Next to these men is a number. Ten hair-like signs, each of which stands for 400 (*tzontli* is "hair" and "400"), represents a quantity of 4,000 in total (as read in the Spanish text). Added to that are two incense bags (*xiquimilli*), each standing for the number 8,000, making a total of 2 x 8,000 + 4,000 = 20,000. So, reading the Spanish and the pictorial text together, one might conclude that this source indicates that 20,000 Mazatecs, Xiuhcoac people, Tlapanecs and Zapotecs were sacrificed at the inauguration of the Templo Mayor.

Interestingly, there is a stone monument dating from the event itself: the so-called Dedication or Inaugural Stone from the Aztec Templo Mayor (fig. 7.9).[67] It contains the Year 8 Reed (which corresponds to 1487) and a scene in which the Aztec rulers Tizoc and Ahuitzotl are shown offering their blood in self-sacrifice to Earth. Both are identified by their name signs: the perforated leg is to be read as Tizoc, whose name means "He who perforates (in autosacrifice)", including a phonetic complement *xo(tl)*, "leg", and the water animal is read as *ahuizotl*.

The Codex Telleriano-Remensis clarifies that Tizoc had died in the previous year, 7 Rabbit (1486), by presenting a painting of his mortuary bundle with a corresponding explanatory alphabetic text. It was his successor Ahuizotl who in the next year inaugurated the temple, but mentions the deceased ruler on the monument to honour his work and devotion. On the Dedication Stone there is no mention of sacrificed subjugated peoples at all, just the rulers themselves and their respect for the Powers of Nature and the Ancestors.

This very different historical testimony from the period and the protagonists themselves compels us to critically re-examine the later colonial version. It is quite plausible that captives from the wars of Ahuizotl's imperial expansion into the State of Oaxaca were executed on the occasion of that ruler's inauguration of the Templo Mayor, but their number does not seem to have been important at the time and seems to be a later reconstruction: 4,000 and 20,000 are general round numbers in the Mesoamerican vigesimal system. Technically speaking, even the reference of the pictorial text of Codex Telleriano-Remensis is not straightforward: the actual killing of the persons is not shown, only their arrival "dressed to be sacrificed", which could be a ritual demonstration of surrender, rather than a mass execution.

---

66 See for example Codex Vaticanus A, f 54v, and Codex Añute (Selden), p. 8-I/II.

67 For publication and interpretation of the Dedication or Inaugural Stone see Seler, *Gesammelte Abhandlungen* (vol. II, 766), and Nicholson and Quiñones Keber, *Art of Aztec Mexico*, 52-55.

Something similar happens with the representation of sacrificial acts in the religious codices. These manuscripts have mostly mantic (divinatory) contents: the depicted acts are not descriptions of acts that are actually taking place but prognostications and warnings. In Codex Yoalli Ehecatl (Borgia), p. 21, for example we see the image of a bound person (captive) being killed in a ball court. This does not register a custom of sacrificing people in ball courts but is a divinatory sign, warning that in this particular period of the calendar violent death may occur (fig. 7.10).[68]

Another interesting case is the representation of an eclipse in the last image of Codex Mictlan (Laud), p. 24. The God of Death is blowing darkness on to the precious disc of the Sun God; at the same time he is killing a white man (fig. 7.11). The scene is explained by information from early-colonial sources about the sacrifice of albinos on the occasion of an eclipse.

> When an eclipse occurred, they make great and fear-inspiring sacrifices (especially if it was a solar eclipses), because they thought that they were going to be destroyed, as they did not yet understand the secret of nature. And they searched for all the white or hairless men and women that they could find, and those they killed and sacrificed to appease the sun. With this act they seemed to recall the death of their gods by the sun... They shouted and screamed loudly at the occasion of a solar eclipse, and equally when an eclipse of the moon happened, or when they saw some other signal or comet in the sky, though not so much as in the case of an eclipse of the sun.[69]

The context of Codex Mictlan suggests, however, that the image has a mantic meaning, which, in turn, points to another possible understanding of Mendieta's colonial text. The mantic genre implies that the meaning of the image is that an eclipse (particularly in the associated time periods) is dangerous for "white and hairless men": the Death God might kill them. In the hostile interpretation by the friar – again: several decades after the end of the pre-colonial period and without a fair intercultural communication – the mantic prediction was transformed into a statement about a supposed practice, suggesting that on the occasion of an eclipse all albinos were rounded up and massacred, while in fact it was most likely a general warning for the population at large about what might happen to some people because of (divine) natural forces.

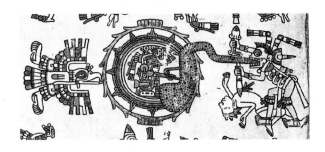

Figure 7.11 The solar eclipse as a death-bringing omen, according to Codex Mictlan (Laud), p. 24.

The image conjured by Sahagún and other colonial sources is not without consequences. It has become a pre-understanding for interpreting Mesoamerican society. Historian Matthew Restall, specialized in the matter, has very well analysed the situation:

> ... the supposed evidence for characterizing Aztec life as built around rituals of slaughter and cannibalism is another example of confirmation bias... Conquistadors and Franciscans, theologians and chroniclers, all seeking to justify some aspect or another of the Spanish invasions, conquests, colonization, and campaigns of conversion, repeated the same denunciations of the Aztecs so many times that they became fact. After several generations, the distortions and lies were widely believed; there was nobody to argue against them. Even the indigenous elite, based on their contributions to Sahagún's great Historia (the Florentine Codex), seemed to believe them (after all, they were now Christians too).[70]

Ancient Mexican visual representations of the act of killing by stabbing a person in the chest are now generally immediately read as human sacrifice, without questioning, which confirms further the idea that such sacrifice was an omnipresent practice. This determines the way Mexican citizens, as well as many tourists and even modern archaeologists still look at the Templo Mayor in Mexico City and at Mesoamerican temple pyramids in general, namely that their main function was that of a place for human sacrifice. In line with this preconceived image and Cortesian lens all artefacts, found at these sites, are understood in this sense: all knives are sacrificial knives, all altars functioned for human sacrifice etc. The site museum of the Templo Mayor, the permanent exposition of Aztec culture in the Museo Nacional de Antropología, and many other archaeological exhibits in the country confirm and promote the same idea.

68   See the edition and commentary by Anders, Jansen and Reyes García, *Templos del Cielo.*

69   Mendieta, *Historia Eclesiástica Indiana*, 101.

70   Restall, *When Montezuma met Cortés*, 88-89.

Consequently many aspects of Aztec iconography are still today generally interpreted as elements of human sacrifice, which reinforces the already established stereotype. A key example is the famous statue of Coatlicue, "She with the Skirt of Serpents".[71] Her name and the presence of many serpents surrounding her are in Mesoamerican terms clearly a metaphoric image of Mother Earth, but evoke to the Christian mind associations with the devil. More specifically, she wears a necklace consisting of hearts and hands, which are in this same paradigm easily interpreted as coming from victims of human sacrifice. However a statement by friar Diego Durán, in a different context, clarifies that during the rite of the month Huey Pachtli the priests dressed in robes that were "painted and decorated with some hearts and hands (with opened handpalms), a sign that meant that with their hands and heart they asked for a good harvest, because it was already the time..." (Durán, *Ritos*: ch. 16). In other words: the necklace of hands and hearts on the Goddess symbolizes a Mesoamerican prayer.

Similarly, sculptures of skulls and other images of death, for example, are immediately supposed to refer to the killing of people in human sacrifice, but modern research suggests that such images may in fact be references to Ancestor worship, which was widespread and important in Mesoamerica.[72]

This makes us also question the meaning of the *tzompantli*, the skull rack or skull altar. On his way to Tlaxcala Bernal Díaz already noted the existence of such monuments:

One certain spot in this township I never shall forget, situated near the temple. Here a vast number of human skulls were piled up in the best order imaginable,--there must have been more than 100,000; I repeat, more than 100,000. In like manner you saw the remaining human bones piled up in order in another corner of the square; these it would have been impossible to count. Besides these, there were human heads hanging suspended from beams on both sides. Three papas stood sentinel on this place of skulls, for which purpose, it was told us, they were particularly appointed. Similar horrible sights we saw towards the interior of the country in every township, and even in Tlascalla.[73]

The most famous *tzompantli* was standing in the Aztec capital, close to the Templo Mayor. Recently (2015) archaeologists discovered its remains. Such skull altars are often interpreted as containing the remains of those who were killed in human sacrifices. Obviously the late medieval Europeans understood this exhibition of skulls as similar to the practice in their own culture of beheading criminals or adversaries (as capital punishment) and then placing their heads on spikes. But actually it still has to be established whether this Aztec monument was indeed some triumphal display of trophy heads taken from slain enemies or if it had a different meaning, for example as a place for worship of dead Ancestors. The description of Codex Vaticanus A suggests the latter:

This was the place where they put all the heads and skulls of the lords who had died in war... this was kept in so much reverence that they called it in their language tlatzolli tzon pantli [tlaçotli tzompantli], wich means: precious or desired death, because even the Devil wanted to have his martyrs, of which the Psalmist speaks, and had convinced them that only those who died in war were going to heaven. And unhappy those people and unlucky the souls of all those others, because they had no remedy but to go to hell, and therefore everyone wanted to die such a death. But here they put the heads of those who were killed, almost like relics, as we have those of Saints in the sanctuaries and churches.[74]

The Nahuatl expression *tlaço(tli) tzompantli* means something like "appreciated or loved place of heads". Clearly this text suggests that it preserved and exhibited the remains of loved ones, as a revered monument of relics, an altar for (collective) Ancestor worship and devotion, anticipating the present-day custom of making altars for the Days of the Dead (October 31 – November 2), which are still an important part of Mesoamerican ritual.

7.5. Ritualised execution
But if the continuity of some pre-Christian ideas and practices was the origin of the notion of witchcraft and if the preservation and worship of ancestral remains was the basis for the allegation of cannibalism in the Caribbean, what was the root element that led to the construction of the stereotype of the 'Aztec human sacrifice'? First of all, we should stress that there was indeed a form of blood sacrifice in pre-colonial Mesoamerica: self-sacrifice, *i.e.* bloodletting from ear, tongue or penis, was frequently performed according to a variety of pre-colonial and early-colonial sources.[75]

---

71 See Pasztory, *Aztec Art*, 157-160, and Matos Moctezuma and López Luján, *Escultura Monumental Mexica*, ch. 3.

72 See for example Fitzsimmons and Shimada, *Living with the Dead.*

73 Díaz del Castillo, *Memoirs*, ch. 61.

74 Codex Vaticanus A, f 57r.

75 Cf. Graulich, *Autosacrifice* and Davis, *Ritualized Discourse.*

In addition, the presentation of food to the images in the temple and the sacrificial killing of animals were common, particularly the decapitation of quails. The custom of sacrificing chicken, for example, remains a prominent element of present-day Mesoamerican religion.[76] These were well-known acts to pay respect to the Gods; they were also related to fasting and visionary experiences.

The pre-colonial Mixtec pictorial manuscripts typically portray the protagonists of their historical narratives as carrying out bloodletting with agave spines or bone perforators, as well as decapitating quails (generally in combination with throwing ground tobacco in the air as an offering), but the famous, emblematic human sacrifice is conspicuously lacking. If rulers such as Motecuhzoma would indeed have insisted so fervently on making sacrifices, as Cortés and Bernal Díaz claim, one would expect the pre-colonial sources (codices, sculptures etc.) to portray them carrying out such actions, but this is not the case. It is therefore more likely that Motecuhzoma was actually insisting on his ritual obligation of bloodletting and sacrifice of quails and/or other animals. But such distinctions were "lost in translation".

But what then about the killing of persons by cutting out their hearts? We find this act represented in pre-colonial manuscripts and other visual art – but how sure are we that it actually was a "human sacrifice"? Clearly it had a religious aspect. The association with temples and statues of the local deities – "demons" according to the medieval Christian worldview – sufficed for the Spaniards as evidence for a connection with the devil. This was the reason that Cortés and the earliest Spanish authors already spoke of it as "sacrifice" and connected it directly with "idolatry", but, as we discussed above, they were mentally conditioned by earlier fanciful accounts of cannibals and witches. On the other hand, the pre-colonial codices demonstrate that this act was not usually part of the native representation of the rituals of the royal persona. Likely there was an element of offering, but this was not the total or primary function or exclusive intrinsic meaning of the killing. What we do find in relation to dynastic history, however, is the slaying of adversaries as a sign of the glorious and victorious character of the ruler. When we try to avoid the colonial gaze and ideological statements about this custom, and focus on the other, more mundane, references, dispersed in different sources, another image emerges. The *Relación Geográfica* of Tequizistlan states:

They venerated the idol Huitzilopochtli and every 80 days they sacrificed to him the Indians that had been condemned to death because of crimes that they had committed.[77]

The *Relación Geográfica* of Teotihuacan (ibid. 236-237) tells us about a temple or altar in front of the Pyramid of the Moon, where wrongdoers and criminals were executed. An example is given: adults who had stolen clothes, feathers, precious stones or other valuable commodities, incurred the death penalty if the stolen good was not returned; but if it was returned, they became slaves for the rest of their lives. Also captives taken in war were killed here, but if they were able to escape before being killed and could climb the temple pyramid they were set free.

There is also an example in the Codex Añute (Selden), an early colonial Mixtec manuscript that is completely painted in pre-colonial tradition. This pictographic book recounts the history of the indigenous dynasty that ruled the city-state ("the mat, the throne") of Añute, now Magdalena Jaltepec in the Mixteca Alta (in the Mexican State of Oaxaca).[78] At a certain moment, in the Year 13 Rabbit (1090 CE), the princess Lady 6 Monkey 'Power of the Plumed Serpent' was going to marry a prince of another town. When she passed by the ancient ruins of Monte Albán two priests shouted to her words from afar: "knife, knife". In accordance with Mixtec custom Lady 6 Monkey interpreted these words as a curse and a threat. With the help of her guiding Goddess she took revenge: supported by an army of warriors she attacked the dwelling of these priests in Monte Albán and took both men prisoner. She then had one killed in her own town, Añute, and the other in the town of her future husband: in both cases the victim was stretched over an altar in the temple court and his heart was cut out (fig. 7.12). Clearly, this was a capital punishment of men who had dared to threaten the princess, in other words: an execution of wrongdoers (Codex Añute, pp. 7-8).

Another example is the murder of Lord 8 Deer, which is represented in a similar manner: Lord 8 Deer is stretched out over an altar and someone is stabbing a flint knife into his chest. In a cognate scene someone is stabbing Lord 8 Deer while he is asleep. The analysis of the context demonstrates that in this case we are not dealing with a sacrifice but with a planned assassination. At a distance

---

76   For example among the Ayuuk people in the State of Oaxaca, Mexico (see Rojas Martínez Gracida, *Tiempo y Sabiduría* y Reyes Gómez, *Tiempo, Espacio y Religión*.

77   Acuña, *Relaciones Geográficas*, vol. 7, 242; The *Relaciones Geográficas* were brief sketches of the situation of the different villages, written for the Spanish authorities around 1580. See Isaac, *Cannibalism among Aztecs*, for a study of the references to anthropophagy in these sources.

78   See our photographic edition and commentary of this codex (Jansen and Pérez Jiménez, *Historia, literatura e ideología*).

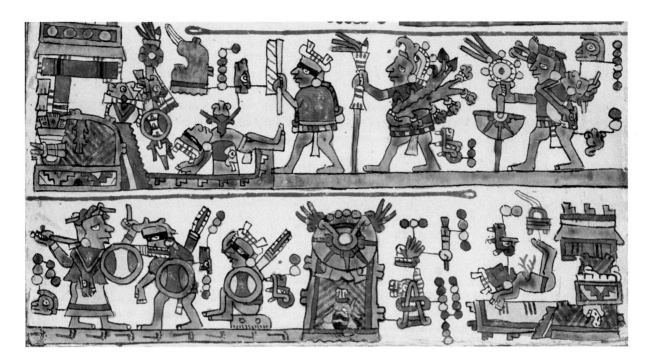

Figure 7.12 (reading from bottom upwards, first row left to right, second row right to left) Lady 6 Monkey takes two men prisoner in battle and has them executed at two different locations, according to Codex Añute (Selden), p. 9. After: Jansen and Pérez Jiménez, *Historia, literatura e ideología*.

Lord 4 Wind is watching; he raises in his hand the sign 'stick and stone', a couplet meaning "punishment".[79] Lord 4 Wind is taking revenge here on Lord 8 Deer for having killed his father and mother. This case shows that the act of heart extraction on an altar is just a pictographic convention for stating that someone is killed.

In accordance with Mesoamerican worldview we understand that taking a life was an act that could only be undertaken with religious respect for the divine forces that had created life in the first place. That explains why the killing was carried out in a ritualised manner, or at least represented that way. The form was similar to that of killing a hunted animal: cutting out the heart as centre of animic power and offering it to the Gods.[80] The palpitating human heart – seat and principle of life – was respectfully returned to the hands and mouths of the (sculptures of the) Creators, who in this way "ate" the killed person. In a similar vein, the Gods drank the blood offered by humans in self-sacrifice and Mother Earth "ate" the body of the deceased that was buried. Indeed there was an awareness of the interdependence of human individuals and the forces of nature, mutually maintaining and nurturing each other, but this was a religious context and paradigm for the (representation of the) way in which someone was killed, not a prime motivation for that killing.

Thinking about the above-mentioned scene in in Codex Yoalli Ehecatl (Borgia), in which the cutting of a tree was painted as a "human sacrifice", we furthermore become aware of the possibility that the heart extraction was not a realistic representation of the act itself but a pictographic image that was to be read as "taking out the life of someone (and returning it to the deities)".[81] An already prejudiced Spanish inquisitor would have understood such idiomatic or metaphorical expressions in Mesoamerican languages, leading to those seemingly realistic representations in visual art, as further proof that such sacrifices of hearts had indeed occurred. In view of the fact that the extraction of a human heart with an obsidian or flint knife implies drastic anatomical and technical difficulties, we should, however, consider the alternative possibility that the person was killed by the act of just stabbing the knife into the chest, without the heart itself being removed.

79 See Codex Ñuu Tnoo – Ndisi Nuu (Bodley), p. 14-I, and Codex Iya Nacuaa I (Colombino), p. 16-II, respectively. For a detailed commentary on the life-story of Lord 8 Deer, see Jansen and Pérez Jiménez, *Encounter with the Plumed Serpent*.

80 See about this connection the erudite monograph of Olivier, *Cacería, sacrificio y poder*.

81 See Hassler's analysis in *Menschenopfer*, 201-213). The same is true for flaying, which likely also had a symbolical aspect (*ibid.* 215-217).

7.6. Conclusion

It is easy to see how in the eyes of non-informed hostile outsiders the (incidental) acts of ritualised killing were convoluted with the customary bloodletting and with the sacrifice of animals: the early colonial sources do not clearly distinguish between them. Consequently, the frequency of the bloodletting ritual could be projected onto the ritualised death penalties and executions, so that a propagandistic image of continuous cruel butchering could be constructed. This representation of the indigenous world as a set of irrational, horrible and inhuman practices served the political interests of the colonial authors to justify the colonial invasion and conquest. When we review and deconstruct that representation in critical retrospect, we find several possible alternative interpretations: the blood in the temples observed by the Spaniards, for example, may well have been that of self-sacrifice and/or that of sacrificed quails and other animals, while the human corpses they encountered probably belonged to executed criminals or war captives.

In this context we also understand that persons sentenced to death were imprisoned in expectation of an adequate ritual event. This explains that the Spaniards encountered persons locked up in wooden cages. Typically they considered this imprisonment as a way of fattening the victims for cannibalistic consumption (analogous to the fairy tale of Hansel and Gretel).

I have still to mention that in Tlascalla we found houses built of wood, in the shape of cages, in which numbers of Indians, of both sexes, were confined, and fattened for their sacrifices and feasts. We never hesitated a single moment to break them down and liberate the prisoners.[82]

The kind reader has now, no doubt, heard enough of this occurrence at Cholulla, and I myself would gladly break off here, but must add a word or two about the wooden cages we saw in this town. These were constructed of heavy timber, and filled with grown-up men and little boys, who were fattening there for the sacrifices and feasts. These diabolical cages Cortes ordered to be pulled down, and sent the prisoners each to their several homes. He likewise made the chiefs and papas promise him, under severe threats, never again to fasten up human beings in that way, and totally to abstain from eating human flesh.[83]

In a similar sense the cited statement of the *Relación Geográfica* of Teotihuacan that those who had stolen

something but returned it in time became "slaves" suggests that "slavery" (or rather obligatory service) functioned as a sort of probation status. Indeed, several accounts state that slaves could be sacrificed, *i.e.* could be killed if their probation period was evaluated negatively, or whenever there was another socially accepted reason. For example, some Mesoamerican societies may have had the custom of killing servants or captives as well as spouses or other specific family members to accompany a deceased important person – master, conqueror, lineage head or ruler – to accompany him/her to the Afterlife to take care of him/her there.[84]

Thus, we conclude, the killing of human individuals through extracting or rather perforating the heart was indeed part of Aztec and other ancient Mesoamerican cultures. Looking at the contextual data we understand that the "human sacrifice" was primarily a form of death penalty for criminals or a way of executing enemies that had been taken captive in battle. We do not propose to idealize or sublimate such practices, but we do propose that what was called "human sacrifice" by the Spaniards was actually a form of ritualised execution or capital punishment, which, in terms of cultural logic and ethics, is obviously something quite different, as such an act is realised in accordance with social norms and a juridical system of laws. In fact, such executions would not have served the conquistadors' purpose of justifying the colonial invasion, as they were also common practice throughout Europe.

The interpretation of the so-called "human sacrifice" as execution or capital punishment also implies that, though the killing of criminals and enemies would not have been uncommon in ancient Mesoamerica, it occurred most likely on a much smaller scale than the numbers mentioned by the colonial authors suggest. The reputed accompanying acts of cannibalism most probably were, as in the Caribbean, fanciful horror stories, which may have been inspired by misunderstood funerary practices, involving secondary burials and the veneration of ancestral bones as sacred relics.[85]

Violence unfortunately has been and still is part of all civilizations in the world. Mass killings have been with us since the expanding kingdoms of the ancient Near East. The Romans had their mad emperors, their fatal gladiator combats and their mass crucifixions, Medieval Europe

---

82   Díaz del Castillo, *Memoirs*, ch. 78, 1844, 187.
83   Díaz del Castillo, *Memoirs*, ch. 83, 1844, 207.

84   Such a custom is mentioned in several Spanish accounts and would explain, for example, the presence of primary burials in an antechamber of a tomb, which apparently accompany the main primary burial in the chamber – see the case of Tombs 1 and 2 in Zaachila (Gallegos, *Señor 9 Flor*). This needs to be investigated further.

85   See our study of Tomb 7 of Monte Albán, which contained such relics as sacred bundles: Jansen and Pérez Jiménez, *Time and the Ancestors*.

its torture, public burnings at the stake, beheadings, flaying, and other forms of cruel execution. Witch-hunt, colonisation and slavery are further reminders of the abuses that European nations were capable of. The past hundred years with two world wars, the Holocaust, atom bombs, civil wars, ethnic "cleansing", genocides, precision bombardments, terrorist attacks, and state terrorism, among others, suggest that the proportions of violence against innocent civilians are only increasing, in spite of consistent efforts to bring about peace and respect for human rights. It is therefore not strange to find acts of violence, war and manslaughter as part of imperial expansion in ancient Mesoamerica. Externally the violence was directed against enemy populations and their leaders, internally it imposed "law and order" through the punishment of individuals who had behaved against the established norms of the state. When the Spaniards arrived, the Aztec expansion had reached its apogee, causing numerous attacks, battles, raids, and ambushes, which probably raised the number of war captives that had to be executed. At the same time the very arrival of the conquistadors likely contributed to a general atmosphere of crisis, lawlessness and desperation, leading to an intensification of bloodshed.

It was in this dramatic context that the hostile colonial commentators constructed the image of human sacrifice and cannibalism as generalized ancient and fanatic practices of pagan peoples. They followed the template of Greek and Latin authors as well as of Biblical and other Christian texts, which presented human sacrifice as characteristic of remote "other peoples", "barbarians", whom they condemned and from whom they distanced themselves. Calling the execution of humans a "sacrifice"

they implied that the primary objective of killing in that pagan and barbarian society was devil-worship: in their opinion it was a bloody and cruel act of a primitive superstitious religion, which imposed on people the need to continuously and irrationally slaughter innocent victims to feed bloodthirsty Gods, and eat the bodies themselves. In this way the European colonisers effectively satanised "the other" as a way of justifying their own violent invasion.

Even today this tendentious image is with us as a *topos* that makes it possible to present the indigenous civilization as monumental and impressive on the one hand, but as fundamentally barbaric and cruel on the other, *i.e.* as interesting to exploit for the macabre fascinations of a large national and international audience and for the tourist industry, but at the same time as something that is alien and something of the remote past that should be overcome. Clearly, this image corresponds to the double mentality, commonplace in Mexico, of admiring and praising the great civilization of the past while at the same time oppressing and discriminating the descendant communities, the indigenous peoples, in the present.[86]

What is needed now is an in-depth historical critique and deconstruction of the sources and data so that we may break with the tradition of taking the reports of Cortés, Bernal Díaz, Sahagún, Durán and other colonial authors at face value, and, instead, start looking for possible alternative interpretations. Only when the colonial gaze and biases are removed can we start to truly appreciate the religious values and symbolism that are present in ancient Mesoamerican art and in the living heritage of indigenous communities today.

---

86   See Pérez and Jansen, *Códices y Conciencia*, and Bonfil Batalla, *México Profundo*.

7.7. References

Acuña, R., *Relaciones geográficas del siglo XVI: México, Volumes 6-8* (Mexico D.F., 1985).

Anders, F. and M.E.R.G.N. Jansen, *Pintura de la Muerte y de los Destinos. Libro explicativo del llamado Códice Laud* (Mexico D.F., 1994).

Anders, F. and M.E.R.G.N. Jansen, *Religión, Costumbres e Historia de los Antiguos Mexicanos. Libro explicativo del llamado Códice Vaticano A (Códice Vaticano 3738).* (Mexico D.F., 1996).

Anders, F., M.E.R.G.N. Jansen, and L. Reyes García, *El Libro del Ciuacoatl. Homenaje para el año del Fuego Nuevo. Libro explicativo del llamado Códice Borbónico* (Mexico D.F., 1991).

Anders, F., M.E.R.G.N. Jansen, and L. Reyes García, *Los Templos del Cielo y de la Oscuridad: Oráculos y Liturgia. Libro explicativo del llamado Códice Borgia* (Mexico D.F., 1993).

Anders, F. and M.E.R.G.N. Jansen, *Libro de la Vida. Texto explicativo del llamado Códice Magliabechiano.* (Mexico D.F., 1996).

Anonymous Conqueror, *Narrative of Some Things of New Spain and of the Great City of Temestitan, México* (New York, 1917).

Arens, W., *The Man-Eating Myth: Anthropology and Anthropophagy* (Oxford, 1979).

Barker, F. P. Hulme, and P. M. Iversen, *Cannibalism and the Colonial World* (Cambridge, 1998).

Bataillon, G., G. Bienvenu, and A. Velasco Gómez, eds, *Las teorías de la guerra justa en el siglo XVI y sus expresiones contemporáneas* (Mexico City, 1998).

Bonfil Batalla, G., *México Profundo. Una civilización negada* (Mexico D.F. 1987).

Bucher, B., *Icon and Conquest: a structural analysis of the Illustrations of Bry's Great Voyages* (Chicago, 1981).

Buvelot, Q., ed., *Albert Eckhout, a Dutch artist in Brazil* (The Hague, Zwolle, 2004).

Cervantes, F., *The Devil in the New World* (New Haven, 1997).

Christensen, B. and Martí, S., *Witchcraft and pre-Columbian paper* (Mexico, 1971).

Churchill, W., *Fantasies of the Master Race. Literature, cinema and the colonization of American Indians* (San Francisco, 1998).

Ciruelo, P., *Tratado en que se reprueban todas las supersticiones y hechicerías* (Barcelona, 1628 / Puebla 1986).

Clark, J. C., *Codex Mendoza* (Oxford, London, 1938).

Cohn, N., *Europe's Inner Demons: An Enquiry Inspired by the Great Witch-Hunt* (Sussex, London, 1975).

Cortés, F., *Letters of Cortes. The Five Letters of Relation from Fernando Cortes to the Emperor Charles V* (New York, London, 1908).

Davis, C.R., *Ritualized Discourse in the Mesoamerican Codices*, M.A. thesis, Leiden University, 2015.

De Bry, Th., *Conquistadores, Aztecs and Incas* (Amsterdam, 1980).

Dehouve, D., *Offrandes et sacrifices en Mésoamérique* (Paris, 2007).

Díaz del Castillo, B., *The Memoirs of the Conquistador Bernal Diaz del Castillo, written by himself containing a true and full account of the discovery and conquest of Mexico and New Spain* (London, 1844).

Durán, D., *Historia de las Indias de la Nueva España e Islas de la Tierra Firme* (Mexico D.F. 1967).

Duverger, C., *La Fleur Létale : économie du sacrifice aztèque* (Paris, 1979).

Evans, S.T., *Ancient Mexico and Central America: Archaeology and Culture History* (New York, 2013).

Fitzsimmons, J.L. and Izumi Shimada, I., eds, *Living with the Dead: Mortuary Ritual in Mesoamerica* (Tucson, 2011).

Gallegos Ruiz, R., *El Señor 9 Flor en Zaachila* (Mexico City, 1978).

García Icazbalceta, J., *Colección de documentos para la historia de México* (Mexico City, 1866).

Ginzburg, C., *I Benandanti: Stregoneria e culti agrari tra Cinquecento* (Turin, 1989).

Ginzburg, C., *Storia Notturna. Una decifrazione del sabba.* (Turin, 2008).

Graham, E. and N. Golson, 'The Faces of Tribute', paper presented at the 71st Meeting of the Society for American Archaeology Meetings (Puerto Rico, 2006).

Graulich, M., *Le Sacrifice humain chez les Aztèques* (Paris, 2005).

Graulich, M., 'Autosacrifice in Ancient Mexico', *Estudios de Cultura Náhuatl* 36 (2005), 301-329.

Greenleaf, R.E., *Zumárraga and the Mexican Inquisition, 1536-1543* (Washington, 1961).

Gunsenheimer, A., 'The Study of Human Sacrifice in Pre-Columbian Cultures: A Challenge for Ethnohistorical and Archaeological Research', in T. von Trotha and J. Rösel, eds, *On Cruelty* (Cologne, 2011), 255-284.

Harner, M., 'The Ecological Basis for Aztec Sacrifice', *American Ethnologist* 4 (1) (1977), 117-135.

Harris, M., *Cannibals and Kings. The Origins of Cultures* (Glasgow, 1978).

Hassler, P., *Menschenopfer bei den Azteken? Eine quellen-und ideologiekritischer Studie* (Bern, 1992).

Isaac, B.L. 'Cannibalism among Aztecs and their Neighbors: Analysis of the 1577-1586 *Relacioners Geográficas* for Nueva España and Nueva Galica Provinces', *Journal of Anthropological research* 58 (2002), 203-224.

Jacobs, J.Q., 'The Cannibalism Paradigm: Assessing Contact Period Ethnohistorical Discourse', term paper, Arizona State University, 2004, http://www.jqjacobs.net/anthro/cannibalism.html).

Jansen, M.E.R.G.N., *La Gran Familia de los Reyes Mixtecos. Libro explicativo de los llamados Códices Egerton y Becker II* (Mexico, 1994).

Jansen, M.E.R.G.N. and T.J.J. Leyenaar, 'De Amate-geesten van San Pablito', *Verre Naasten Naderbij* 9.1 (1975).), 29-60.

Jansen, M.E.R.G.N. and G.A. Pérez Jiménez, *Encounter with the Plumed Serpent. Drama and Power in the Heart of Mesoamerica* (Boulder, 2007).

Jansen, M.E.R.G.N. and G.A. Pérez Jiménez, *Historia, literatura e ideología de Ñuu Dzaui. El Códice Añute y su contexto histórico-cultural* (Oaxaca, 2013).

Jansen, M.E.R.G.N. and G.A. Pérez Jiménez, 'Tiempo, Religión e Interculturalidad en la Colonia: los catecismos pictográficos de México', in M.E.R.G.N. Jansen and V. Raffa, eds, *Tiempo y Comunidad. Herencias e interacciones socioculturales en Mesoamérica y Occidente* (Leiden, 2015), 65-101.

Jansen, M.E.R.G.N. and G.A. Pérez Jiménez, *The Mixtec Pictorial Manuscripts. Time, Agency and Memory in Ancient Mexico* (Leiden / Boston, 2011).

Jansen, M.E.R.G.N. and G.A. Pérez Jiménez, *Time and the Ancestors: Aztec and Mixtec Ritual Art* (Leiden, Boston, 2017).

Jesse, C., 'The Spanish Cedula of December 23, 1511, on the subject of the Caribs', *Caribbean Quarterly* 9.3 (1963), 22-32.

Jiménez Moreno, W., *'Primeros Memoriales' de Fray Bernardino de Sahagún* (Mexico D.F., 1974).

Keen, B. *The Aztec Image in Western Thought* (New Brunswick, 1971).

Klein, C.F. 'Death at the Hand of Strangers. Aztec Human Sacrifice in the Western Imagination', in J.M.D. Pohl and C.L. Lyons, eds, *Altera Roma: Art and Empire from Merida to Mexico* (Los Angeles, 2016), 257-312.

Kramer, H. and J. Sprenger, *The Malleus Maleficarum* (New York, 2007).

Lantigua, D., 'Religion within the Limits of Natural Reason: the Case of Human Sacrifice', in D.T. Orique and R. Roldan-Figueroa, eds, *Bartolomé de las Casas O.P. History, Philosophy, and Theology in the Age of European Expansion* (Leiden, 2019), 280-309.

Las Casas, B. de, *Historia de las Indias* (Caracas, 1986).

López Luján, L., and G. Olivier, eds, *El sacrificio humano en la tradición religiosa meso-americana* (Mexico D.F. 2009).

Madsen, W. and C. Madsen, *A Guide to Mexican Witchcraft* (Mexico, 1999).

Mandeville, J., *The Travels of Sir John Mandeville* (London, New York, 1900).

Mason, P., *Deconstructing America: Representations of the Other* (London, New York, 1990).

Mason, P., *Infelicities. Representations of the Exotic* (Baltimore, London, 1998).

Matos Moctezuma, E. and L. López Luján, *Escultura Monumental Mexica* (Mexico D.F., 2012).

McCafferty, G.G., 'The Cholula Massacre: Factional Histories and Archaeology of the Spanish Conquest', in M. Boyd, J.C. Erwin, and M. Henderson, eds, *The Entangled Past: Integrating Archaeology and History* (Calgary, 2000) 347-359.

Mendieta, G. de, *Historia Eclesiástica Indiana* (Mexico D.F., 1971).

Meszaros, J. and J. Zachhuber, *Sacrifice and Modern Thought* (Oxford, 2013)

Nájera, M. I., *El don de la sangre en el equilibrio cósmico* (Mexico City, 1987).

Nicholson, H.B. and E. Quiñones Keber, *Art of Aztec Mexico. Treasures of Tenochtitlan* (Washington, 1983).

Nutini, H.G. and J.M. Roberts, *Bloodsucking Witchcraft: An Epistemological Study of Anthropomorphic Supernaturalism in Rural Tlaxcala* (Tucson, London, 1993).

Olivier, G., *Cacería, sacrificio y poder en Mesoamérica. Tras las huellas de Mixcóatl, 'Serpiente de Nube'* (Mexico, 2015).

Olmos, A., *Tratado de hechicerías y sortilegios* (México D.F., 1553 / 1990).

Oosten, J., 'The prime mover and fear in Inuit religion. A discussion of native views', in M.E.R.G.N. Jansen, P.L. van der Loo, and R.A.G.F.M. Manning, eds, *Continuity and Identity in Native America: Essays in Honor of Benedikt Hartmann* (Leiden, 1988), 69-83.

Pasztory, E., *Aztec Art* (New York, 1983).

Pérez Jiménez, G.A., and M.E.R.G.N. Jansen, 'Los códices y la conciencia de ser indígena', *Revista Mexicana de Ciencias Políticas y Sociales* 97 (1979), 83-104.

Pico della Mirandola, G.F., *La Strega, ovvero degli inganni dei demoni* (Milano, Udine, 2012).

Quiñones Keber, E., *Codex Telleriano-Remensis. Ritual, Divination, and History in a Pictorial Aztec Manuscript* (Austin, 1995).

Restall, M., *Seven Myths of the Spanish Conquest* (Oxford, 2003).

Restall, M., *When Montezuma Met Cortés. The True Story of the Meeting that Changed History* (New York, 2018).

Reyes Gómez, J.C., *Tiempo, Espacio y Religión del Pueblo Ayuuk, México* (Leiden, 2017)

Rojas Martínez Gracida, A., *El Tiempo y la Sabiduría en Poxoyëm. Un calendario sagrado entre los Ayook de Oaxaca*, PhD dissertation, Leiden University, 2012.

Sahagún, B. de, *Florentine Codex, General History of the Things of New Spain*, edition and translation by Arthur J.O. Anderson and Charles E. Dibble (Santa Fe, 1950-1978).

Sandstrom, A.R., *Corn is our Blood* (Norman, 1991).

Seler, E., *Gesammelte Abhandlungen zur Amerikanishen Sprach- und Alterthumskunde* (Graz, 1960-1961).

Silva Tena, T., 'El Sacrificio Humano en la Apologética Historia', *Historia Mexicana* 16.3 (1967), 341-357.

Solis Salcedo, J.O., *Les Sacrifices Humains chez les Aztèques: la construction du discours colonial espagnol d'après les sources du XVIe siècle*, M.A. thesis, Université de Sherbrooke, 2009.

Sued Badillo, J., *Los Caribes: realidad o fábula. Ensayo de rectificación histórica* (Río Piedras, 1978).

Torquemada, J. de *Monarquía Indiana* (Mexico D.F., 1975-79).

Van Groesen, M., *The representations of the overseas world in the De Bry collection of voyages (1590-1634)* (Leiden, Boston, 2008).

Vervoort, R. and Dries Vanysacker, *Bruegel witches: witchcraft images in the Low Countries between 1450 and 1700* (Utrecht, 2015).

Watts, J., Sheehan, O., Atkinson, Q. D., Bulbulia J. and Gray, R.D., 'Ritual human sacrifice promoted and sustained the evolution of stratified societies', *Nature* 532 (2016), 228-231.

Widengren, G., *Religionsphänomenologie* (Berlin, 1969).

Winkelman, M. 'Aztec Human Sacrifice: Cross-Cultural Assessments of the Ecological Hypothesis', *Ethnology* 37.3 (1998), 285-298.

Zuluaga Hoyos, G., 'La Discusión sobre el Canibalismo y los Sacrificios Humanos en la Disputa de Sepúlveda con Las Casas (1550-1551)', *Cuadernos de Filosofía Latinoamericana* 30, núm. 100 (2009), 39-46.

Chapter 8

Death and new life

An intimate relationship

Pieter ter Keurs*

8.1. Introduction

Among the very few certainties in human life there are two moments that stand out as the most important ones: birth and death, the beginning and the end. The world before birth and after death belongs to the world beyond, a universe we cannot comprehend. When, at the end of the eighteenth century, Western philosophy finally made a clear-cut distinction between what we can observe with our senses and understand with our rational abilities, the empirical world as it shows itself to us, and what we can never understand (the world beyond, or the Kantian *das Ding-an-sich*) the European sphere of influence distinguished itself from many other areas in the world. To many people there is no clear-cut separation between the two spheres, as Western philosophers after Immanuel Kant – such as Arthur Schopenhauer – also quickly recognised.

This balancing act between the known and the unknown stands at the basis of human artistic, symbolic, and religious expression. And creating and guarding a balance in society and in the universe is, apart from coping with the world beyond, a second constant, essential and universal trait of human culture. It is around these two basic human needs, coping with life and death as well as finding a balance in personal and communal life, that this text will develop.

The subject of sacrificing fellow human beings to the gods, hoping for the return gift of new life, is fiercely debated in scholarly literature. Why should one kill and offer the most precious thing we have, life itself, for an uncertain outcome, since we can never be sure of the willingness of the gods to return the gift? To tackle this question we should keep in mind at least four issues that usually tend to blur the discussion. I will focus on the phenomenon of head-hunting, a specific type of human sacrifice. My remarks may therefore be of limited use to other types of sacrifices, but I do think that the basic principles I will discuss are relevant to our attempts to comprehend the general idea of offering life to get new life in return.

Sacrificed human beings are often slaves or enemies, not our closest friends or relatives. There are many examples of headhunting raids, or stories about headhunting raids, aiming to capture enemy heads, which will be ritually transformed to play a meaningful role in ritual practices of the receiving society. This transformation makes the hunted head, the hunter's prey, from something strange that comes from outside the local community into something that supports, and is even essential to, the local community. As Maurice Bloch formulates it, a transformation takes place from *Prey into Hunter* (1992). Taking strangers or slaves as offering to the Gods means that ritualised human sacrifices

*Leiden University

are less disruptive for society than in the case of offering relatives or direct neighbours.

A second issue that should be taken into consideration is the fact that stories about human sacrifices are often exaggerated. The discourse of exchanging life for new life is a very powerful discourse, so even when human sacrifices or headhunting raids do not actually take place, it is important to keep the discourse alive. One does not want to take the risk that the gods will blame people that they actually stopped offering 'real' human beings. It is also clear that headhunting practices and warfare enhance the prestige of men and without the prestige of men and the life-giving force of women there can be no continuation of society. So here as well, one has to keep the stories about headhunting alive to ensure a proper relationship between men and women and the creation of new life.

Apart from pleasing the Gods and enhancing the prestige of men, another reason for spreading around stories about human sacrifices and headhunting is the wish to keep foreign intruders out of the region. Probably, this technique has often been used to keep the European coloniser out, at least for some time.

So, stories about headhunting are more widespread than the actual practice. One can find many examples. Speaking of Kupang, the capital of Timor, Janet Hoskins wrote:

> I heard rumors that the new influx of long-haired European and Australian tourists signaled that heads would be taken and used to fortify the building of international hotels.[1]

This is in line with the traditional practice of supporting new houses with hunted skulls to secure prosperity of the house and its inhabitants. I have heard similar stories in the 1990s about the large, new skyscrapers in Jakarta. Here too, the creation of a cosmological balance is crucial for the well-being of future generations.

Finally, we should keep in mind that Western idealism has also sometimes blurred discussions on human sacrifices and headhunting. If one sees 'the other' as an, in essence, good person (the echo of Rousseau) one is not inclined to see the violent aspects of a foreign culture. In addition, since headhunting raids have seldom been documented, some authors have doubts whether they really took place. Sometimes anthropologists are so involved in the societies they study that they are not willing to see the aggressive and violent aspects of the group in which they were so well accepted. It may be that particularly anthropologists who have been trained in the 1960s and the 1970s (in the context of the student movements stressing social relations based on goodness and lacking dominance and violence) were receptive to such sentiments.[2]

8.2. Killing and creating new life among the Asmat

To illustrate how the relationship between taking life and renewing life is seen and ritualised, I will shortly describe some ritual practices of the Asmat of Southwest New-Guinea (now part of Indonesia). Until the 1960s the Asmat were feared as headhunters, by neighbouring groups and by the Europeans (mainly Dutch) who represented the colonial authorities. There was hardly reliable information on Asmat culture available, although Dutch museums already possessed impressive Asmat woodcarvings, collected during a military expedition in the beginning of the twentieth century. It was Major A.J. Gooszen who, in the 1910s, sent large collections to the Netherlands, avoiding the existing regulation which stipulated that collections should be sent to the museum of the Batavian Society of Arts and Sciences in Batavia (now the National Museum of Indonesia in Jakarta).

Gooszen's collections are still seen as the best Asmat collections in the world and they have stimulated generations of researchers. Adrian Gerbrands, who was very familiar with the Gooszen collections in Leiden, did groundbreaking research on the creativity of Asmat woodcarvers of the village Amanamkai, in 1960-1961. His book *Wow-Ipits* (1967) became a classic in the anthropology of art. Gerbrands showed convincingly that Asmat art can only be understood within the context of Asmat society and he showed that symbolism related to headhunting explained, to a large extent, the choice of designs and the ritual practices in which the carvings were incorporated. For information on headhunting Gerbrands relied heavily on Father Zegwaard, a priest who worked in the area for a long time and published a thoroughly documented article on Asmat headhunting in *American Anthropologist*.[3]

The main reason to practice headhunting was to stimulate fertility and there are indications that the women urged the men to go on a headhunting raid. Gerbrands witnessed and filmed a conflict in Amanamkai with men threatening each other with axes. In the film Matjemos (1966) it is clearly visible that the women push the men to show more ferocity. Apparently, some men were not inclined to escalate the conflict, but they were pushed back

---

2   In discussions with colleagues I sometimes encountered fierce, even aggressive, denial of headhunting practices, based on the fact that raids have never been documented in 'their' (meaning the anthropologists') society. Of course this does not mean that they did not take place.

3   Zegwaard, 'Headhunting Practices'.

---

1   Hoskins, *Headhunting*, 32.

by the women. Female fertility is only possible when there is male status and prestige, so the women have an interest in urging the men to show the strength and the courage to hunt for preys and to kill.

When Asmat men embarked on a headhunting raid they did not deliberately aim for a victim with a high status. They tried to attack a village by surprise and capture the persons who did not succeed to get away in time. Very often it concerned women or children. The victim lost his or her own name when the head was carried into the village of the headhunters. The victim, the slain enemy, had to be incorporated in the ritual practices that were planned to re-vitalize the village of the headhunters. For this purpose the hunted head received a new identity, with a new name. The prey was welcomed in the village by the women singing and dancing.

Contrary to what early travellers and colonial officers thought, not all skulls in Asmat society were slain enemies. In the men's houses many ancestor skulls were on display. Therefore, the scale of headhunting practices may have been overestimated by early travellers. Photographs of Asmat warriors resting with a skull as a pillow actually show ancestor skulls and not hunted skulls. The difference is clearly recognisable since ancestor skulls still had the lower jawbone and were usually elaborately decorated. Hunted skulls could also be decorated, particularly when they were incorporated in ritual practices and thus in the receiving society, but they always lacked the lower jawbone.

The importance of Asmat headhunting was and is also illustrated and justified in powerful symbolism. Gerbrands documented the role of the *wènet*, the praying mantis, in decorations on woodcarvings.[4] The *wènet* design is found everywhere, which suggests a central role in Asmat thought. Here, it is important to realise that the female *wènet*, in captivity, bites off the head of the male during sexual intercourse. This powerful symbolism – which includes the relationship between death and new life – actually supports headhunting practices in Asmat society and makes it understandable that the *wènet* designs appears on drum handles, canoe prows, spears and many other material expressions.

Examples of this design are not difficult to find in museums collections. A combination of two overlapping *wènet* designs are depictions of ancestors. In addition, the *wènet* looks like a living piece of wood, a walking stick. Note that the term Asmat (As-amat) means 'people of wood'. Fruits on trees are seen as 'the heads of the tree' and fruit eating animals, such as the black cockatoo, are seen as headhunters.

Images of slain enemies are also carved on *bisj* poles, large wooden statues with several ancestor images used

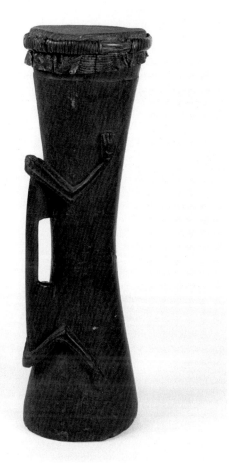

Figure 8.1 Asmat drum. The handle is carved in the shape of a *wènet*. Collection National Museum of World Cultures (NMWC), Leiden, RV 5029-1.

as architectural elements in men's houses or as statues for rituals in which the hunted heads were received in the village. Normally the image of the slain enemy was carved close to the genitals of an ancestor, illustrating the relationship between killing life and renewing life.

All this shows how incrusted headhunting, and its symbolism, is in Asmat society. Even if raids no longer take place, it is important to keep the stories about headhunting alive, because these stories represent essential elements of Asmat life: male prestige and female fertility. Without these two elements, society will not survive. I will show below that this is not only the case among the Asmat. It seems to be a general human phenomenon.

8.3. Slain enemies and ancestors

There are indications that victims of headhunting raids are symbolically transformed into ancestors to be able to support society in creating new life, but often this

---

4   Gerbrands, *Wow-Ipits*.

transformation is not explicitly mentioned.[5] On Enggano island, southwest of Sumatra (Indonesia), there are no stories known about headhunting practices. Yet, there are ample symbolic indications that headhunting used to play a crucial role in Engganese culture in the past.

It is impossible to reconstruct ancient Engganese culture. Apart from the fact that there are no written sources, there was a dramatic population decline in the nineteenth century. It is estimated that there were around 8.000 to 10.000 Engganese people in the beginning of the nineteenth century. In the beginning of the twentieth century there were only 300 left.[6] Part of the population had mixed with migrants from mainland Sumatra or Java, but most people had died from diseases that were imported by Europeans as well as Chinese and Buginese traders. It is likely that particularly smallpox and cholera decimated the population. Although the Dutch colonial authorities sent several researchers and medical doctors to the island to find out what was happening, they were never able to control the situation and to stop the devastating mortality rate. By 1903, when the Protestant Mission arrived, there must have been a general amnesia of a dying culture. In 1994, when I visited Enggano, several informants said that they were now good Christians or Muslims and that they knew virtually nothing about traditional Engganese culture. Yet, based on some stories that have survived, museum collections, and documentation of nineteenth century travellers, we can reconstruct at least something of the old ritual practices.

The book *L'isola delle donne. Viaggio ad Engano* (1894), an account by the Italian traveller Elio Modigliani (1860-1932) about his stay on Enggano Island, is an important source. His work is of significance not only because of what he wrote, but also because of the collection he brought to the Ethnographic Museum in Florence. This is by far the most important Enggano collection in the world.

In the 1930s the German linguist Hans Kähler spent some months on the island. The stories he collected (and published in 1975) also throw some light on Engganese ritual practices, particularly on the *eakalea* (the great feast), a large-scale feast to re-vitalise society involving several villages.[7] Bringing in the hunter's preys was an important part of the *eakalea*.

On Enggano hunters' preys are mostly wild pigs.[8] Even in the 1990s wild pigs were roaming around in the forest and were sometimes frighteningly close by. In one of the villages I saw a young man heavily wounded after he was attacked by an aggressive pig. And when travelling from one village to another one had to be on the alert constantly, not only for pigs, but also for snakes. In the past, when large amounts of food were necessary for the large-scale feasts, the village square was renamed 'the place where the head is cut off' when de hunters returned from their raids in the forest. The hunters' preys were welcomed by the women who were extensively adorned for the occasion. The women were dancing and threw young coconuts in front of the houses, to stimulate fertility. An important detail is the women's headdresses. These small wooden cylinders usually had a carved image of a slain enemy as main decoration. The headdresses themselves were further decorated with chicken feathers. Several examples of these unique objects have survived in museum collections.[9]

The ritual welcome of the preys, including slain enemies, by the women was not the end of the ceremony. In the middle of the village square there was usually the house of the village leader. These houses are called beehive houses, since the shape resembles a beehive.[10] They were not meant for an extended family, only for a couple with one or maximum two young babies. The houses were too small for more people.

Under the floor of the beehive houses an impressive carving of a slain enemy was attached, to support the house and to symbolically support the community. It is likely that here the slain enemy is transformed into an ancestor who supports the kin group with his or her blessings. Unfortunately we have no ethnographic data to corroborate this hypothesis. It does, however, confirm the important role of the slain enemy in re-vitalising society: the women are adorned with the slain enemy and the houses are supported by the slain enemy. Without such as ritual, in which 'the wild' from outside is brought in and 'civilised' is essential for the well-being of the group. Only by killing life one can guarantee continuation of society's fertility and welfare.

8.4. Headhunting as trope

As mentioned above, stories about sacrificing human beings or headhunting practices are not always factual. However, even as a figure of speech they need to be taken seriously. Even if headhunting no longer takes place it is still important to find a way to enhance male prestige. It is not uncommon to achieve this by showing off. In European society it can regularly be observed,

---

5   Bloch, *Prey into hunter*; Hoskins, *Headhunting and the Social Imagination in Southeast Asia*.

6   For more information, see ter Keurs, *Condensed Reality. A Study of Material Culture*.

7   Kähler, *Texte von der Insel Enggano*.

8   For more detailed information on ritual practices and house construction on Enggano, see ter Keurs, 'Eakalea. a ritual feast on Enggano Island', *Condensed Reality, and 'Beehive houses on Enggano Island'.

9   The most impressive examples are in Florence, Leiden and Jakarta.

10 In 1994 these houses no longer existed, although some floorparts were still kept by some families. The last beehive house was probably demolished in, or shortly after, 1903. See ter Keurs, 'Beehive houses on Enggano Island'.

Figure 8.2 An Engganese woman's headdress, with an image of the slain enemy. Collection National Museum of World Cultures (NMWC), Leiden, RV 712-1.

preferably on a beautiful summer's day, that some men (nowadays also women) find a lot of satisfaction in driving ostentatiously in an expensive sportscar with open roof.[11] This secures a lot of attention from bystanders and also suggests extensive financial means of the driver: the hunter who brings in considerable wealth. Stories about courageous behaviour during headhunting raids serve similar purposes.

Secondly, aggressive images supported by stories about human sacrifices and headhunting have certainly served to keep out foreigners as long as possible. And they have served this purpose well. The threat of violence has indeed prevented explorers to continue their journeys. This way local populations have successfully kept out European colonisers, at least for some time. A good example is the Central Sumatra expedition in 1877-1879, meant to map the area, both geographically and ethnographically, and to explore the possibility of exploiting the natural resources of the region. At a certain point, however, the expedition members were threatened to be killed if they went on.[12] After ignoring the warning one time they were again

summoned to hold. This time the expedition gave in and changed course.

Farther north on Sumatra, the Toba succeeded to keep the western coloniser out of the area for some decades. Stories about human sacrifices and aggressive warriors were part and parcel of this.[13]

It has already been mentioned above that stories about the necessity of headhunting still roam around in contemporary cities such as Jakarta. In the 1990s, when travelling extensively in several parts of Indonesia, I was twice, jokingly, reminded that this was the time to kill the foreigner (me): once on Ambon, while talking about Seram, and once on Enggano Island. In both cases I was in an isolated situation, with limited transport opportunities. I was the ideal victim. I did not feel threatened for a moment, because I knew the people who made these remarks well and considered them to be my friends. However, I can imagine how these stories may have impressed and influenced early travellers and colonial officers. It can be very uncomfortable to be alone in a hut in the forest, surrounded by strange noises and threatening warriors.

8.5. Concluding remarks

Although the separation between male and female worlds has blurred in contemporary society, we can still recognise the basic principles that are important for rituals related to human sacrifices and headhunting practices. The hunt for status and prestige and to be recognised as a successful person is more alive than ever. I already mentioned the sportscar driver, but there are many other examples to give. People who search for the right person for a, usually high-level, job are called headhunters. They are after your head, to be incorporated in a new job environment, to fertilise it. In films and advertising sexuality and human fertility are stressed again and again. One does not need to search long for examples. We are constantly overwhelmed by these types of images: usually powerful male and seductive female characters. Only when these two elements are brought together society can flourish.

It seems to be a general human phenomenon to stress prestige and fertility as essential elements for society's continuation and well-being. At the same time the other essential element, keeping a balance in the cosmos by killing and creating new life is more complicated to identify nowadays. One has to kill life to create space for new life. One has to give something very valuable in order to receive something very valuable in return. Contemporary societies however tend to exclude death from our daily lives. People live longer than ever before and as a consequence are no longer willing to include

---

11   See also Baudrillard, *The System of Objects*.
12   See Veth, *Midden-Sumatra*; Ter Keurs, 'Collecting in Central and South-Sumatra', 85-87.

13   Ter Keurs, *Au nord de Sumatra*, 17.

the possibility of death in their worldview. Advertising is focusing on the extension of life as long as possible. Preferably we thrive for eternal life, although we know this is impossible. In advertising mothers often look like their daughter, as if they have not aged. They may have matured, but they do not look older.

This lack of balance, between male and female, culture and nature, life and death, is broadly felt in contemporary society.[14] And in some periods, such as during the corona crisis of 2020, it is felt even stronger. Here, the study of human sacrifice practices can help us even nowadays. Morally we disapprove of killing life for the benefit of younger, new life, and rightly so. There is no moral justification for killing people and we know from European history how things can go wrong if we do not live according to moral standards that prevent killing on a small or large scale. The concentration camps during the Second World War are extreme and powerful examples of a disregard for killing. However, there is a contradiction here. The moral and legal prohibition to kill may lead to a disregard for death, to a denial of death, to marginalising death. This means that the necessary balance to keep humanity 'on track' is lost or, at least partly, replaced by symbolic killings, by headhunting as a trope. As I said, we usually do not kill people to create space for others, but in present-day society many phenomena serve to replace the actual killing. This is where the study of human sacrifices and headhunting can help us nowadays, to understand what we need and what we should do to keep a balance in human life and in society: in order to ensure a healthy, fertile, sustainable and safe future.

8.6. References

Baudrillard, J., *The System of Objects* (London, New York, 1996).

Bloch, M., *Prey into hunter. The politics of religious experience* (Cambridge, 1992).

Gerbrands, A., *Wow-Ipits. Eight Asmat Woodcarvers of New Guinea* (The Hague, Paris, 1967).

Hoskins, J., *Headhunting and the Social Imagination in Southeast Asia* (Stanford, 1996).

Kähler, H., *Texte von der Insel Enggano* (Berlin, 1975).

Keurs, P.J. ter, 'Eakalea. a ritual feast on Enggano Island, viewed from a regional perspective. *Indonesia and the Malay World* 30 (2002), 238-252.

Keurs, P.J. ter, 'Collecting in Central and South-Sumatra', in S. Endang Hardiati and P. ter Keurs, eds, *Indonesia. The Discovery of the Past* (Amsterdam, 2005), 85-89.

Keurs, P.J. ter, *Condensed Reality. A Study of Material Culture* (Leiden, 2006).

Keurs, P.J. ter, 'Beehive houses on Enggano Island. Western Indonesia', in R. Schefold, P. Nas, G. Domenig, and R. Wessing, eds, *Indonesian Houses. Survey of vernacular architecture in western Indonesia* 2 (2008), 465-486.

Keurs, P.J. ter, *Au nord de Sumatra. Les Batak* (Paris, 2008).

Modigliani, E., *L'isola delle donne. Viaggio ad Engano* (Milan, 1894).

Veth, P., ed., *Midden-Sumatra. Reizen en onderzoekingen der Sumatra-Expeditie, uitgerust door het Aardrijkskundig Genootschap*, 4 volumes (Leiden, 1882).

Zegwaard, G., 'Headhunting Practices of the Asmat of Netherlands New Guinea', *American Anthropologist* 61 (1959), 1020-1041.

---

14 Here, one can refer to public figures and writers such as Al Gore, Naomi Klein, Greta Thunberg and many others.

About the Authors

Jacobus van Dijk (Dutch) was an associate professor of Egyptology at the University of Groningen, The Netherlands. He worked for many years as a philologist/epigrapher with the joint mission of the Egypt Exploration Society, London and the RMO Leiden to the New Kingdom Necropolis at Saqqâra (1981-2003), the Cambridge Expedition to the Valley of the Kings (2006-2008), and the Brooklyn Museum Expedition to the Precinct of Mut at South Karnak (1986-present). Since his early retirement in 2013 he works as an independent scholar. Website: www.jacobusvandijk.nl.

Brien Garnand (American) is an Assistant Professor in the Classics Department at Howard University. His interdisciplinary research interests straddle the Greco-Roman and Near-Eastern Mediterranean, its languages and literatures, its archaeology and history. In particular, he focuses on interactions between Greeks and Phoenicians in the Central Mediterranean and North Africa, comparing their diffusion of city-state urbanism, alphabetic literacy, and trade networks. He has undertaken extensive archaeological fieldwork and archival research, including excavations at Mt. Polizzo in Sicily, and he is currently preparing the final archaeological reports for the ASOR Punic Project excavations at the *tophet* of Carthage.

Karel Innemée (Dutch) studied History of Art, Archaeology and Egyptology at Leiden University. He worked as an assistant professor at the department of Art History, at the Faculty of Archaeology in Leiden, and at the department of Ancient History of the University of Amsterdam and as a visiting professor of Coptic Studies at the American University in Cairo. Currently he is a research fellow at the University of Amsterdam and the University of Divinity in Melbourne. His field of research in general is Eastern Christianity and more specifically monastic culture in the Nile valley. He is director of the project The Mural Paintings of Deir al-Surian.

Maarten E.R.G.N. Jansen (Dutch) is emeritus professor of 'Heritage of Indigenous Peoples' and 'Mesoamerican Archaeology and History' at the Faculty of Archaeology, University of Leiden, The Netherlands. Recently, he was also awarded a position as Distinguished Emeritus Professor for Mesoamerican Studies at the University of Bonn, Germany. Combining cultural historical research with ethnographic fieldwork in Mexico, he has published extensively on the interpretation of ancient Mexican visual art, in particular the Aztec and Mixtec pictorial manuscripts and the famous treasure of Tomb 7 of Monte Albán (Oaxaca).

Pieter ter Keurs (Dutch) is professor of Museums, Collections and Society at the faculties of Humanities and Archaeology of Leiden University, the Netherlands. As an anthropologist he did fieldwork in Papua New Guinea and Indonesia. Previously, he was a curator at the National Museum of Ethnology (now World Cultures) in Leiden and head of Collections and Research at the National Museum of Antiquities. Ter Keurs is also Academic Director of the LDE Centre for Global Heritage and Development. He was project leader of several museum-based cooperation projects and he made exhibitions in Leiden, Amsterdam, Jakarta, Paris and Brussels. Pieter ter Keurs is particularly interested in material culture and museum studies. He focuses on the phenomenon of collecting.

Theo J.H. Krispijn (Dutch) is a (retired) lecturer of Sumerian at the department of Ancient Near Eastern Studies (ONOS) / LIAS of Leiden University. He studied Theology and Semitic Languages (Assyriology and Hebrew) in Leiden with F.R. Kraus and with D.O. Edzard and C. Wilcke in Munich. He specialised in the Sumerian language and literature, the earliest lexical tradition in Mesopotamia, the Elamite language, and Mesopotamian religion. Another important theme of his research is music and musical instruments of the ancient Near East. He mainly publishes in the field of ancient music and Sumerian language, lexicography, and literature. He is national secretary of the Ex Oriente Lux society and editor of its magazine Phoenix.

L. Bouke van der Meer (Dutch) was born in Leeuwarden in 1945. After military service he studied Classical Languages at the University of Groningen. He was a teacher at the Johannes College in Den Helder for one year. He taught classical archaeology at Leiden University from 1973 until 2010. He got his PhD at the University of Groningen in 1978. He wrote several books: on Etruscan urns from Volterra, the Bronze Liver of Piacenza, the Etruscan language (with prof. Rob Beekes), Etruscan mirrors, stone sarcophagi, rituals, the Liber Linteus Zagrabiensis, and on in situ inscriptions at Ostia (Ostia speaks). He is a guest researcher at the Faculty of Archaeology of Leiden University since 2010.

Gabina Aurora Pérez Jiménez (Mexican), born in Chalcatongo, Oaxaca, Mexico, has taught Mixtec language and culture at Leiden University in the Netherlands. Actively involved in several scholarly projects, she has published a Mixtec course book and dictionary, while also being co-author of a set of commentaries on Mixtec pictorial manuscripts. By participating in meetings at the United Nations and other forums in the 1980s and 1990s, as well as through multiple lectures and consultancies, she has contributed to raising international awareness about the heritage and rights of Indigenous Peoples.

Printed by Printforce, United Kingdom